FRANK A. GOLDER

AN ADVENTURE OF A HISTORIAN
IN QUEST OF RUSSIAN HISTORY

by

Alain Dubie

EAST EUROPEAN MONOGRAPHS, BOULDER
DISTRIBUTED BY COLUMBIA UNIVERSITY PRESS, NEW YORK

1989

EAST EUROPEAN MONOGRAPHS, NO. CCLXVIII

Contents

Photographs

Maps

FOR

Richard Kent Mayberry

in memoriam

Acknowledgments

Writing Golder's story was a labor of love and—labor. It was historian Charles B. Burdick who first suggested that I undertake the endeavor of bringing Golder's story to light. His keen sensitivity for historical investigation, insights into the historical process, and stylistic considerations—"History is a good story," proved to be invaluable resources as I pieced together this mosaic. Historians Dimitrije Djordjevic, Joachim Remak, Irma Eichhorn, Alexander DeConde, and Al Lindemann read either all or parts of the manuscript in various stages of its composition, offering me a number of useful suggestions. A variety of archives provided me with documents related to Golder's life, particularly the Hoover Institution, where a treasure of Golder memorabilia resides, as well as the Department of Special Collections at Washington State College, the Herbert Hoover Presidential Library, and the National Archives in Washington, D. C. Most valuable to me were my interviews with Golder's former colleagues, Thomas Bailey, Harold Fisher, Carl Brand, Stuart Graham, Thomas Barclay, and Mabel Junkert, and the letters I received from Golder's relatives and students; they gave the past that irreplaceable human dimension. Lastly, I must acknowledge most gratefully Nancy Anne Dubie, whose encouragement and gentle nudging kept body and soul together and moving forward. In the final analysis, though, I am responsible for the story, and therefore, am, regretfully, responsible for any flaws and errors.

A. D.

Writers have too often confounded an
explorer, like Perry, with a hunter, like
Deshnef. The former has an ideal to draw
him on, the latter has no such high purpose.
Although possessed of an equal amount of
endurance, the hunter has less perseverance;
he is easily discouraged. In navigating he
keeps close to land and at the first sign
of danger runs there for protection. He is
always ready to turn back. Why should he
risk his life? Money has far less power
over him than is usually supposed. The
hunter is more like the ambitionless native
. . . than the enthusiastic explorer.

> —Frank Golder

The students who have contributed anything
of value to [Russian studies] could be
counted on one's fingers.

> —Archibald Cary Coolidge

That Golder, that Golder, I find his traces
all over the world.

> —Mr. Henry, a collector for the
> New York Public Library

I am living through a tremendously interesting
period, which I am just beginning to understand
a bit.

> —Frank Golder

Chapter I

The Beginning: Among the Aleuts

Frank Alfred Golder was born on 11 April 1877 in Odessa, a Ukrainian port city on the Black Sea. The Ukraine, under Tsarist Russia's control, had a high Jewish population at the time of Golder's birth. Many of these Jews lived amid poverty in specially designated areas, and suffered from anti–Jewish pogroms, or organized violence against Jews by the local population, a situation which was tolerated and even instigated by the police. The first major pogrom in the Russian Empire occurred in Odessa in 1871. Frank's parents, of German origin, sought an avenue to escape such cruel persecution, and, like thousands of Jews, immigrated to the United States in 1885, taking a long, unhealthy, and hazardous voyage to the country they believed offered tolerance, opportunity, and freedom. The family of three survived the voyage, and settled down at Bridgeton, New Jersey, a city swarming with immigrants from the Old World. Frank's father, a Talmudic scholar who occasionally suffered from attacks of asthma, found steady employment at any work a continual hardship in this competitive environment. The resultant lack of income forced Frank, at a tender age, to participate in helping his family by selling miscellaneous wares on the crowded, noisy Bridgeton streets.[1]

One day, Richard Minch, a Baptist minister, came across this youngster on the street, and his determination to assist his parents impressed Minch. He decided to aid the family with a modest financial contribution so that Frank could attend elementary school. Thus, Frank entered an insular world of learning instead of being involved with a tumultuous one on the street. The family stayed in Bridgeton for several years, and then moved on, trying their fortunes at Vineland, New Jersey. There Jewish immigrants had been buying inexpensive farmland. Frank's parents bought a few acres of farmland, although they had no previous experience with farming. After moving to Vineland, the father struggled to cultivate the farmland in spite of his asthma, and the mother, Minnie, a salty, jovial, and strong–willed woman, raised a family that had an additional two sons and four daughters.[2]

From the outset, the Golder family's experiment with farming proved to be a disastrous one because of the soil's insufficient richness. The family's supply of food dropped so low at times that sympathetic neighbors had to give them butter, bread, and milk. Despite the hard circumstances, Frank managed to go to school, and at the age of sixteen he qualified for admission to Georgetown College, a preparatory school in Kentucky. How Frank's parents paid for his education at a private school is a mystery, but Reverend Minch, who had attended the same school, may have provided the money. Frank left for Kentucky in 1893, and his departure constituted his first separation from parental control. His parents, highly valuing education, viewed the separation as a necessity rather than as a joyless occasion. That same year, 1893, Frank's parents faced new challenges themselves. They abandoned their farming adventure and moved to a city environment, Philadelphia, which had a large Jewish community, and they lived there the rest of their lives in humble surroundings.[3]

Frank graduated from Georgetown College in 1896. From Kentucky, he moved to Lewisburg, Pennsylvania and entered Bucknell University. He took a variety of courses in the sciences and the humanities, earning a high scholastic average. Although he did well in every subject, Frank showed a preference for history and literature. In his leisurely hours, he read widely in literature with a voracious appetite, feeding his fanciful and imaginative mind.[4]

After Frank received his degree in 1898, a two year program which qualified him to teach, he traveled to Philadelphia and stayed with his parents. He could have taught school in Philadelphia, but the restless graduate had different ideas, wishing to experiment with an unconventional way of life. He had a revulsion for the city of Philadelphia—its crowded streets, its profusion of buildings, and its smoky factories, and therefore sought a life in the wilderness, close to nature. He had read with enthusiasm such authors as Jean–Jacques Rousseau and James Fenimore Cooper, whose romanticization of nature strongly appealed to him. Frank thought that the teeming wilderness of Alaska would satisfy his conception of nature, and, in July 1899, he applied for a teaching position there through the Department of the Interior. The following month, Frank received a letter from William Hamilton, the Assistant Agent for Alaska Education, who offered him a teaching assignment at Unga Island. The news brought the romantic twenty–two–year old Frank Golder immense joy.[5]

Golder thus became a participant in America's version of Kipling's "White Man's Burden." In 1867, the United States government had purchased Alaska from Russia, a transaction which brought about the closing of a number of schools run by the Russian or Eastern Orthodox Church and Russian trading companies. For years, the United States government neglected the region. In 1884, Congress passed a bill directing the Secretary of the Interior to provide education for Alaskan children. The Secretary entrusted this task to Sheldon Jackson, a deeply religious man, who had campaigned in the 1870s and 80s for the introduction of law, religion, and education to Alaska. Jackson became the General Agent for Education in 1889, and opened up a number of schools in the vast region in order to bring American culture to the Alaskan natives, with the primary purpose of teaching them the English language so that they would be useful to Americans in Alaska who were involved in mining, transportation, and the production of food.[6]

Golder had no awareness of the realities involved in teaching in Alaska. When he applied for the teaching job, Hamilton, the Assistant Agent for Alaska Education, failed to give the young applicant an accurate picture of what life was like for an American teacher in Alaska. Hamilton wrote Golder:

> Unga is an attractive village in Western Alaska. It has at least one general store, possibly more. There is monthly mail the year around, and the climate is not vigorous. The salary would be $100 per month for the nine months of the term; there is a building in Unga that the teacher can occupy free of rent.[7]

In fact, because of the adverse conditions in Alaska, there was a high turnover of teachers. Glen Smith writes, "Salaries were low and the risks, both physical and psychological, were great. Several teachers died in Alaska either of accidents, disease, or occasionally at the hands of irate natives."[8]

The trip to Unga Island involved traveling almost 5,000 miles. Anxious to begin his trip, Golder boarded the train in August 1899 at Philadelphia and traveled across the plains and over the mountain ranges of the North American continent to Seattle, Washington. At Seattle, the gateway for traveling by sea to the settlements, villages, and towns of Alaska, he embarked on the steamer, *City of Topeka*, for a nine day voyage to Sitka, a large island. Along the way, he experienced glass–like seas and the irreplaceable beauty of sculptured glacial horizons. At Sitka, he transferred to the *Excelsior*, the mail steamer which sailed west as far as Bristol Bay in the Bering Sea.

During the following eight days, the steamer traveled along the lengthy, curving Aleutian Island chain that stretched out into the Pacific Ocean. Golder found this part of the trip unpleasant; several days of stormy weather forced him to stay in his cabin. When the *Excelsior* approached Unga Island, the continuing stormy weather prevented the Captain from docking at the dangerously exposed harbor at Unga Village. After blowing the steamer's whistle three times, the Captain steered the ship to Squaw Harbor, a few miles from Unga Village and a less perilous landing site. The Captain, after his ship had arrived at Squaw Harbor, observed that Golder seemed to be depressed and, hoping to cheer him, explained that he had blown the whistle to attract someone to guide him safely to Unga Village. The Captain's reassurance, while providing Golder with some comfort at first, faded before long as he waited in the heavy rain for two almost unbearable hours without sighting anyone on shore. Finally, he spotted a hazy figure on shore struggling against the wind, a sight which brought him instant relief.

Several crew members rowed Golder to the shoreline, and the stranger waded into the sea to assist in pulling the unsteady boat ashore. After leaving the boat, Golder greeted this welcomed stranger, a rough–looking Caucasian dressed appropriately in hip–high boots and oil skins. This stranger, who identified himself as Pete Nelson, no doubt came close to chuckling as he sized up Golder's appearance: a young man wearing city clothing—a suit and dress shoes. The two men then proceeded in the direction of Unga Village, by way of the Apollo Gold Mine, and Golder had trouble staying astride Nelson as they marched over hills of thick mud. After they arrived at Nelson's residence, a room in the rear of a saloon, which belonged to Nelson, he took pity on the inexperienced newcomer and hung his soaked clothes to dry, fixed him a meal, and provided him with a warm bed. Golder thoroughly appreciated Nelson's hospitality that first night, but he changed his attitude toward Nelson the following day. Golder, extremely moralistic in his youth, wrote:

> Deep runs influences of early prejudice, for when later in the day I discovered that Pete Nelson was the saloon keeper of the village and that I had spent the night in the back room of the saloon, I felt, in spite of myself, quite angry with him. . . . He must have caught the change of my attitude, because when I announced that I would move into the government quarters provided me, he did not pressure me to stay longer with him as he had done earlier.[9]

That day, Golder moved into his new home, a separate room in the government schoolhouse. This schoolhouse, located on a slope, overlooked a cemetery, underground sod huts that dotted a creek, and white wooden structures. After moving in, Golder began to acquaint himself with his new, unfamiliar world. Unga had a polyglot popula-

A View of Unga

tion of Aleuts, Russians, Americans, and Creoles—persons of mixed Russian and native blood. The native Aleuts fascinated Golder in particular since they reminded him of the Indians in Cooper's fiction. In Golder's view, the Aleuts were self-sufficient, living off sea life; they were in harmony with nature, understanding the behavior of the sea, the geography of the land, and the climate of the island; they were unassuming, spoke an unembellished language, and acted with kindness and generosity. Because of these initial impressions, Golder jotted down in a notebook that he had "found what the eighteenth century philosophers dreamed of." [10]

During the tranquil summer weather of early September, Golder adapted with relative ease to his island environment. He tapped the seemingly unlimited supply of fish and game as he fished in the streams and shot ducks around the lakes. He plucked the fowl and cleaned and scaled the fish for the meals that he cooked for himself. His new independence from materialism, superficial values, and a congested city existence gave him moments of intense joy. Golder believed he had attained his ideal of living in harmony with nature. [11]

Soon, though, Golder's idyllic impressions of his life on Unga Island began to slip away. He wrote, "I did not leave civilization in a huff; I had not cut off all tender ties behind me; I still look forward with pleasure for letters." [12] He expected the mail ship, *Golden Gate*, to arrive at the harbor sometime around the 20th of October. At first, he did not attach too much concern over the ship's arrival, but when it failed to appear by the 25th he became disconcerted. Almost daily thereafter, Golder would trudge up a mountain top with a sweeping view of the ocean opening up before him and scan the sea for the *Golden Gate*. But the ship would always fail to appear. After the sun sank below the horizon, he would wearily plod down the mountain and in despair follow the glimmering, yellow oil lamps to the village.

While Golder waited for the mail ship, he had started teaching the village's children at the schoolhouse. Before long he developed his share of complaints about standardized teaching methods. Even though he taught the children at Unga rudimentary math, English, history, and geography and made considerable progress in teaching these subjects, offering prizes to the best students, Golder criticized the Bureau of Education for its lack of awareness in understanding the different cultural and social experiences between American children and children raised in Alaska. He saw no advantage in the learning process if one took the teaching methods of another culture and superimposed them over a foreign one. For example, Golder found the study of U. S. history, based on ideals and lofty principles, completely alien to an Alaskan culture that stressed admiration of heroic deeds. He stated in a report,

> History is . . . a difficult subject to the class, since much of the subject matter is unfamiliar and almost beyond their imagination. The textbooks are far from satisfactory for these pupils.[13]

As a result, Golder had to teach history in terms of heroic deeds, telling the students about "some feat of strength or daring" of Daniel Boone, Andrew Jackson, Abraham Lincoln, and George Washington.

Soon after Golder began teaching, the community added to his work load many extra duties, a circumstance which especially applied to teachers in Alaska. The natives, illiterate for the most part and without the normal services provided for in a modern society, expected Golder to perform such services as sanitation officer, lawyer, social worker, post office employee, physician,[14] and minister. He performed these extra assignments without complaint in order to help the village, although he was not paid for this work.

Golder's public functions started in a curious manner. One day a Creole boy stopped him in the schoolyard before the opening of class. The boy said to Golder, "I can't come to school today. My father is dead." The boy, he noted, showed the emotion of pride rather than sorrow, as if he had proudly witnessed the killing of a long–elusive bear. Golder dismissed the boy, but the memory of his behavior lingered in Golder's mind. He opened the schoolhouse and completed the morning instruction, and in the afternoon, the boy's older sister handed him a letter she had written to her uncle in Nova Scotia and asked him to correct any mistakes. He perused the note, "Dear Uncle, we had an accident last night. Father died." The word "accident" further picqued Golder's curiosity.

After closing school that day, Golder paid the family a respectful visit. What he saw astonished him. The family had placed the corpse in the house but no one revealed any expression of loss. He investigated further, trying to find out why the family acted as if nothing had happened to them. As Golder looked around "[he] was greatly shocked to find an Aleut whose relations with the dead man's wife were of very dishonorable nature calmly making the coffin and acting as chief mourner."[15] Golder assumed that this Aleut had murdered the dead man, but, since the authorities lacked any proof, nothing could be done. Golder left this scene in a bewildered state of mind.

The following day, several of the community's members asked Golder to conduct a burial service for the dead Aleut. Although he had misgivings, he agreed to do so. Thus began Golder's public community service. At the grave site, he delivered a funeral oration. After his final words died away, the deceased Aleut's family and relatives released a flood of emotions and wailed profusely. This heavy display of emotion, a native social custom, personally touched Golder, even though he still harbored suspicions regarding the nature of the Aleut's death.[16]

As Golder's romantic perceptions of Alaska were challenged by firsthand experience, he finally received a number of letters after the mail ship arrived at the harbor on 4 November. These letters consoled him for a few weeks. Then, around the 24th of November, the first snow of winter settled on the terrain.[17] Pete Nelson had warned Golder about the psychological hardships of loneliness during the winter season. As winter unfolded this year, Golder kept busy to counter the depression brought on by the howling wind (sometimes he had to crawl to get anywhere), the bitter cold, and especially the long dark days. Besides teaching, he consumed in leisurely moments a wide variety of literature, such authors as Dickens, Emerson, and Wordsworth, in order to satisfy his intellectual curiosity as well as distract himself. He also visited friends,[18] played cards, attended dances and masquerade parties, developed photographs, and wrote scores of letters. On top of these activities, he worked in the post office, conducted burials, doctored the sick, and acted as counselor. And yet, in spite of all these distractions, Golder's environment conspired to drive him into a profound depression. Loneliness and gloom, or as he euphemistically called his unpleasant companion, "old Harry," harassed him day and night.[19]

Golder waited with intense impatience for the arrival of springtime. When spring finally did arrive, he noted with particular relief that the sun appeared more frequently, that the icy, powerful winds subsided, and that heather covered the terrain where the snow had melted away. In late April, Golder wrote in his diary how enthusiastically he embraced the refreshing seasonal change:

> Was up at 9 a.m. Went for a long walk to the lake and then to the marsh. There the scenery was grand. A beautiful and musical waterfall greeted me. On each side were snow covered mountains. The brook on its way to join the sea sang very sweetly. I was overjoyed by the whole scene. I sang, I jumped, unconscious of what I was doing.[20]

With the arrival of springtime, Golder forgot his mental anguish, as if a thick veneer clouded over a horrible dream. The pleasures of spring and summer, filled with hunting, fishing, and gathering wild berries, living in peaceful relaxation and contemplation, compelled him to stay another year as a teacher in Alaska. Had he deceived himself again?

That September, Golder opened the schoolhouse doors to twenty–four students. He wrote in his diary, "Felt happy to be at work again."[21] A few days later, a measle epidemic broke out and forced him to close the schoolhouse because of so many sick children. The measle epidemic soon covered the village's life with a torpor. During the epidemic, he called on the village's stricken members and did what he could to relieve their symptoms. This epidemic, dangerous to an unexposed aboriginal, also gave him a reason for sober reflection. He wondered why he had elected to stay in Alaska, so near the proximity of death. He wrote in his diary on 22 September, "Makes me feel as if I wanted to get away from here."[22] By 1 October, the epidemic subsided enough so that children reappeared at the schoolhouse. That day, Golder wrote, "Feel much better by being occupied."[23]

Then, the beginning of winter made Golder again acutely aware of his vulnerability in Alaska's harsh environment. As a result, he accelerated the tempo of his activities as he had done the previous winter, trying to insulate himself against too much self–destructive isolation. He even held school sessions on Saturdays to prevent his isolation and to shield the children from crude behavior in the village.

Somehow, Golder managed to endure this winter, too, and in May 1901, he traveled to Belkovsky on the peninsula where he had planned to teach summer school. After being there only one week, he found himself besieged with an urgent request. The village Chief and a few other natives told him that they had learned from a trader that a trapper named Tom Williams had died and lay unburied at Thin Point, a remote, deserted area. The trader had not buried Williams because stormy weather had forced him to leave, and the Chief feared that if he and other villagers buried Williams, white authorities might accuse them of having murdered Williams. The Chief urged Golder to supervise an expedition to bury Williams. Before making a decision, Golder inquired about Williams from a few natives, and they informed him that Williams had been a civil war veteran, had drifted west full of dissatisfaction with himself and civilization, had made a living in Alaska as a hunter, and had been a heavy drinker. They said that Williams had had two partners, whose sudden disappearance led them to believe that Williams had murdered them. As a consequence, the community had avoided Williams, and this ostracizing behavior had compelled him to live alone at Thin Point, where he had trapped animals. After gathering this information, Golder hedged over taking the trip to a desolate area and finding a body, dead for several days, of a man whose reputation had been so tainted with controversy.

Golder tried to persuade the only permanent white resident in the village, a fisherman, to undertake the expedition, but he refused to go. The Chief now strongly urged Golder to make the trip and offered him the use of a kayak and two Aleut guides to paddle him to Thin Point. Golder, who had never ventured anywhere in a kayak, appeared to have no choice. He agreed to go. Then the fisherman, hearing of Golder's decision, sympathized with him, and volunteered to go along, offering his sailing boat for the voyage.

During the boat trip, Golder suffered from seasickness most of the way and arrived at Thin Point with relief, momentarily. When the burial party located Williams' hut, it was half underground and had one small window. Golder wrote, "I shall never forget the ghostly sight that struck us as we entered. He had turned black and his glassy eyes stared at us."[24] Golder looked around for a piece of writing which Williams might have left behind to explain what had happened. Golder found none. The calendar clock that hung on the wall indicated that it had stopped on the 26th, but one could not determine if this was the 26th of February, March, or April. He found flour, sugar, and tea in the hut, but no evidence of cooking. There was no water. At first, he thought that Williams had died of starvation, having been too sick to feed himself. After searching his bunk, Golder then discovered a half loaf of bread and a mug with Williams' hand around it. And he lay there with all his clothes on. The circumstances surrounding Williams' death continued to baffle Golder. This mysterious death, as well as Williams' decomposing body and the forsaken area, nauseated him. Golder could hardly wait until the party buried Williams.

Soon, the party dug a grave in the sand pit close to the hut. After burying Williams, Golder repeated a few memorized references from the Bible and had the Aleuts sing some of their funeral songs.

The funeral ended at twilight. Even with Williams underground, Golder felt an overwhelming depression. He wrote:

> To shake off the depression . . . I climbed one of the ridges only to behold cold, bleak, gloomy, lonely snow covered mountains. I don't believe that I fear death more than the average run of people, but somehow after the charm of the wilderness had worn off I would catch myself praying, "Good God, I am willing to work here but don't let me die here, it is so cold, gloomy, lonely and away from everybody." And as I stood up there in that cold solitude this feeling came over me with such force that I almost cried out.[25]

Golder then returned to the camp, close to Williams' hut, where

he found supper ready and tents and sleeping gear set up for the
night. Before long everyone in the camp had fallen asleep, except
Golder, who dwelled restlessly on the unnerving day as he listened to
the nighttime sounds—the repercussions of sea–breakers, the howling
of wind, and the barking of foxes. To divert his mind, he lit a candle
in his tent and began reading a book by Robert Louis Stevenson, *The
Merry Men*, which he had hurriedly snatched before leaving. Golder
read until he came to a paragraph that made him shudder:

> Here was a grave . . . what manner of man lay there? I
> knew . . . his imperishable soul was . . . far away among
> the raptures of the everlasting Sabbath or the pangs of hell;
> and yet my mind misgave me . . . with a fear, that perhaps
> he was near . . . guarding his sepulcher and lingering on
> the scene of his unhappy fate.[26]

Golder wondered, "Why of all the books in the world, I should have
brought this one to read under such weird circumstances is one of the
mysteries which I cannot explain."[27]

The party had breakfast early the following morning. Then the
fisherman and the two Aleuts climbed to a neighboring hill to observe
the sea's condition for sailing. The sea appeared to be too rough to
the fisherman. When he returned to the camp, the fisherman tried to
discourage Golder from crossing the turbulent bay. Golder consulted
one of the Aleuts, and this Aleut anticipated a safe crossing in the
kayak that he had brought on the fisherman's sailboat, in spite of
the fiercely blowing wind. The fisherman advised against taking the
risk. But Golder, preferring intuitive rather than rational reasoning,
trusted the Aleut's judgment. The fact that the memory of Williams'
burial still lingered in Golder's mind also weighed substantially in his
decision to reject the fisherman's advice.

Before embarking, the Aleuts carefully examined the kayak for
holes and then ballasted it with rocks. Golder and the Aleuts then
put on waterproof jackets and twisted themselves into the three man-
holes. Golder sat between the two Aleuts, his legs stretched out in
the hull. He now observed his seemingly precarious situation: the
kayak, 18 inches in width, had only an inch or two of freeboard because of the weight of three people, the guns tied to the kayak, and
the ballasting, and if the kayak capsized, placing one under water, he
believed he would not be able to extricate himself from the manhole's
tight squeeze.[28]

As soon as the sailing party launched themselves to cross the bay,
the excitement grew intensely, with the Aleut sitting aft watching
for a big wave to come along. After finding one, he would issue a

command so that the two Aleuts could swiftly paddle in order to set the kayak on the wave's crest and ride it out. While riding these waves, the Aleuts had to be constantly on the lookout for waves that might upset the kayak. But, as Golder wrote, "To know the Aleut at his best one must see him handle his boat in rough weather under unfavorable circumstances."[29] Repeatedly, the one Aleut shouted to his partner to brake water in order to avoid running into a high wave about to collapse. Golder wrote:

> The sea, however, was so bad that in spite of all [the Aleuts] could do we were often caught and literally buried under the water for a second, but so skillful was the boat handled that it did us no harm. One moment we were on top of a wave, a second later we looked up to waves 20 to 30 feet above us. The excitement was so intense that I don't believe I even thought [of the danger].[30]

After struggling four hours to cross the bay, the two Aleuts received a respite when the wind died down, and they glided easily toward Belkovsky.

After the haunting Williams' experience and the wild sea ride, Golder returned to the less exciting world of teaching summer school at Belkovsky. Perhaps this peaceful setting again induced Golder to stay for still another year of teaching in Alaska. However, Golder's request in a letter to Hamilton that he would prefer to teach on Kodiak Island revealed his unhappiness with Unga Island. In contrast to Unga Island, Kodiak, a teeming commercial center, had a cultural life, contact with the outside world, and a less rigorous climate. With disappointment, Golder learned in a letter from Hamilton that another instructor had been appointed to teach at Kodiak Island.[31]

Toward summer's end, Golder returned to Unga Village, and began his regular teaching assignments. At the same time, he became deeply disturbed by the rise of murder, rape, and fights at Unga, for which he chiefly blamed Caucasian traders who took advantage of the defenseless natives, after no one had replaced the marshall, L. L. Bowers, who had quit that summer without informing the proper authorities. Moreover, the U. S. Commissioner for the Shumagin Islands, of which Unga was one, had resigned from his office. That October 1901, Golder complained to the governor of Alaska, John Brady, "There are two saloons here and many degraded white men, and their doings, at times, are both shameful and criminal. Several natives have recently died under circumstances that should have been investigated."[32] Golder's letters to John Brady, the governor of Alaska, as well as to Sheldon Jackson and to a judge, M. C. Brown, describing the lack of authority on Unga Island and the upsurge of violence, failed to bring about any new appointments. They could not find someone competent, trustworthy, and willing to accept the low pay. Finally, in April 1902, Golder received the august, if unenviable appointment, of U. S. Commissioner for the Shumagin Islands.[33]

In a familiar way, too, Golder had trouble coping with his environment. He suffered more from that winter's isolation than from the previous two. He wrote:

> It is not the cold, the lack of fresh fruit and vegetables or overwork that the white men scattered in the isolated parts of Alaska suffer, but the long dark nights, gloomy sunless days, and the indescribable loneliness which drives one almost to despair.[34]

He recalled that during the first winter he had read with great delight the works of Tennyson, Wordsworth, Emerson, and other poets. During the second winter, he became so depressed that he locked up his books because the sight of them became so distasteful to him. The contemplative life lost all meaning for Golder, and his values deteriorated to the point where he "craved for the morbid and wicked." In retrospect, he wondered why he had not lost his mind. Toward the third winter's end, he became afraid of himself and often reviewed his acts of the previous few days to determine if they were rational. Sometimes a whole week would go by, and he would have contact with no one except the children. Still worse, he dreaded meeting anyone and when he did see someone coming, he felt extremely uncomfortable. He would have sought company in order to end his loneliness and resultant paranoia, but the Caucasian hunters and fishermen who made up the white population often boasted about sexual conquests, which only heightened his loneliness. Golder wrote:

> Above all I hated myself. Those long winter nights when I could neither read nor sleep were nights of hellish torture. All the mean things that I ever did in my life loomed up like big mountains, and my diseased brain punished me until I dropped asleep from mere exhaustion only to wake up in a horrible nightmare.[35]

After Golder departed Unga Island, he wondered what had maintained his sanity. He then thought the extra duties the community had asked him to fulfill had been his salvation. They had given him fleeting moments of escape.

The Schoolhouse at Unga

At times, though, Golder's extra duties only reminded him of his cruel environment. He had a good friend, Daniel Walpert, a native of Germany, who had immigrated to the United States, settling in Iowa. The thought of making a fortune had lured Walpert to the vast wilderness of Alaska. Golder wrote, "Some of the saddest sights in Alaska are the hundreds of men who having left home, love, and good positions come to Alaska in search of gold."[36] He stated that few miners actually discovered gold; while many of them returned home wiser men, some of them were too proud to leave and remained in Alaska, sinking into a rut of dissipation and sloth. But a few who stayed led righteous lives, and "some when on the verge of realizing their hopes [found] sudden death."[37] Walpert belonged to this third category.

Walpert had endured many hardships after his arrival in Alaska before finally staking a promising claim in Nome in the summer of 1901. During the winter months, he could not work his claim because of the heavy snowfall, and consequently had traveled to Unga Island for employment at the Apollo Gold Mine. After Golder met Walpert, he compared the miner to himself; the saloon had no attraction to Walpert; he lived a quiet, unassuming life; and he always helped out in a crisis. That winter at Unga, Walpert was saving his money in order to invest it in his mine at Nome, where he planned to return in May.

One April night, as miners lowered Walpert and two other miners down the mine shaft, a piece of ice dislodged the elevator and Walpert fell to his death. Just moments before the accident one miner had stepped off the elevator. The mine's physician, having traveled to San Francisco on an urgent call, had left Golder in charge of medical emergencies. Miners summoned Golder to the mine, where he sadly found out that Walpert had been killed in a mine accident.

The following day, Golder, as the new U. S. Commissioner and ex–officio coroner, held an inquest and discovered that Walpert had lived in Cedar Rapids, Iowa. He wrote to this town inquiring about Walpert, and received several letters. One of them read:

> I am very sorry to hear of the sad news about Daniel Walpert's death. I wrote a letter to him one year ago addressed to Nome City, Alaska, but don't know if he had received it. There may have been a mistake. I didn't get his letter. If Choly Chifman is there, then perhaps he would know it and something about Walpert as they were together at a time, so I was told. I would ask some more questions but am not able for sorrowfulness of the loos [sic] of my faithful Daniel. I am his girl . . .[38]

Golder wrote:

> Both of them were good, hard working, honest, true Germans. He went to Alaska to make a fortune in order to prepare a home for her; in the meantime, she was working as a servant girl, waiting patiently . . . for Daniel, who alas, she was never to see again in this world.[39]

Such a tragic death perhaps reminded Golder of what fate might be his if he stayed longer in Alaska.

Golder's public functions, however, did provide him with humorous experiences. He recalled with amusement the first couple he united in marriage. One day a squaw, Mary Guscov, who had a discredited moral reputation and had been married three times, visited Golder, and complained that her common–law–husband, John Caton, who had an equally disreputable past, had been beating her. Golder sent for Caton; when he visited Golder, he denied the charges and offered counter ones. Golder wrote:

> They perhaps did not realize how helpless I was to punish either of them, for as U. S. Commissioner, according to law, I had any amount of power, but in fact I had neither jail, marshal, nor any other means of enforcing the law which Congress had made without making equal provision for its enforcement.[40]

As an alternative, Golder suggested to the acrimonious couple that they might live with less turmoil together if they married each other. Caton said that the suggestion was all right with him, but Guscov refused to go along. Golder gave Guscov twenty–four hours to make up her mind. Two days later, she told him that she was willing to marry Caton. Golder wrote, "I really hoped that perhaps by legalizing the already existing union marriage would have some good influence on their lives, for the other men might respect their marriage."[41] The next day, Caton straggled into the schoolhouse with his hands in his pockets "as if it was a daily occupation of his." Guscov wandered in a few minutes later. Golder, in the presence of three witnesses, placed the couple side by side. When he administered the wedding vows, the couple replied in a matter–of–factly tone. Then Golder attempted to impress the couple with the sacredness and seriousness of the binding occasion. But Golder's subsequent experience with the couple proved him wrong. He wrote, "[I did not succeed because] marriage to [them] was like changing one coat for another."[42]

Finally, in the summer of 1902, Golder decided to return to the "moral and spiritual" values of civilization. Before he departed from Alaska, he reached what he jokingly referred to as "the highest point of my varied public career—I made a Fourth of July speech."[42] He was teaching summer school at Belkovsky. No one in the village could understand English but nearly everyone understood Russian as a result of Russian expansion in Alaska. The villagers, though, did know that the *Amerikansky* celebrated the Fourth of July, and Golder thought that the village should celebrate the occasion. He filled a bucket with candy, and drilled the children in singing "America" and Christmas and nursery songs which they had learned the previous year. He then announced to the village that the children would sing on the fourth and that he would give a Fourth of July speech. In the meantime, he distributed small American flags to the villagers.

When Golder looked out the window at 7 a.m. on the Fourth of July, he saw flags over many of the native homes and the whole village seated on a hillock near a creek, waiting for him to open the school. He opened the school an hour early, and the children came running to Golder with bunches of wild flowers, their way of greeting him every day before school. Golder gave the children soap, towels, and combs, and they all went down to the creek to wash. He wrote, "The children would wash and comb each other, and did their best to make their old rags look as respectable as possible."[43] They then assembled in the schoolhouse. While the children sang their well-rehearsed songs, the villagers stood outside the schoolhouse, listening attentively.

After the children finished singing, Golder gave them candy and flags, and, as he wrote, "they were truly happy as happy can be."[44] The men then filed into the schoolhouse, and Golder spoke of the American purchase of Alaska from Russia in 1867, of how America now ruled Alaska, and of the fact they were all Americans. He spoke slowly, in the simplest Russian, and noted their perfect attention; his heart swelled with pride over his oratorical gifts. Golder's speech lasted for about a quarter of an hour and then he announced that they could go. No one moved as they sat as quiet and as motionless as statues for several minutes. Golder became confused, and dismissed them again, but they would not leave. Finally, the village's Chief came to his rescue, saying that the villagers were waiting for candy. Golder wrote, "My pride had a terrible fall."[45]

At the end of the summer, Golder prepared to leave Alaska. At this time, he took stock of his experience there. He extolled the summer days when "the winter seemed like a forgotten nightmare and the mind was as pure as air."[46] Furthermore, the Aleuts as well as Caucasians had shown consideration toward him on many occasions. A few days before his departure, several hunters embarked on a hunting expedition for venison and trout so that he would have provisions to take with him. On the day of his departure, villagers interrupted their daily work in order to see Golder off. He wrote:

> I believe they really felt sorry to see me go. To some the
> Aleuts may be "dirty" but to one who has come in daily
> contact with them during three years . . . I learned to love
> them and I try to think that three years was not too high a
> price to pay for that.[47]

Chapter II

From Harvard to Russia

Golder traveled back to Philadelphia in August 1902, after a three year absence. He received an emotional welcome by his family, and moved in with his parents, brothers, and sisters, who treated him like a celebrity because of his unusual Alaskan adventure. Golder found the household atmosphere exhilarating, and he thrived with contentment on his mother's home cooked meals, the warm conversation with his parents, and the playful bantering with his younger brothers and sisters. To Golder, civilization seemed precious now.

During his stay in Philadelphia, Golder also had to consider his future. He had carefully saved his money while teaching in Alaska, where he had lived rent free and had often supplied his own food. Before his departure from Alaska, he had applied to graduate school at Harvard University. In Philadelphia, he learned that Harvard's history department had accepted his application, and he decided to undertake the new challenge, a challenge which offered him opportunities his still financially deprived parents had never known.[1]

After a brief stay with his parents, Golder, in September 1902, moved to Cambridge, Massachusetts so that he could begin his studies. His Alaskan experience, fresh in his mind, influenced him to choose history as his field of specialization. Despite Golder's troubled experience in Alaska, his contact with the Land of the Midnight Sun inspired him to seek knowledge of foreign lands, their cultures and peoples.[2] His interest in Alaska, his fluency in Russian, and his parent's European background drew him to study European and American history. He now embarked on a Master's Degree in history, while remaining uncertain about what career he would pursue after graduation.

In 1903, Golder, while still a student, was offered the position of superintendent of Alaska reindeer stations by Sheldon Jackson, the General Agent for Education in Alaska. These stations supervised the reindeer herds which Jackson had introduced from Siberia to Alaska on the premise that they would improve Alaska's economy. Golder would be involved in traveling over magnificent wilderness from one reindeer station to another inspecting the herds. Golder, although lured by the offer, wrote Jackson that he would take the position for only one year and after he finished his M.A. Jackson did not hire Golder, wanting someone to fill the position on a permanent basis.[3]

Golder went on to finish his M.A. program in one year. The experience proved to be intellectually rewarding, so much so that he decided to enter the Ph.D. program in history at Harvard. He thus headed in a direction that would preoccupy him for the rest of his life—studying history, teaching, and traveling. Beginning the Ph.D. program in 1903, he undertook the study of modern Russian history, general European history, and American history. Golder's experience in Alaska and his knowledge of Russian influenced him to complete a dissertation on Russian expansion in the Pacific, a study which involved Vitus Bering's voyages of exploration during the age of Peter the Great. Fortunately for Golder, he studied with two leading historians: Edward Channing, who wrote an authoritative, multi-volume history of the United States, and, more importantly, Archibald Cary Coolidge, who had developed the first academic courses on Russian history in the United States.[4]

During the first year in the program, Golder took a full load of courses which gave him a deeper understanding of European and American history.[5] The following year, 1904, he traveled to Paris for research, language study, and sightseeing. He settled down in an inexpensive, small hotel in the Latin Quarter, and, before long, Paris greatly appealed to his intellectual appetite. Throughout the year, he studied French at the University of Paris, becoming fluent in the language. He also began researching the Paris archives for primary source materials regarding his dissertation; he spent many hours at the Archive de la Marine, looking at the Delisle manuscripts of letters, copies of journals, charts, reports of conversations, newspaper clippings, and other materials that shed light on Russian expansion in the Pacific in the seventeenth and eighteenth centuries and on such adventurers as Vitus Bering.

During his stay in Paris, Golder also absorbed Paris' two major cultural institutions: the theater and the opera. He wrote in an article regarding Paris, "to the Parisians these institutions are not luxuries but necessities,"[6] a view which he retained as his lifelong philosophy of culture. He saw the famous actress Sarah Bernhardt and classical plays at the *Comedie Francqise* and listened to such classic operas as Faust at the Opera House. Golder recalled, "while watching these artistic performances there came fleeting moments when the soul gets a glimpse of a higher, beautiful, and spiritual world of which I had no conception before."[7]

The city of Paris became special to Golder in another way, too.

He thoroughly admired the Parisians' child–like playfulness.[8] To illustrate this point, he remembered an incident which occurred one evening as he was walking to the Pantheon, a church in Paris. He suddenly saw men and women rush out from alleys and onto sidewalks, carrying boxes, papers, and straw. They threw this debris into a pile in the street, ignited this combustible pile into a bonfire, and danced and sang around the flames. Golder joined this lively frolicking, which, he admitted, had been designed not only to have fun but also to tease the police. As expected, the police appeared to investigate the fire, and everyone, including Golder, scattered gleefully down side streets. He wrote, "How could anyone, even a cold–blooded Anglo–Saxon, resist this gay spirit."[9]

After staying a happy academic year in Paris, Golder spent the summer in Berlin. He studied German at the University of Berlin, and gained fluency in this language. At summer's end, he returned to the United States with many memorable experiences, a knowledge of French and German, and bundles of information from the Delisle manuscripts. He also returned almost penniless, in need of a job to save money for another research trip to Europe. To meet his financial goals, he accepted a teaching appointment at Arizona State Teacher's College at Tempe, Arizona,[10] arriving at this desert community in September 1906. That year, he taught classes on American history, ancient, medieval, and modern European history, as well as political science, and earned $1,100 for the year, not an inadequate salary for those times.

While at Tempe the campus newspaper wrote about Golder: "It is agreed by all that in his quiet, unobtrusive manner Mr. Golder worked his way into our school and before we realized it he had established himself as a powerful influence."[11] He started the campus's first student newspaper, the *Tempe Normal Student*, and his efficient business management and guidance of a handful of student journalists turned the paper into a success. He also took charge of the Tennis Club, which suffered from insufficient funds, and he inspired the Club with new life; the tennis team became solvent after a number of profitable tournaments. Furthermore, Golder, an amateur anthropologist who had collected folklore tales while in Alaska,[12] established the American Folklore Society's Arizona branch, which collected the folklore of indigenous Indians in Arizona before their priceless oral history vanished forever.

Golder's energy and intelligence, as well as his affable, congenial, and understanding personality accounts for his successful undertakings at Tempe. Most students that he came in contact with respected and admired him. One time, though, Golder found himself the victim of a student revolt. As a teacher, he proved to be very demanding. In his American history course, for example, he required his students to recite every week, outline chapters in the textbook, read the daily newspaper and primary current events magazine, *Outlook*, fill in an atlas, write essays, and complete research projects. Not unexpectedly, his students complained of the heavy workload. But he had no idea that they would try to bring action against him. In a memorandum to the Board of Directors, an entire class signed this document:

> We have become so overburdened with his work that we find it necessary to ask the Board to take some action toward compelling [Mr. Golder] to lighten it . . . because they have kept us bent and cramped over a study table when we should be taking some outdoor exercises. We . . . have not taken this action with any ill feeling toward Mr. Golder, for we personally like him . . . , but we do think the work and time required by him to be spent unreasonable and unjust.[13]

The Board voted not to take any action against Golder. The campus newspaper wrote, "to come up to the high standards as set by him required unusual time and effort and some were unable to reach it."[14]

After saving a portion of his salary, Golder resigned from Arizona State in the spring of 1907. During the summer, the adventuresome young man rode on horseback all over the Arizona desert and visited the Hopi Indian tribe. Then, that fall, he returned to Paris. At Paris, he went as often as possible to the *Bibliotheque Nationale*, the equivalent of the Library of Congress in Washington, D. C., gleaning information for his dissertation from rare books and especially from a rich collection of maps. He also enrolled at the University of Paris in order to expand his historical knowledge and devoted a full academic year to studying a variety of history courses. The combination of research and academic study kept him extremely busy.

When Golder ended his course of study at Paris, he moved on to Berlin for further dissertation research. He also wished to travel to St. Petersburg, Russia's capital, Moscow, and Siberia in order to explore pertinent archival materials involving Russian expansion in the Pacific, but lacked the money for such a trip; he had tried to obtain financial support for the undertaking from the Carnegie Institution in Washington, D.C., but this organization did not come to his aid. In spite of this gap in his research, he still had a large depository of information from Paris, Berlin, and the Library of Congress in the United States.

After returning to the United States in 1908, Golder began to painstakingly write his dissertation. He progressed slowly and with

Frank A. Golder, around 1907

frustration because he had to earn a living, which consumed valuable time. While writing, he taught history at the University of Missouri, but, in 1909, he managed to complete the project, entitled: "Russian Voyages in the North Pacific Ocean to Determine the Relation between Asia and Alaska." This work constituted the most up-to-date scholarly treatment of the subject by a non-Russian.[15]

Golder now faced the far less arduous task of employment as a professor of history. There were a plethora of openings available for a Ph.D. graduate at various schools of higher learning. He shopped around after leaving the University of Missouri in 1909, teaching for a semester at Boston University and for a year at the University of Chicago. He always detested a city environment, though, with the exception of Paris; these universities, located in major cities, had no appeal to him since he desired space, fresh air, and peacefulness. His Alaska experience had given him an abiding love of the outdoors, as well as a rugged disposition for hiking in the mountains or riding horseback in the desert. This fondness for nature and peace and quiet encouraged Golder to accept a history professorship at Washington State College in Pullman, Washington, an agricultural school with a small rural community surrounded by fields of wheat and close to the mountains and the desert. He arrived at Pullman in 1911 where he began a nine year teaching relationship with this college.[16]

During the next three years at Washington State College, Golder taught a heavy combination of European and American history courses, political science, and civics for $1,500 per annum. While his salary did bring him average affluence, he occasionally complained that he should be earning a higher salary because of his rigorous workload. Teaching, rather than material considerations, though, provided him with self-satisfaction. He gave his students challenging assignments, while offering them his time, concern, and advice. His courses became the most popular at Washington State, and this popularity spread to the community in Pullman. Golder became well known for his many examples of kindness and generosity. A community member wrote, "We used to say . . . that those who enjoyed Golder's friendship possessed the finest thing the school had to offer."[17]

Although Golder enjoyed teaching at Washington State College, he remained watchful for new challenges involving himself in the world at large. In December 1913, he received an opportunity to go to Russia. The Carnegie Institution in Washington, D. C. inquired if he would put together a catalogue of documents, located in St. Petersburg's archival centers, which had a bearing on Russo-American relations, Russian exploration of the North Pacific, and the Russian settlement of Alaska. Golder accepted this assignment, since he would be able to work for a prestigious American institution and research topics of interest in the Russian archives which he could later turn into articles. He could also extend the research on his dissertation to the Russian archives, for which he would receive permission to sift through the key documents, and look forward to the publication of a book. Such scholarly goals nourished his intellectual curiosity, but the thought of gaining new experience in Russia, a country in which he had not had any personal contact, also excited him. He had studied the history of Russia for the previous eight years.[18]

One cannot determine from the evidence Golder's sophistication of Russian history. But Tsarist Russia in January 1914, the year Golder departed for this country that covered one–sixth of the earth's surface, had undergone a number of changes from its traditional static history of many centuries. For hundreds of years, Russia had been under the rulership of autocratic Tsars, who, for the most part, re-sisted political and economic change. At the turn of the nineteenth century, Russia experienced a surge of capitalistic development, at-tributable in part to loans from France, which placed this traditionally non–developed country on the path of modernization. The resulting new wealth in Russia widened the ranks of the middle class, and this middle class wanted political power commensurate with its economic power. The middle class, in reaction to autocracy, advocated such western ideas as constitutionalism and national representation. The Tsar, though, governed Russia with a vast bureaucracy, and its mem-bers jealously guarded this system of government against any political reform.

In 1905, socially deprived Russians tried to bring about reform in Russia. Factory workers, who also wanted a share of the new prosper-ity as well as political representation, drew up a petition of grievances which demanded an eight hour day, a minimum wage of 50 cents, an end to the Tsar's bureaucracy, and a democratically elected govern-ment. Several thousand workers took this petition and assembled in front of Tsar Nicholas II's Winter Palace in St. Petersburg, appeal-ing for justice; they naively believed the Tsar to be above the wicked capitalists and the stony, unsympathetic officials. In the confusing scene, however, the Tsar's soldiers fired on the crowd, killing several hundred.

This event, Bloody Sunday, set off waves of protest in Russia. Peasants overran the land of the gentry and the St. Petersburg Soviet, a workers' council, declared a general strike: railroads stopped, banks closed, and newspapers ceased to appear. With the government par-alyzed, Nicholas II issued his October Manifesto, promising a consti-tution, civil liberties, and a Duma or parliament. These concessions, along with the use of force, stopped the widespread protest. Soon after Nicholas gained control of his country, he asserted sovereignty, limiting the Duma's powers to the point where the Duma had no legal power to check the Tsar's and his bureaucracy's conduct. The conflict between government and society continued to be a major affliction of Tsarist Russia, and inspired a number of very radical political organizations, such as the Bolshevik Party. This party did not want mere constitutional reform, but a revolution which would bring about the political and economic transformation of Russia—freedom from state authority, freedom from class domination, and independence of modern society from the irrational demands of production and competition. In the meantime, Russia expanded as an economic power against a background of political backwardness. [19]

Golder entered this world of a changing Russia in February 1914 when he arrived by train in St. Petersburg. He sublet a room in a house owned by a Russian couple because he wished to speak Russian in order to perfect his usage of the language. While he developed a friendly relationship with the Russian couple, he had problems with their son, a young man who lived with them. Golder found out that when the young man had attended a university he had participated in conspiratorial activities. Now he led a sedentary existence, suffering from tuberculosis and festering because autocracy had not fallen and materialism seemed to be dominating society. Resentful of the affluent professor, he acted imperious and condescending toward Golder, who wrote in his diary:

> Russian students . . . take themselves seriously and talk down to their auditors which is irritating. It is true with them . . . that "a little knowledge is a dangerous thing." He seems to get a great deal of delight in criticizing others for not doing something which he himself is unwilling to do. [20]

The two intellectuals had several debates that irked Golder, who had few bourgeois pretensions, to no end. He wrote:

> One day this man came to me and expounded Rousseau's philosophy of the social contract, though he gave the impression that he was saying something new and original. After going on for a time he turned to me with this question: "How many suits of clothes have you?" I said, "Three." "Are you a Christian?" he asked again. "Yes," I replied. "If you are," he went on, "why don't you follow the teachings of Christ and give the two extra suits to the poor?" It was a hard question to answer and I did what most people under the circumstances, that is to say, I put the same question

to him. "How many suits have you?" I asked. "Three," he said. "Why don't you give two of them to the poor?" I followed up. "Because I live in a state of nature and keep what I have," he replied.[21]

The youth irritated Golder to the point where he decided to live elsewhere in St. Petersburg, and this decision led to a series of embarrassing incidents as he attempted to cope with an unfamiliar society. He asked several of his Russian friends, whom he had recently met, to notify him if they learned of a family who wanted to sublet a room. One day, Professor Alexander Danilevsky, a prominent Russian historian and fellow at the Russian Academy in St. Petersburg, sent Golder a note alerting him to a Russian army officer and his wife who were advertising a vacant room. When Golder located the house, he observed a policeman standing at the door. Thoughtlessly, he assumed that all Russian officers had a small retinue of guards. He inquired if Captain Troianovsky lived there. The policeman responded affirmatively and led Golder into a waiting room. Before long, a man in a uniform strode in, and Golder explained that he wished to sublet a room. The Captain excused himself. In a few minutes, he returned with his wife. The couple scanned Golder's appearance, which they approved of, and showed him a small, immaculate room, which seemed appropriate to Golder. He agreed to take the room, and moved his belongings from his former infernal place of residence with welcomed relief. He was confident that he had made a wise decision.

During the next several days, Golder's busy schedule prevented him from closely examining the Captain's household. One day, Danilevsky unexpectedly appeared at the Captain's house and embarrassingly explained to Golder that he had settled down at a district police station. Danilevsky's errors of omission and commission in recommending this residence and his own lack of observation amused Golder. Guilt–ridden, Danilevsky offered to find him a new residence. Golder, who did not mind being unconventional, said that he wanted to think the matter over.

In the meantime, many of Golder's new friends, who thought his residence a serious discourtesy, rushed in to express their sorrow and to recommend suitable quarters. He appreciated their consideration, but refused all offers. After Golder had thought about his situation, he decided that the police station was a perfect haven. He wrote, "In a country so full of police and spies as Russia is it would do me no harm to live under the roof of the guardian of the law."[22] Golder could not complain about his future treatment by the policemen; with unobtrusive goodwill, they brushed his clothes, polished his boots, and opened doors and ran errands for him, and gave him protection.

Despite the thoughtfulness and respect of the Russian police, Golder's living accommodations soon developed severe drawbacks. The Captain and his wife slept so late that he could not practice speaking Russian at the breakfast table; the servants neglected their duties and prepared distasteful meals, and a colony of flies always seemed to be circling the dining room. Even when Golder dined with the Captain and his wife, the experience proved to be unpleasant. At first, the Russian couple asked him thoughtful questions. After a few meals, however, the couple began to quarrel. Golder who liked cheerfulness and interesting conversation during his meals, remained angrily silent during the quarrels. Moreover, whenever one of them left the room in indignation, the other defended his or her version of an argument. To avoid alienating them, Golder always offered his sympathy.

After two months of trying to assimilate himself into the family, Golder reached the point where he could no longer tolerate them. He wrote in his diary, "I was ready to forego all knowledge to be gained in that circle." [23] But Golder, who did not wish to appear to be rude and leave abruptly, waited for the opportune moment to exit gracefully from the police station. This decision to wait turned into a learning experience for Golder; the Captain, who personally liked Golder, took him on long, meandering walks and entertained him with insights into police corruption and spying on revolutionaries in the capital.

Then, one day, Golder discovered that the St. Petersburg police department had promoted the Captain, an event which required him to transfer to another district. Golder, seizing this opportunity, informed the Captain that his new residence was too far from the archives. This time, he moved into a boardinghouse. Although absent of family life and of close contact with Russians, he at least had relative peace of mind there.

Besides housing problems, Golder also experienced embarrassing moments at the archives. Before he ventured into the archives at St. Petersburg, Golder inquired from Danilevsky about the rules of etiquette regarding tipping. Danilevsky had replied that one tipped the man who brought the documents to the table, vaguely adding that there were exceptions, which he failed to identify.

After Golder had researched materials for several days at the Ministry of Foreign Affairs archive, he decided to reward the assistant who carried the documents to his table and handed him a generous tip. At first, the assistant stared uncomprehendingly at the note. When he realized that the note constituted a tip, the assistant reacted with alarm and anger. Golder tried to explain the reason for the tip, but the assistant stalked out of the room. A few minutes later, the archive's director, an elderly man, walked up to Golder, grumbling. He said, "You think this is America. In Russia we do not bribe or tip gentlemen."[24] Behind the director, the assistant and two other archive employees added a few derisive remarks. In response, Golder defended himself against this violence of etiquette, but convinced no one. He wrote in his diary, "They made me feel that I had committed the unpardonable sin."[25] Golder, taking such matters very seriously, left the archival building in despair.

Golder then related the incident to Danilevsky, fearing that the director might not let him use the archives. Danilevsky phoned the director, who, having calmed down, agreed that the incident had resulted from a misunderstanding and consented to forget the matter. After this conversation, Danilevsky said to Golder, "In the archives never tip the man in civilian clothes. He is an official. Tip the man in the uniform. He is a servant."[26] This advice was so utterly uncomplicated that Golder never gave it another thought.

Golder returned to the Ministry of Foreign Affairs archives, where he again thrived on exploring the documents there. He wrote:

Working on . . . correspondence makes me realize how very human are kings, emperors, and others to whom we unconsciously look up to. It is such a temptation to turn from my task and peep into the correspondence of Alexander with Napoleon, Metternich, and others. It seems to be the only way to study history. I am learning much by absorption and by getting the atmosphere.[27]

Golder, who preferred the storytelling and human side of history, worked diligently for several more weeks at the Foreign Affairs archives. When he neared finishing his work there, the formerly abrasive director, perhaps feeling guilty over his rash criticism of Golder, volunteered to speak with the Ministry of Marine's director about letting Golder do research at this archival center.

One day, a messenger, dressed in a splendid uniform, approached Golder at the Foreign Affairs archives and asked if he wished to use the Marine archives. Golder said that he had made such a request through the director of the Ministry of Foreign Affairs. The messenger then stated, "You have been granted the desired permission." After delivering this message, he lingered, asking Golder a variety of questions on what documents he would be researching at the Ministry of Marine. Golder thought the messenger was stalling because he wanted a tip. Thinking that a proper tip would assure a harmonious beginning with the Marine's archives, Golder handed him some money. The messenger looked at Golder in surprise and said, "I am the director of the archives." Golder wrote in his diary, "I wished that I were a thousand miles from St. Petersburg."[28] He quickly explained his blunder, and this director, less emotional than the Foreign Affairs director, accepted Golder's explanation without any complications.

Such experiences were the price Golder had to pay in adjusting to Russia. Before long, though, he developed a sensitivity for his environment. While at the archival center for Russian industry and commerce, he observed the archives' two curators who sat leisurely at their desks, during the two hours they kept the archives open, smoking incessantly, sipping tea, and indulging in local gossip. They also passed the time putting rare stamps in their albums. Taking notice of this hobby, Golder bought a few interesting stamps and gave them to the curators. This generosity earned him their undetachable friendship.

One day, Golder stated to the two curators that the archives' time restriction of being open for only two hours was delaying his research. The two curators led him outside to the main entrance, where they revealed to him a hidden nail. One curator said, "This is where we hang the key. Should you come earlier than we, you will find it here. Should you leave after we are gone, you will hang it here." Their lax regulations seemed unbelievable to Golder. Thereafter, he opened the archival center at 9 a.m. and closed it around 5 in the evening. Golder, who essentially became the archives' third curator, mused in his diary, "Is there another country in the world where such a state of affairs exists?"[29]

While in St. Petersburg, Golder also took advantage of the city's rich cultural and social life. For example, every Friday night Danilevsky's wife invited Russian professors and foreign scholars to her home for an evening of intellectual inquiry. During these evening gatherings, the hostess asked a newcomer to deliver a lecture and afterwards a discussion took place. The evening then became less formal, concluding with a tea party, which permitted everyone to mingle. After Golder's first visit and lecture, he gained the reputation as a familiar and popular figure at these gatherings, a fact attributable to his affable personality and curiosity.

One evening, Golder met George Vernadsky, a young Russian historian who became a highly respected scholar at Yale University after he immigrated to the United States following the 1917 November Revolution. The two scholars shared a mutual interest in the colonization of Siberia, whose history Vernadsky happened to be researching at the time. They often saw each other at the Marine archives, where they exchanged ideas and advice. Vernadsky, who had a lively intel-

lectual appetite, took Golder to learned societies, where they listened
to a variety of scholarly presentations. Such occasions extended the
list of Golder's Russian acquaintances, as he met university professors and politicians and scholars, many of them liberals, who brought
him closer to contemporary Russian political reality, since they were
sharp critics of the Tsar's oppressive bureaucracy that kept them from
having influential political power.[30]

Golder's social life also brought him into contact with the *nou-*
veaux riche, whose numbers had skyrocketed because of Russia's modernization. He wrote:

Since coming here I have been fortunate enough to become
acquainted with a rich family of merchants. They are, of
course, not permitted to mingle with the official class but
in their way they try to live in the same style. . . . Their
house is decorated with precious works of art, their table
covered with the best foods and wines, their women covered
with pearls; they have their automobiles, and their box in
the theater adjoining to one of the nobility—and yet with
all that I cannot find that they possess a real appreciation
of art, music, or literature. There are many such families.
It is theaters, balls, dinners, suppers, cards, races, etc.[31]

To Golder, these privileged Russians not only had a superficial
lifestyle, but also had a shallow awareness of those who suffered from
poverty in St. Petersburg, many of whom lived in crowded, unsan-
itary urban ghettos. He saw many of these lower class Russians on
the streets begging for money. This seamy side of life alarmed him,
and he had reason to be so.[32]

The Tsar's Minister of Internal Affairs, Peter Stolypin, had ini-
tiated a program of agrarian reform in 1906, dismantling the village
communes and allowing individual peasants to appropriate lands in
order to recapture the peasants' loyalty for the regime and to bring
about efficient farming. But thousands of peasants, who could not
secure land were and attracted by factory jobs, had migrated to the
city. This migration had a negative effect on the social stability of
urban Russia, a situation which Stolypin had no intention of creating. Unlike the village, the city placed the underprivileged workers
in obvious contrast to the privileged and made the workers painfully
aware of their deprivation. New factory workers faced deplorable industrial conditions without any unions to protect them: long hours,
low wages, and no safety regulations. The urban poor developed
a certain solidarity from living together, and this manifested itself
through their growing radicalization. But what the future bode, how

The Nevsky Prospect during Pre-War Tsarist Russia

fate would resolve lower class bitterness, Golder could not predict.[33]

An inkling of the future did occur in July 1914 when a number of strikes broke out in St. Petersburg. A trip that month to the Monastery of Valaam, located on an island in Lake Ladoga, a large lake in northwestern Russia, prevented him from staying abreast of the growing class tension;[34] Golder wished to go there to look over the papers of a Russian missionary party which had traveled to Alaska. After Golder departed St. Petersburg, he took the train to Truslov, Finland and stayed the weekend with Danilevsky, who had a summer house overlooking the Gulf of Finland. During his stay, Golder took long, aimless walks on the beach with Danilevsky, and they eagerly discussed literature, philosophy, and history.[35] At the conclusion of this delightful visit, Golder then proceeded on to the shores of Lake Lodaga. When he arrived, dusk had blackened the harbor's boarding area. But the many cries and shouts that filled the air indicated considerable human activity. He walked up the gangplank to a steamer's deck, where he waded through compact masses of pilgrims who were also traveling to the monastery. He then searched for a place to sleep on the crowded deck but could not find one. The ship's Captain spotted Golder, whose clothes contrasted with the pilgrims', and, realizing his predicament, improvised a bed for him in the lounge.

During the next three days, the lounge became Golder's domicile, separated from the groups of pilgrims, who rapidly adapted to their cramped sleeping conditions with what he thought surprising ease. On the third day, he walked out on the deck during the early hours of a Wednesday morning. While the pilgrims stood around him in their disarrayed smocks, he gazed through the fog and observed the monastery's hazy outline. After several minutes, he could see a large church quite clearly and anticipated his arrival at this retreat from civilization. The steamer, by ten o'clock, reached the island's harbor, on which stood a crowd of monks and guests of the monastery. They welcomed the steamer with prolonged, intense shouts of joy, which gave Golder a feeling of equivalent joy.

The following day, Golder examined the monastery's archives regarding the missionary expedition to Alaska. He discovered that church scribes had attempted to disguise the fact that hostile Alaskan natives had murdered every missionary. Instead of revealing this disaster, the scribes had glowingly written about the high number of natives the missionaries had converted to Christianity.[36] Without any authentic historical data to occupy him at the monastery archives, Golder finished his work there in less than a day. All of a sudden, he had the luxury of two weeks of relaxation at this timeless sanctuary.

Golder was thoroughly fascinated by his new home. He had an

austere but curious cell for lodging and an abundance of food, all of which cost him nothing. During his stay, he came across many vacationing Russians, some who were highly educated and others desperately poor; everyone respected each other and helped the enterprising little community by volunteering, without pay, to aid in the production of food, tools, clothes, and shoes. Golder thought this social harmony and unselfish cooperation an ideal which civilization ought to emulate. He also found the monastery's environment an oasis of tranquility. In the church, he listened to the rapturous singing of the many worshippers; he walked on the shoreline and watched monks, quiet, serene, and immobile who sat fishing on the lake's edge; and he gazed at undulating boats, rowed by monks, with lay members aboard, sailing in the calm water to different shrines. He was not inclined to reject the secular world, but, after staying at the monastery for two happy weeks, he regretted that he had to leave.[37]

After Golder departed the Monastery of Valaam, he arrived at St. Petersburg on 30 July to continue his research. Little did he know that he had returned to a European world on the verge of flames. At St. Petersburg, he found out that Austria–Hungary, two days earlier, had declared war on Serbia after the assassination of the Austrian, Archduke Francis Ferdinand, at Sarajevo, Bosnia by Serbian conspirators. The assassination had given the Austrian monarchy the opportunity to subdue Serbia, whose independence from the Ottoman Empire in 1878 had inspired separatist agitation among ethnic groups within the Austro–Hungarian Empire. On 30 July, Russia, having ethnic, economic, and diplomatic ties with Serbia, began mobilization. The following day, 31 July, Austria–Hungary mobilized against Russia, and Germany, allied with Austria, demanded that Russia stop its war measures. Later that same day, France authorized its own mobilization, and two hostile European camps, the Allied governments and the Central Powers, faced each other in a rivalry that had intensified at the turn of the century over imperialistic conflicts, entangling alliances, and ethnic attachments. Then, on the first of August, Germany, fully aware of its vulnerability in a two–front war, struck first, declaring war on Russia. Suddenly, Golder lived in the capital of a country at war with a formidable enemy, a war which in the next few days would release a flood of nationalistic madness as Great Britain, France, and Austria–Hungary entered the conflict.[38]

On that fateful day when Germany declared war on Russia, Golder went to the Nevsky Prospect, a fabulous boulevard, in the early morning. There he witnessed the city transform into a patriotic emotional center, as large crowds cheered the dawn of war. He then walked to the Ministry of Marine's archival center and saw greater evidence of Russia's preparation for war. Rows of reserve units were lined up in front of the Ministry building, and he observed wives and children clinging in pathetic desperation to soldiers, a scene which gave the nearness of war a chilling reality.

Golder worked that day at the Marine archives until late in the afternoon. When he left the building to go home, he followed his customary route, which took him to the Nevsky. On this boulevard, he encountered masses of Russians carrying Russian flags and cheering ecstatically for the Tsar, the Russian army, and Holy Russia. Captivated by the crowd's enthusiastic spirit, he marched along with it as a detached observer. He had proceeded only a short distance when someone broke the patriotic solidarity by singing the Internationale, a revolutionary song strictly forbidden in Tsarist Russia. A number of marchers joined the dissenter in his rebellious song, an act which encouraged others to sing. The mounted police, patrolling the Nevsky, reacted swiftly, riding their horses toward the center of this disturbance. Before the police reached the area, the singing faded away and marchers began singing an innocent church hymn, which appeased the police. But the marchers' boldness struck Golder as a disturbing event at a time of patriotic fervor, as if previous dissatisfaction with the Tsar's regime lingered on.[39]

The following day, a Sunday, Russia plunged into a war that would be the most ferocious in history until World War II. Certain Russians, like Golder, did not let patriotism consume them. Russians, observing the sadness of war, flocked to church services on this Sunday. Golder attended a service at the Kazan Cathedral, the most resplendent cathedral in the city, where he saw worshippers bearing an unusually deep religious demeanor. As he wrote in his diary two days earlier, "These people have lived through the bitterness of war too many times to take it lightly the way we do in America."[40]

Golder, a foreigner in a country committed to fighting in a major war, did not take his situation lightly. He had to consider if he would continue to receive his paychecks, and if he would be able to leave Russia by November so that he could resume his teaching at Washington State. After the church service, he proceeded to the American Embassy to find out what transportation routes would be available for traveling. As he proceeded to the embassy, he noted that zealous Russians had engaged in destroying property owned by Germans, and he viewed this destruction with disgust. Then, at the American Embassy, he confronted crowds of desperate German aliens who clutched the hope that American authorities, neutral during the war's outbreak, would secure them transportation for escaping Russia, since Russians were attacking the German Embassy. The Germans and

Golder received little comfort from the embassy, learning that the mobilized Russian army had requisitioned almost every train to carry thousands of soldiers to the eastern front. Escape would be difficult. Golder's predicament brought him a terrible forboding, especially the thought of trying to survive in a war–preoccupied society without a paycheck.

In spite of this forboding, Golder, as a historian, keenly observed that the euphoric response to war among Russians outpaced any piety over its tragedy by the 2nd of August. Patriotism had pervaded every class in Russia. For example, the workers' movement, a few days earlier, involved in a general strike, now supported the Tsar, and liberals, many of them perpetually in opposition to the Tsar, pledged to withdraw their criticism. The national unity at this time placed the Tsar, Nicholas II, at the pinnacle of his power. Like thousands of Russians, Golder headed for the Tsar's Winter Palace, where Nicholas II would announce a formal declaration of war, an event a historian on the local scene could ill afford to miss.

When Golder reached the spacious square below the Winter Palace, the crowd, spilling onto the street, pushed him haplessly about. Above the broad sea of people in the square, he saw hundreds of hoisted holy icons, flags, and banners. In this same square, in 1905, the Tsar's soldiers had fired on reverent petitioners, igniting a new era of protest against autocracy. Now, in August 1914, when the Tsar and his wife, Alexandra, stepped onto the Palace's balcony, Golder watched the crowd below kneel with unwavering respect. The Tsar lifted his arm and spoke of continuing the war until the Russian army had driven every enemy soldier from Holy Russia. The Tsar then lowered his head and the crowd sang the Imperial anthem. Golder observed this display of unity, loyalty and devotion with awe, a patriotism which spilled over into the night. He wrote in his diary:

> All during the night there were processions. At each street corner on the Nevski there are little groups of men and women, discussing the coming campaign and dividing up the Central Empires.[41]

Golder had noted only the day before Russians singing the Internationale.

After this exciting day, Golder returned to his archival work. He still had to go through materials for the publication of his dissertation, future scholarly articles, and a guide to Russian archives during the months of August, September, and October. He also expected his next paycheck to arrive sometime in September so that he could comfortably afford to leave Russia for his return trip to the United States.

While he waited for his paycheck, the curious historian could not discipline himself. The patriotic processions, the nationalistic speeches, the uniformity of belief, the alterations of lifestyles, the sudden emergence of numerous soldiers, the movement of troops, the success or failure of battles, and the latest economic and political developments pulled him away from the archival table. Golder now led a double life—one in the archives and the other on the street.

By November, though, Golder did manage to finish all his projects. This release from his archival responsibilities signified the end of his stay in Russia. He now had to worry about his exit. Transportation by train had reached the point of paralysis. The German front, which slashed a jagged line across East Prussia, cut off escape through Germany. Masses of German refugees trying to flee to Sweden closed off the Baltic Sea route. Golder booked passage on a steamer at Archangel, the Arctic Ocean route, but the steamship company abruptly cancelled his reservation. There remained only one alternative—the Trans–Siberian route, a 6,000 mile journey through European Russia, across the Ural mountains, and over the unbelievably vast wasteland of Siberia to the coastal city of Vladivostok at the Pacific Ocean.

Golder went to the Nicholas train station, and the clerk at the ticket window tried to discourage him from embarking on the Trans–Siberian railway, stressing the train's reputation for leaving passengers stranded in desolate areas. The clerk's warning certainly affected Golder, but he had little choice. His paycheck had failed to arrive so that he could barely afford forthcoming transportation, hotels, and food expenses.[42]

The Trans–Siberian train, scheduled to leave the capital the following day, prompted Golder to be at the station early so that he could buy a precious ticket. When he arrived at the station, he saw only a few travellers who lingered around the platform. In dismay, he waited two hours for the ticket window to open while no one seemed inclined to take the Trans–Siberian line. He bought a ticket but wondered if he would be embarking on the most perilous train journey of his life.

When Golder boarded the train, he could not find an empty space in a compartment because so many passengers had crowded onto the train at other stations. To Golder's relief, he finally found a compartment occupied with just one person, a male Russian student from Moscow. The train pulled out of the station. In a short while, the train reached a culminating speed, moving further from the feverish war atmosphere in Petrograd—the capital's new, Russian–sounding

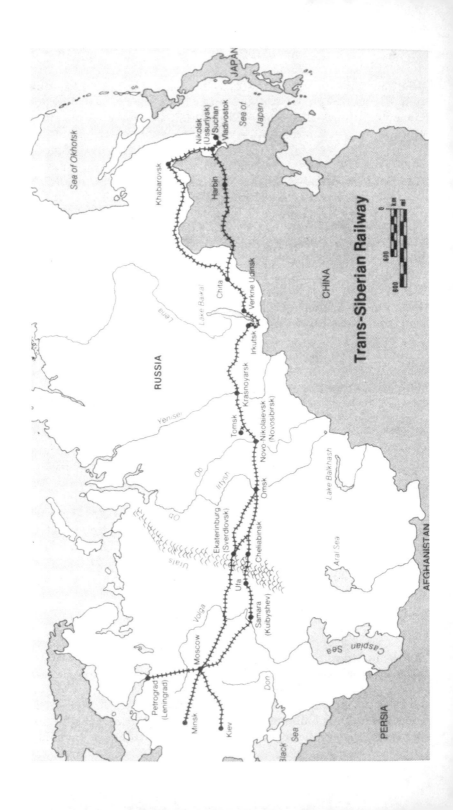

Trans-Siberian Railway

name. As the train's movement jostled Golder, he noticed the stunning beauty of the morning's sunlight illuminating the countryside. His train continued on, passing mile after mile of terrain as clouds covered the sky during the afternoon. By evening, the train ran into a snowstorm, and Golder soon became cold. He put on his jacket, but its flimsy material provided him with little warmth. The Russian student, sympathizing with Golder's discomfort, handed him a heavy sheepskin coat. This coat proved to be too warm, and that first night Golder could not sleep, as he listened to the train's wheels grinding through the snow and as he conjured up images of being stranded in a wild, forsaken region.[43]

Two days later, a severe cold plagued Golder. On top of this, he had to transfer to another train car, which lacked private sleeping accommodations, after railway workers detached his car from the train. He foresaw few moments of boredom among his fellow passengers—civilians, soldiers, and an old woman. Soon after his transfer, the old woman, seventy-two years old, related to him how her adventuresome son had settled down in the Siberian town of Chita, a bustling, boom town not unlike those of the 1849 gold rush in California, to strike his fortune. She said that she would be living with this son before long, and eagerly looked forward to a new life of luxury after a grueling one. Golder viewed her prospects with skepticism, but did not discourage her. The old woman was not entirely lost in her dreams, though, because she became very concerned over Golder's extremely pale complexion. She attributed his ill-health to insufficient nourishment and offered him an apple. He politely declined it, which prompted the old woman to comment, "We have come to a sad state of affairs when a young man is afraid to eat a bit extra."[44] The old woman would not accept Golder's refusal. With pride and a sense of personal accomplishment, she rattled off a list of cold remedies which she claimed had successfully cured her own children. Having heard her mention only one son, Golder asked the old woman how many children she had. She said fifteen, but admitted that fourteen of them had died. He decided to let his cold expire without her aid.

The other passengers in the train car also distracted Golder from boredom. They were lively and talkative, and their debates often centered around Russia's war effort and the Tsarist government. He wrote in his diary on 20 November, "they all had something unkind to say about the government, and many were pessimistic about the outcome of the war and the future of Russia."[45] He also wrote two days later, "Our little family talks of nothing but the wickedness of the government and the cruelties of the war."[46] This lack of patriotism caught Golder's interest, since affection for the Tsar had been so widespread in Petrograd during his war declaration.

As Golder no doubt knew, Russia had suffered a crushing military defeat at the beginning of the war. Russia's backwardness in comparison to dynamic Germany had played a decisive role in this defeat. Short of rifles, munitions, clothing, doctors, nurses, medical supplies, transportation, and competent soldiers and military leaders, the Russian army was trapped by German forces in East Prussia on 18 August during the Battle of Tannenberg, in which 300,000 Russian soldiers lost their lives. General A. V. Samosonov committed suicide, two of his army corps surrendered, and General P. K. Rennenkampf, a reputedly gallant cavalry officer, deserted his troops, fleeing into Russian territory. Such an inglorious defeat encouraged Russians once again to view critically the Tsarist regime—the inefficiency of the Tsar's bureaucracy, the Tsar's lack of imagination, and the court intrigue. The old corrupt world of Tsardom had returned to center stage.[47]

At night, Golder could dwell at length on the little family's controversial opinions about the Tsar's government and the war, since the mail passengers had the habit of always smoking cigarettes, whose drifting smoke often kept him awake at night. One particular night, he thought that he would suffocate from the smoke's density and became restless because of a passenger who lay snoring beneath him. He ached to escape the train car for a moment of peace and fresh air. When the train stopped at Krasnoyarsk, the midway point between Moscow and Vladivostok, he exited the car and breathed reviving fresh air. He then strolled along the platform. As he approached a baggage car, he saw soldiers struggling to unload a cumbersome object. Curious, he moved closer to them. They heard his footsteps and two soldiers, as if caught in the act of stealing something, swirled around and thrust rifles with fixed bayonets dangerously near his chest. They ordered him to move on, which he did without hesitation. Golder had no wish to test their resolve.[48]

Golder returned to his train car, and the train departed the station, transporting him closer to his destination—Vladivostok. During the next few days, the car in which he traveled became emptier and emptier as each member of the opinionated little family reached his disembarkation point. Finally, only Golder and the old woman remained in the large, steel car, and to pass the time they traded jokes, stories, and observations. At one stopping point, he bought a roasted chicken, a bottle of milk, bread and butter from station vendors and the old woman filled a teapot with hot water from boilers. Inside the car, he prepared the meal and the two travelers feasted with relishment. Sharing company and meals with the old woman upheld

Golder's morale. Then, the train arrived at Chita. There the old woman bid Golder a sad goodbye, and the train slipped away with a loneliness that brought him to despair.[49]

Golder reached Vladivostok on 2 December after traveling for sixteen days. He wrote:

> The cost of the journey, including the railroad ticket, food and such accommodations as I had, is 130 rubles. This leaves me 50 (about twenty–seven dollars) for returning to America. I wonder how far that will take me.[50]

For the moment, though, he repressed all gloomy thoughts, prepared to enjoy himself after the exhausting trip. In this slow–paced city, far from the fighting on the eastern front, he checked into a comfortable hotel, where he caught up on his sleep. He then celebrated for the next three days, squandering money on food and beer. Only on the third day did Golder acknowledge his foolishness.[51]

Golder lacked enough money for traveling to the United States. He decided that he would travel as far as Shanghai, China, where he had two friends; he hoped to borrow money from at least one of them. He had not heard from them in several years, and he considered, with some fear, the likelihood of their departure elsewhere. In spite of this apprehension, he boldly stuck out on 5 December on the steamship *Poltava*, after paying for a ticket, which left him with one dollar.[52] The first day out at sea, he experienced calm weather, a delightfully blue sky and a refreshingly warm sun, which put him in good spirits. As if to celebrate the smooth sailing, he ate a number of spicy foods for dinner. The following day, a storm broke out, rocking the steamship incessantly, and he became extremely seasick. All day long, he confined himself to bed. The next day, a Monday, someone announced the sighting of Nagasaki, Japan, and this news brought Golder out onto the deck. His curiosity of Japan, a country he had never seen before, made him eager to take a glimpse of the city's port life, so much so that his seasickness, which had agonized him the previous day, did not seem to affect him now.

After the steamship docked, Golder disembarked and entered the port's environment. He had always thought of Japan as a land of people full of gentleness and refinement and now, amid this bustling port, he saw crude laborers, boisterous seamen, shady characters, and drunks. He continued to wander aimlessly in the dockyard, observing heaps of cargo, long coils of rope, wooden cranes, and collapsed hauling nets. Then he heard the *Poltava's* shrill whistle, a signal for all departed passengers to return. As Golder headed back toward the steamship, several Japanese prostitutes spotted the unaccompanied foreigner, and they attempted to entice him. After the initial shock, he was humored by the attention, perhaps even tempted to indulge in sensual pleasure, but the steamship's near departure and his low funds put an end to any wishful thinking.[53]

Golder sailed another day before the *Poltava* drew close to Shanghai. Worry failed to bother him over the dismal prospect of not locating his friends. He awoke early the morning that the steamship sailed down the Yangtze River in the direction of Shanghai, and looked on in fascination at the bamboo huts built just above the waterline, the small, fragile docks, and the many Chinese junks in the softly undulating water. When the *Poltava* docked at Shanghai, he grabbed his suitcase and hurriedly departed the steamship. On the dock, he roamed around, now in uncertainty, looking for transportation. He finally found an unoccupied rickshaw and handed the owner a portion of his last dollar. He then passed through the chaotic, crowded city to the Grand Hotel. After entering this hotel, he borrowed a phone. One friend, a schoolmate of Golder's at Harvard University, worked at the American Embassy. Golder phoned the embassy and learned that his friend no longer worked there. He next called Gilbert Reid, a missionary who directed a religious institute at Shanghai. The receptionist did not know if Reid had come to the institute. Golder waited for a few tense moments, when, suddenly, he heard Reid's voice, and he exuberantly related his tale of ruin. Reid took the tale to heart, promising to loan the footloose, reckless professor two hundred dollars and invited him to take a week's vacation at the institute.[54]

Chapter III

Dramatic Year: Revolution in Russia

In January 1915, Golder returned to the United States in debt to his friend Reid, but rich in experience regarding Russia's archives, classes, people, values, culture, and government. He wanted to go back to Russia as soon as possible because of his attachment to that country, his research interests, and his curiosity over Russia's involvement in the war. But Golder would have to patiently wait for another opportunity in order to visit Russia again. In the meantime, he resumed his teaching duties at Washington State, and, during his spare time, he wrote several articles that established him as a scholar.[1]

While in Petrograd, Golder had taken notes of many documents in the archives, largely unexplored by American scholars, and now he experienced the joy of publishing articles based on original research. Several of his articles were published between 1915 and 1917, and two—"The Russian Fleet and the Civil War" and "Catherine II and the American Revolution"[2]—appeared in the *American Historical Review*, the most prestigious historical journal in the United States. He also fulfilled his commitment to the Carnegie Institution, which published his *Guide to Materials for American History in Russian Archives*. Furthermore, he expanded his dissertation with his research materials from Russia, and a publishing company brought it out under the title of *Russian Expansion on the Pacific, 1641–1850*.[3] Thus, Golder joined a small circle of American scholars on Russia— Archibald Cary Coolidge, Samuel N. Harper, and George Kennan (the uncle of the diplomat).

There were so few American scholars in the field of Russian history because Russia, autocratic, isolated, feudalistic, had little appeal to professors or students. Golder's guide to Russian archives served as an attempt to stimulate interest in Russian studies. American students who pursued European history studied England and France, and, to a lesser degree, Germany. But the outbreak of World War I would change this minimal interest in Russia. United States diplomatic and economic ties with Russia during the war would bring about increased contact. A number of American missions would travel to Russia, and some of their members would later write about Russia.

Woodrow Wilson would bring attention to Russia when he hailed the Provisional Government, after the fall of Tsardom during the 1917 March Russian Revolution, as a victory for democracy. Then, after the Bolshevik Revolution in November 1917, when Russia emerged as the first socialist state, the American government would perceive Russia as a threat. The Bolshevik Revolution would also compel a number of Russian scholars, like George Vernadsky,[4] to immigrate to the United States, where they would enter university teaching and write about Russia. Such factors would increase interest in Russia, and Golder, through his contact and keen interest in Russia's history, would be a leader in developing Russian studies in the United States.

After being in the United States for two years following his 1914 trip to Russia, Golder received another opportunity to return to Russia. The American Geographical Society asked him to find in the archives at Petrograd the journal of Georg Steller. Steller, a German mineralogist, had accompanied Vitus Bering on his second voyage along Alaska to discover the benefits to be derived from Russian commercial and territorial expansion. Only extracts of the journal had been published. The Geographical Society wanted Golder to translate a complete version for publication. Golder accepted this assignment, relishing the idea of finding the journal; the opportunity would also afford him the chance of further researching Russo–American relations, seeing his Russian friends, and noting the changes that had happened in Russia since the outbreak of World War I, a war whose savagery continued on and on in a war of attrition[5]

Only a few days after receiving this new assignment, Golder, in February 1917, hurriedly departed Pullman for his trip to Russia. From Seattle, he crossed the Pacific Ocean on a steamer, docked at Vladivostok's port, and boarded the Trans–Siberian train that would carry him across Siberia to Russia's capital. In spite of massive railway confusion brought about by the war, Golder managed to reach Petrograd on 4 March 1917 without any long delays. At the station, he met his friend, George Vernadsky. The two historians traversed the snow–covered streets, until they arrived at the apartment of an upper–class family at 60 Bassenaia. There Vernadsky had arranged for Golder to sublet a room.

During the cold train ride and the walk on the chilly streets, Golder looked forward to the comfort of a heated room. To Golder's surprise, he discovered that this upper–class family had neither coal nor wood to heat their apartment. This case was not unusual. Most Russians in Petrograd suffered from the cold weather since the war had upset the normal channels for the distribution of fuel.[6]

The next day, Golder noticed another change in the capital. Everywhere, on the streets, in streetcars, and at public places, he encountered Russians who spoke bitterly of the Tsar's mismanagement of the war and his administration's ineptitude. He wrote later, "In the archives where I worked, which was almost under the very noses of the Imperial family, the criticism [of the Tsar] was as open as in private homes."[7] In 1914, while traveling on the Trans–Siberian train to Vladivostok, Golder had listened to Russian passengers complain about the Tsar; now, in 1917, the criticism seemed to have penetrated every class in Russian society.

As Golder found out, Russians had many valid reasons for complaining. Since 1914, two million Russian soldiers had been killed, wounded, or captured in the war. The war had uprooted thousands of Russians; they flocked to Petrograd, overcrowding the city; vacant rooms and apartments were scarce and expensive. The war, which brought chaos to Russian railway operations, made the delivery of food to Petrograd haphazard; black bread could often only be bought after standing in long lines for hours. Not only was food scarce but other items completely disappeared—boots, shoes, galoshes, fabrics, soap, and medicine. Moreover, the Tsarina, Alexandra, aroused suspicions because of her German origin. She also alienated Russians with her superstitious behavior; she took advice, some of which had political ramifications, from the debauched holyman, Rasputin, because he had miraculously stopped the bleeding of her only son, a hemophiliac and heir to the throne. The liberals in the Duma objected to this state of affairs. The Tsar and his reactionary advisors, however, turned a deaf ear and hoped to close the Duma forever. To many Russians, then, the Tsar represented corruption, favoritism, incompetence, and intolerance.[8] Golder wrote, "I remembered quite vividly how the same people cheered the Emperor when he had declared war."[9]

The pervasiveness of this anti–nationalist spirit astounded Golder. But a revolution, bringing the Tsar's downfall that very month, was for him, as for almost everyone in or out of Russia, a scarcely imaginable possibility. Russians did speak of revolution, but only after the war, for they feared that a revolution during the war would bring a German victory.[10] But, as Golder soon found out, Petrograd would transform itself into high–pitched levels of protest, culminating in a spectacular revolution before the war's end. Through fortuitous circumstances, Golder had arrived in Petrograd just in time to witness one of the most momentous events in history since the French Revolution in 1789—the March Russian Revolution,[11] a revolution which occurred spontaneously. As Golder wrote, "The Revolution came as a surprise to us all."[12]

The first day of the revolution took place on 8 March, four days after Golder had reached Petrograd. On this day, International Women's Day, many women abandoned their work in several textile factories in the Vyborg district, a large industrial area, and marched to neighboring factories, shouting, "Bread." While their husbands and sons fought at the front, these women sometimes worked as long as thirteen hours, earned low wages, and stood in long lines for hours to buy black bread. Male workers, who demanded higher wages, also joined the women demonstrators. They formed shapeless, large groups, and moved along the city streets, stoning the few automobiles, smashing some windows, and clashing with police. Perhaps as many as 56,000 workers became involved in the demonstrations. Golder noted, though, that the mounted police easily controlled the crowds. He had no idea that this day marked the beginning of the March Revolution, since strikes had occurred in January and February. He wrote, "Such acts were more or less common and no one paid much attention to them."[13]

The following morning, 9 March, Golder noted that the crowds had become bolder as he walked the city streets toward the archives. They mixed yesterday's economic protest with political protest. Protesters chanted for more bread and higher wages as well as sang unlawful revolutionary songs and occasionally waved red flags. But Golder did not believe that the crowd's boldness threatened Tsarist political order. Policing authorities seemed to have the upper hand.[14]

When Golder finished his research that afternoon, he walked to the Nevsky Prospect and entered the wide boulevard. As he walked along, a number of Cossacks galloped past him, headed for a crowd approaching Fontanka Bridge, which they wished to cross in order to march on the Nevsky. The day before, the police had forcefully prevented protesters from reaching the Nevsky. After Golder arrived at the bridge, he learned that a bizarre skirmish had just taken place. Policemen, who had accompanied the Cossacks, had used whips and swords to disperse the demonstrators while the Cossacks had refrained from doing so. The Cossacks then took exception to the policemen's brutality, and attacked them with such decisiveness that they fled from the scene. But this discord within the ranks of Petrograd's policing authorities failed to shake Golder's conviction of the crowd's weakness. He wrote:

> It was no secret that there was bad blood between the Cossacks and the police; the Cossacks complained that while they were suffering and fighting at the front, the latter were having an easy time, enriching themselves by graft, and oppressing the soldiers' families.[15]

After the Cossacks had dispersed the police, Golder saw demonstrators pat the Cossack horses, while shouting cheers. The Cossacks begged the people to move on. In response, a number of them, the majority being young, women students, repeated in affectionate voices, "Comrades, come over to our side. Our cause is your cause." Golder observed that the Cossacks looked at each other with anxious glances, torn between loyalty for the Tsar and sympathy for the people. Their confusion, Golder noticed, paralyzed them to the point where they could only plead, "Please go away, go home."

Suddenly, Golder saw an officer take charge. He ordered the Cossacks to regroup, and they did so obediently. They then rode into the middle of the crowd and Golder watched in stunning amazement as the Cossack riders majestically spun their horses in a widening circle, forcing the crowd onto the sidewalk. In the meantime, another company of Cossacks formed a line from wall to wall along the street and charged. The demonstrators came back and even cheered. From this scene, Golder realized that the crowd had developed a fondness and trust for the Cossacks—the romantic heroes of Russia's past. On the other hand, he believed that the demonstrators could not depend on the Petrograd garrison's sympathy. This garrison, numbering around 170,000 soldiers, constituted the Tsar's personal army for protecting Petrograd against insurrectionary protest.[16]

Chaos in Petrograd grew to an even greater extent the following day, Saturday, 10 March. On Friday, local revolutionary organizations had ordered a three day general strike. On Saturday, Golder noted its effect: "Streetcars were not running, telephones were barely working, factories and shops were closed, banks and stores were locked, there was little to eat, for the only provision on hand was water."[17] On this day, he also saw factory workers, many of whom had stayed away from demonstrators the past two days, swarm through the streets since so many factories had closed down. Now, there were over 200,000 demonstrators. Students, white–collar workers, and teachers also joined the workers' demonstrations. Golder especially noted the students, who urged the crowds to overthrow the Tsar. Like certain dauntless workers, they assumed spontaneous leadership roles.

As Golder would note in a few days, this revolution happened without the leadership of long–standing, professional revolutionaries, many of whom lived in western Europe. For example, Vladimir Lenin, the Bolshevik party's leader, who lived in Zurich, Switzerland, had not returned to Tsarist Russia because officials had introduced heavy repressive measures against radicals to mold conformity during the war. Lenin had remained in Zurich since 1914, discouraged over the

The Nevsky Prospect during the March Russian
Revolution

initial nationalistic response to the war (the majority of socialists in Germany and France had voted for war credits), wondering if he would live long enough to see his dream of a social revolution in Russia.[18]

Little did Lenin know that at the moment matters in Petrograd had become quite serious, and the Tsar's ministers were panicking. They even threatened to resign so that the Tsar could appoint ministers acceptable to the Duma, an act which they thought might quell the disturbances. They also advised the Tsar, who had departed Petrograd a few days earlier for the Russian army's general headquarters, to return to Petrograd because the absence of his authority seemed to be responsible for bringing chaos to the capital. The Tsar, however, refused his ministers' advice, preferring the role of military leader. Instead of returning, he telegraphed a message on 10 March to General S. S. Khabalov, commander of the Petrograd Military District, to end the disturbances, an order which implied the use of arms.[19]

The next day, Sunday, Golder attended services at the British–American church on a sunny winter day. After the service, he walked along the streets, covered with soft snow, and came across posters that warned Russians not to gather in the streets because soldiers would shoot to restore order. In addition to the posters, he saw few people on the streets, for the city had turned into a military camp overnight, with soldiers everywhere—in front of buildings, at intersections, at bridges, and at railway stations. Squads of cavalry patrolled the streets and policemen armed with rifles stood at their posts. Golder thought that the combination of the poster's warning and the military atmosphere had intimidated the demonstrators so much that the disturbances might not occur again.[20]

After a luncheon, Golder decided to visit a friend. On the way, he passed by the Volynsky regiment, a training detachment of the Petrograd garrison. He saw these soldiers, for the most part experienced in warfare, load their rifles with live cartridges, shoulder their weapons, and march off toward the Nevsky. Golder followed the soldiers for a while, perhaps fearing that violence would occur if any demonstrators did dare try reaching the Nevsky.[21]

When Golder finished visiting his friend, he headed for the Nevsky. At the boulevard, he saw that he had thoroughly misjudged the posters' intimidating influence. Demonstrators, in the late morning, again appeared on the streets, marching festively, singing revolutionary songs, and shouting subversive slogans. Golder saw in front of him soldiers who had cordoned off the intersections, while the demonstrations took place on the Nevsky. Determined to enter the Nevsky, Golder passed through the cordon after he showed a soldier his American passport. Once on the Nevsky, he saw Cossacks, less sympathetic than previously, galloping their horses at full speed in the protesters' ranks, chasing some of them away. Other people rushed around in a frenzy. Then someone told Golder that soldiers and machine gunners had killed many civilians. The Volnysky regiment Golder had seen marching off had killed forty people at Znamenskaya Square, a popular public speaking area of the Nevsky. After hearing the shocking news, Golder returned home. But the cacophony failed to die away. He wrote, "Sunday night was full of excitement and fear and there were not many who slept soundly. Firing was heard at different times but what it portended, none of us could tell."[22]

While walking to the archives the following day, 12 March, Golder again came across excited groups of people. He learned from them of an event central to the Tsar's overthrow: the Volynsky regiment had revolted. Golder wrote: "There were so many rumors afloat it was not easy to know what to believe."[23] The previous night, a platoon of the Volynsky regiment had decided to refuse to take up positions at Znameskaya Square the next day. That morning, while this platoon stood in formation in the barracks, one soldier shouted at the company commander, "We will no longer shoot . . ." and killed him after he left the building. These rebellious soldiers scattered to other regiments, inciting them to insurrection. The Tsar's garrison was disintegrating.[24]

At four o'clock that afternoon, Golder left the archives and approached the Nevsky for crossing. In contrast to Sunday, there were neither guards posted nor many soldiers patrolling the boulevard. After Golder walked freely onto the Nevsky, he heard gunshots ring out. In the distance, he saw curls of smoke ascending above buildings. All these scenes confused Golder.[25]

As Golder proceeded, walking on the Nevsky, the minister of the British–American church, Robert Clare, drew up beside him. Golder wrote: "We were discussing the situation, . . . and perhaps the word revolution passed our lips but neither of us nor those about us took it seriously."[26] While absorbed in conversation and in the chaotic scene around them, a gate flung open. About two dozen soldiers passed through it, heading for the crowd. Intimidated, protesters began to clear out of the street. But the soldiers waved for them to stop running and shouted they would not shoot. This scene revealing the soldiers' sympathy for the crowd brought Golder closer to the realization that he was witnessing a revolution. Still, he would not commit himself to this view until he had more convincing evidence.[27]

Golder and the minister continued on. After they walked a short distance, a machine gun let loose a burst that came close to them. Golder wrote, "I found myself sticking like a poster against the wall,"[28] and he watched the fleeing demonstrators, observing that everyone seemed to escape being hit. He then tried to locate the machine gun in one of the many building windows but could not do so. After the firing let up, the emboldened Golder ventured farther along the street, while the minister, rationally fearful of more gunfire, disappeared down a side street. Golder's path took him near the Nicholas railway station as demonstrators returned to the open street, chattering. Suddenly, Golder saw soldiers coming from the station. Their presence would have normally cleared the street. But these soldiers failed to evoke fear on this occasion, since scores of civilians had joined the soldiers, as if in kindred spirit. As Golder saw, they were in a rebellious mood, as they shouted, "Down with the government," and attacked loyal officers, disarming them. Golder wrote, "Then it dawned upon me that the revolution was on in earnest, that the anarchists . . . had become the heroes of a great cause."[29]

On that day, 12 March, traditional authority in Petrograd melted away. Soon, middle class leaders demanded the dismissal of the Tsar's ministry and the formation of a new one responsible to a majority of the Duma. In response, the Tsar ordered the Duma to disband. Duma members then selected politicians from the defunct Duma, forming a special committee, and this committee called for the Tsar's abdication. In order to take command of his city, Nicholas II tried to return to Tsarskoe Selo, his palace near Petrograd. Disloyal troops, however, stopped the Imperial train and sent it back to the front. The army in the field had taken sides with the revolution, and the generals, realizing the soldiers' disaffection, advised Nicholas to abdicate. He did so, almost as an act of resignation.[30]

The news of the Tsar's abdication on 15 March thrilled Golder. He wrote, "How fortunate for me that I came just in time to see it all."[31] He, like so many Russians, despised the Tsar for his mismanagement of the war, for the scandals surrounding Rasputin, and for ministers, like Protopopov, who discredited the regime with their excessive conservatism. Golder wrote, "so worthless had the monarchy become . . . that it toppled over like a rotten tree."[32] And once this tree had fallen, Golder watched the parades of celebration, with regiment after regiment of soldiers, sailors, and Cossacks, colorful in their regimental uniforms, jubilant and carrying revolutionary flags, marching along the streets. Army trucks filled with soldiers, red handkerchiefs tied to their bayonets, drove wildly up and down streets. Crowds, intoxicated with joy, ran through the streets, waving red flags and singing the Marseillaise. Bonfires blazed, burning Imperial eagles, crowns, and other insignia of royalty. Golder wrote,

"It was a Glorious Revolution (relatively bloodless) . . . and I hope a successful one."[33]

To replace the Tsarist government, the Duma Committee elected a Provisional Government to govern Russia, until a constituent assembly could determine a permanent form of government. This new Provisional Government was composed of a body of ministers, who had a wide range of political views, from the liberal democrat (Cadet), Paul Miliukov, the Minister of Foreign Affairs, to the socialist, Alexander Kerensky, the Minister of Justice. The ministers, in general, though, had a conservative outlook; they favored winning the war at almost any cost and remained committed to the Allied governments' imperialistic war aims, as well as Russia's own, the annexation of Constantinople and the Straits as a reward for Russia's war effort. Another political body, the Petrograd Soviet of Workers' and Soldiers' Deputies, also arose in juxtaposition to the Provisional Government. Composed of Russians with a socialist background, the Soviet acted to pressure the Provisional Government to bring about social reform, an acknowledgment of the powerful influence of socialism in Russia following the 1905 Revolution. Yet, this body, although renouncing Allied and Russian imperialistic war aims, had a policy of defensism. The Soviet wished to fight the war while trying to rally European socialists to pressure the Allied governments into negotiating a peace. Neither the Provisional Government nor the Soviet advocated separate negotiations with Germany, fearing a draconian peace.[34]

Most Russians greeted the new governmental institutions with enthusiasm. Even though Golder shared their enthusiasm over the collapse of Tsardom, he believed the Provisional Government had a large burden on its shoulders in terms of solving the problems of war, food, fuel, transportation, and industrial and land reform at a critical juncture in Russia's history. Worse still, the Provisional Government had no real authority to do so, lacking tradition, a bureaucracy with administrative skill, an army with widespread loyalty, and a police force. Golder thought that the war would create the greatest problem for the Provisional Government. This sentiment had a powerful truth to it, for all other reforms, such as land distribution, could not be resolved until the war had passed into history. One could not embark on land distribution with the army's majority composed of peasants. Golder lamented, "If only the war was over. It was the vacillation of the Tsarist government in the war . . . that helped to bring its downfall."[35] In his estimation, as Russia descended into the hydra of national division over the war, governmental stability would suffer immeasurably.

After the creation of the new dual government, Golder tried to follow a regular work schedule at the archives. But in light of the war, he found leading a quiet, contemplative existence in the archives almost meaningless. He wrote, "It hardly seems fair to bother with such things when thousands of good people are dying at the front."[36] He even wanted to share the soldiers' hardships at the front.

> A Russian friend of mine and I are planning to spend two summer months at the front doing Red Cross work. It is too soon to know whether it will work out, but . . . if I go I shall be able to tell whether the machine guns of the Germans are worse than those of the ancient regime.[37]

In the meantime, Golder decided to give up archival work. Instead, he followed the swirling events in the capital and collected documents, such as books, newspapers, pamphlets, posters, and other materials, regarding the revolution. Current history seemed far more relevant to him than the remote past.[38]

During the months of late March, April, and May, Golder observed the initial popular enthusiasm for the revolution turn into disillusionment. As Golder feared, the Provisional Government could not cope with the war; the army won no great victories and suffered more and more from disaffection. The working class population in Petrograd became increasingly restive over the war, food rationing, and the high cost of living. The peasant began to overrun rural districts, burning and looting, since the Provisional Government had failed to redistribute land. As defeats and demoralization spread to the front, peasant soldiers deserted in great numbers under the illusion that they would share in the promised distribution of land. Golder wrote on 12 April, "Trains from the front are full of deserters on their way home to be on hand when the land is divided."[39] The army was literally melting away. The Provisional Government seemed helpless, paralyzed by the magnitude of its obligation without having any substantial power. Golder viewed Russia as groping in a dark vacuum of power.

In Zurich, Lenin sensed the governmental paralysis, and searched for a way of returning to Russia. Before long, he arranged with the German government to travel through Germany in a sealed train car. The German government authorized this arrangement because of its belief that Lenin, as a pacifist and revolutionary, would further disorganize the Provisional Government's war effort. On 16 April, Lenin arrived at the Finland station at Petrograd, and he, like a thunderbolt, offered to the soldiers, sailors, and workers around him a new epoch of social revolution and the slogan: Peace, Bread, and Land.[40] Golder wrote, "The trouble with Russia is that the population is tired of the war. At the front the soldiers are in a mood to listen to anybody who will promise them peace."[41] Golder believed that Lenin's decisive slogan represented a powerful weapon in a country with the majority of the population wanting an end to the war, a restoration of the economy, and a redistribution of land. Other American observers in Petrograd, such as the historian Samuel Harper, failed to foresee the tide turning against the Provisional Government.[42]

On 14 May, Golder received an opportunity to view the Provisional Government's desperation up close. He, along with Charles Crane, a conservative American industrialist, and Lincoln Steffens, a liberal, muckraking American journalist, had an interview with Kerensky, who had moved from Minister of Justice to Minister of War in a recent government shakeup. In early May, the Provisional Government had suffered a major crisis because Paul Miliukov, the Minister of Foreign Affairs, had steadfastly supported Allied and Russian war aims. Massive street demonstrations, decrying war aims, drove Miliukov from office, and a new coalition government, which included socialists from the Soviet, came into existence. Kerensky wished to give the Provisional Government a fresh image; he wanted to publicize Russia's war involvement with the Allied governments as an honorable fight against German imperialism in order to rally Russian patriotism and fighting spirit. He therefore asked Steffens to take a message to President Woodrow Wilson, who appeared as an idealist to Russians, which requested him to pressure Britain, France, and Italy to give up their imperialistic war aims.

Golder, who had a good deal of common sense, must have thought Kerensky's suggestion a fanciful illusion. Five weeks earlier, Wilson had brought the United States into the war, on 17 April, because of wide-ranging economic ties, involving loans and war equipment, with Britain, France, and Russia and the approaching collapse of the western and eastern fronts. Wilson, in 1917, did not wish to disunite a concerted war effort by calling for a revision of war aims; such a revision, he envisioned only after the war. But Wilson did plan to aid its desperate Russian ally with loans and war equipment in order to increase its fighting ability. Between 1914 and 1916, Tsarist Russia had spent millions in the United States on railway rolling stock and war materials. Two days after Golder's interview with Kerensky, Wilson approved 100 million dollars in credits to assist Russia in the war. This loan, as stated in a special contractual clause, had to be used for buying war and railway materials in the United States.[43]

A few days after Golder's interview with Kerensky, he became involved in the United States economic assistance to Russia. David Francis, the U. S. ambassador to Russia, summoned Golder. Francis asked him to travel to Vladivostok, meet the John F. Stevens' Advisory Commission there and act as Stevens' interpreter. Wilson had assigned this group of engineers to increase Russia's railway efficiency and to provide advice for the purchase of railway equipment in the United States. Golder, who had wanted to help out in the war, volunteered to act as Stevens' interpreter.[44]

As Golder realized, Russia had become mired in a railway crisis. Before the war, Russian railways had been barely adequate for the transportation of people, food, coal, industrial equipment, and other supplies, even though Russia's industrialization period had greatly improved railway service. The war interrupted Russia's railway expansion, and the war's burdensome railway demands of moving men, ammunition, and food to the front strained the railways to the point of paralysis. The winter of 1917 had been especially critical to the railways; 1,200 locomotive boilers had frozen or burst and heavy snow drifts had stopped 57,000 railway cars. Supplies of flour, coal, and wood trickled into Petrograd, and food, clothing, medicine, and war materials sporadically arrived at the front. Ambassador Francis hoped to prevent Russia's defeat at the front and collapse from internal disintegration by improving Russia's railway efficiency.[45]

Golder, on 17 May, arrived at the Nicholas station to embark on his assignment to meet the Stevens' Mission. At this time, he needed a change of environment and a period of relaxation. His friend, Vernadsky, who accompanied him to the station, wrote, "Golder was smiling with his usual soft smile, but his face, however, was very pale."[46] The privation of food because of the food shortage in Petrograd and sleepless nights from preoccupation with political developments had exhausted Golder. Downcast, he wrote on the day of his departure,

> If I am not much older in years, I see the world differently since the Revolution here. Our joy has turned to sorrow. I could not imagine that a country could go to pieces in such a short time and the end is not yet.[47]

Chaos in the city had also spread to the railway station. Golder had to confront crowds and unruly soldiers everywhere. After he boarded the train, he soon escaped the tumult for a journey to Vladivostok— thousands of miles from restive Petrograd.[48]

Ten days later, Golder reached Vladivostok and took his sleeping quarters at the Hotel Oriental. He found the city and its population playful, happy, and mischievous. For three days, he relaxed, exploring his environs, a graveyard of war materials from the United States; he spoke with a number of Russian radicals from the United States returning to their homeland to advocate a socialist transformation of

Russia; and he bought shoes and flour for his unfortunate friends in Petrograd.[49]

The Stevens Mission came by rail to Vladivostok on 31 May. Golder joined the mission and met Stevens, whom he embraced with admiration. He wrote, "Stevens is a sturdy American, helped build the Great Northern Railway, and is a well read man with a kindly heart."[50] At Vladivostok, Golder participated in the inspection of 700,000 tons of railway materials, nitrate of soda, high explosives, shells, barbed wire, phosphate, metals, equipment, food, and raw materials which had arrived from the United States and Britain and had piled up in conspicuous neglect all over the city—in vacant lots, in side streets, and on hillsides. Some of this material had been wasting away for as long as two years because of a lack of coordinated railway supervision, train cars and locomotives, loading equipment, and motivated manpower.

Along with the Stevens Mission, Golder, on 2 June, boarded a special train car, the Tsar's former accommodations of his Imperial train, to begin the journey back to Petrograd. En route, the mission inspected key railway centers, looking at rolling stock, tracks, repair shops, water tanks, and coal bins. Golder saw firsthand the phenomenal deterioration that these railway centers had suffered due to the war and weather damage. He also found general apathy prevailing among railway workers, who, responding to weariness with the war and the Provisional Government's lack of authority and effectiveness, refused to work on a regular basis, engaging in idle chatter and speechmaking against the government. Such observations prompted Golder to believe that credits, war materials, railway equipment, and sanguine words (a function of another U. S. mission, the Root Mission, in Russia simultaneously with the Stevens Mission) could not prevent Russia's disintegrating spiral.[51]

After reaching Petrograd on 12 June, Golder remained with the Stevens Mission. He expended many hours with its members as they haggled with Russian railway experts over railway requirements, orders, operations, and supervision. Soon, he became weary of playing the secondary role of translator and being constantly on the move, pursuing objectives that led nowhere. He wrote, "I cannot satisfy myself that I am making the best use of my time. About all I do is drive around all day, eat expensive meals, and help a bit."[52] He dreamed of escaping the noise and confusion of the city and the many pointless debates Stevens had with Russian railway experts; he urged to return to a rustic environment. He nostalgically wrote, "How sweet it would be to hear the murmur of trees and live in God's world. When tired I just close my eyes and wander once more on my horse over the desert and in the mountains."[53]

Golder's unhappiness also stemmed from the bleakness of Russian politics. The Petrograd Soviet, as well as the Provisional Government, still entered blind alleys regarding a solution to the war; the Soviet futilely depended on a general European socialist conference to compel statesmen to cease plundering each other when they were fanatically committed to winning the war; the Provisional Government futilely depended on a miraculous victory at the front. As the war dragged on, transportation stagnated, labor discipline flagged, peasant disturbances spread, food shortages grew alarmingly high, and manufactured goods disappeared more and more. During May and June, a growing percentage of factory workers sought solace with the Bolshevik Party that seemed to liken itself to destiny with such slogans as "All power to the Soviets," (with the Bolsheviks in control of them) and "Down with the war." On 1 July, 300,000 disgruntled protesters jammed the streets, chanting Bolshevik slogans and waving Bolshevik banners. Golder, politically conservative, did not sympathize with extremists, whom he viewed as demoralizing the army and the country. Extremist agitation, combined with the dual government's drifting, only magnified Golder's pessimism regarding the March Revolution.[54]

But Golder soon received a jolt. Kerensky yielded to British, French, and American pressure, as well as popular Russian opinion and the Soviet's insistence for a stronger Russian war effort. The Soviet, failing to win a negotiated war settlement through an international socialist conference, concentrated more on the military solution. Kerensky ordered an offensive along the Galician front. Many Russians feared a massive German invasion of Petrograd, and, having a deep longing for peace, responded jubilantly to Kerensky's directive for an offensive against the enemy. Russians, at the moment, clung to the illusion that Russia could triumph over the combination of Austrian and German forces superior in tactics, trained soldiers, equipment, and fighting spirit. On 2 July, only one day after the upsurge of protest, the demonstrations faded away. Golder saw exultant crowds flow into the streets singing nationalistic songs, carrying patriotic flags, and hoisting banners with Kerensky's portrait.[55]

Three days later, Golder departed Petrograd with the Stevens Mission. He had elected to continue his involvement with the mission since it would be traveling in the direction of the Russian front. Golder first traveled to Moscow, where the mission conducted a railway inspection. From Moscow, he moved on to the Donetz Basin in the Ukraine, a major coal mining region. There he came across particularly insubordinate railway workers. The few operating cars, plus the apathetic workers, prevented the necessary tonnage of coal from reaching the cities. Then, on 11 July, the mission train, traveling north from the Ukraine, arrived at Mobilov, the general headquarters of the Russian army. Stevens, who had remained at Petrograd because of his hospitalization on 3 June with erysipelas, now rejoined the mission for a conference with General A. A. Brussilov, the Russian army's commander–in–chief. At Mogilov, Golder learned that the 8th Army of General Kornilov had broken through the Austrian lines on a twenty mile front, but General Brussilov, Golder noted, seemed unemotional over this early Russian success in the field; the General no doubt believed that a challenging counteroffensive could expose the Russian army's weaknesses—low morale, inadequate equipment, and insufficient provisions. As Golder observed, the euphoric atmosphere in Petrograd did not correspond to any enthusiasm at headquarters. One wondered how long the offensive would last until the German army came along and routed the Russians.[56]

The next day, the Stevens Mission traveled on in a northernly direction to Vitebsk, a small city on the Dvina River. As the train pulled into the station, Golder observed on the station platform a crowd of people marching after an elderly–looking man with grey hair and a moustache. The mission party surmised that the crowd had captured a German spy, and perhaps were taking him to a terrible fate. After the train stopped, Golder decided to investigate the matter. He found out that the presumed German spy happened to be Paul Miliukov, who had run afoul as the Provisional Government's first foreign minister. Even though no longer in office, Miliukov had embarked on a speechmaking tour, trying to inspire flagging Russian enthusiasm for the war with new life.[57]

As Golder stood on the station's platform, a member of Miliukov's entourage approached him and stated that Miliukov had missed his train. He wondered if Miliukov might travel with the Stevens Mission. In a few minutes, Golder obtained Stevens' permission, and Miliukov stepped aboard the train car, proceeding to a compartment. The crowd had followed Miliukov to the car and stood curiously in front of it, as if waiting for a farewell speech. Meanwhile, Golder informed Miliukov of the news that the Russian army had broken through the Austrian lines. This news overjoyed Miliukov, and he walked outside to the train car's platform, announcing the Russian army's initial success and calling, with excitement, for three cheers for Kerensky, the Russian army, and the Allies. The crowd responded with a volley of cheers.

After Miliukov withdrew from the platform, the train started up the tracks, heading in the direction of Petrograd. Miliukov, a professional historian like Golder as well as a politician, visited the American in his compartment. While Golder enjoyed talking with this controversial politician, the Russian officer in charge of the special train interrupted them, asking Golder to step outside the compartment. The officer, who perhaps had anti–war beliefs and disliked the Provisional Government, informed Golder that Miliukov had to leave the train because of the haranging speech at Vitebsk and non-membership with the Stevens Mission. Golder differed with the officer, stating that one did not treat a prominent politician disrespectfully.

In spite of Golder's defense of Miliukov, the officer would not change his mind. Golder then hoped that Stevens might intercede. Miliukov, as foreign minister, had been instrumental in admitting the Stevens Mission to Russia. But Stevens would not interfere, claiming that the Russian officer had sole authority over the train. Stevens' decision incensed the historian. He returned to the officer and threatened to accompany Miliukov if forced to leave the train. The officer still would not change his mind, which settled Golder's course of action.

When the train stopped in the night at a dilapidated station, the officer ejected Miliukov from the train. Golder, still upset, also got off, without Stevens' permission. The station, hidden in darkness, was full of destitute, ill–clad, and weary travelers who were trying to sleep. As soon as someone found out the news of Miliukov's presence at the station, travelers gathered around the two new–comers, a famous, controversial politician and an American professor, awestruck. For over an hour, the they asked the two celebrities dozens of questions, holding a seminar in this dark and deserted region of Russia, until the train to Petrograd came in. Miliukov and Golder boarded the train, secure in the thought that they were on their way home. But Golder, hypersensitive from the previous excitement, did not sleep all night long.

At two o'clock in the afternoon, Golder's train arrived at Petrograd. The two fatigued men left their train car and went in separate directions, but Miliukov would not forget Golder's help. The same day, 12 July, Golder visited Franklin Reading, a member of the Stevens Mission and in charge of payroll, at the Hôtel d'Europe. Reading informed Golder that Stevens had fired him. The decision affected him more with relief than with angry surprise. He had expected Stevens, who had the habit of making unreasonable demands on the Minister of Ways of Communication, such as arresting insubordinate workers and placing the Trans–Siberian railway under American control, to become involved in further conflicts. And Golder wanted to bring his archival research to an end so that he could depart Russia in August.[58]

Golder's separation from the Stevens Mission occurred at a critical point in the March Revolution. On 13 July, Petrograd again stood on the threshold of chaos. By this time, the vaulted Russian offensive had turned into a disaster; German shock troops had struck at the Russian forces in Galicia, creating a disorderly rout. The Russian army, reaching its lowest point in morale and disorganization, became ever more susceptible to Bolshevik propaganda involving a separate peace, something neither the Provisional Government nor the Soviet under its current non–Bolshevik leadership would permit. The army's demoralization had even spread to the Petrograd garrison, whose soldiers also became susceptible to the Bolsheviks' peace program. The civilians in Petrograd, too, suffered discouragement; the illusion of peace through victory at the front had burst, bringing to mind that no progress had been accomplished not only toward peace, but neither toward the scarcity of food nor toward the labor and land questions. On the 16th of July, thousands of demonstrators poured into the streets, angrily demanding the Provisional Government's overthrow and even attacking the Soviet for its irresolution. Many Bolshevik sympathizers were in the crowds, but Lenin had dissuaded Bolshevik leaders from trying to ignite a revolution. He patiently waited for a larger disintegration of the army, the dual government, and the peoples' morale.[59]

Late in the evening of 16 July, Golder walked among the masses who filled the Nevsky, staying clear of the wildly driven automobiles. No sign of authority existed anywhere. He then heard the discharge of a machine gun, and soldiers and civilians fled in panic; some of them dropped flat on the street, lying very still. A few moments later, he saw a group of nervous soldiers aim their rifles at bright lights in window buildings, firing at non–existent targets. Fearful of the danger, Golder ran off, seeking safety at the Hôtel d'Europe. He had not traveled very far when the machine gun fired again. Golder raced into a courtyard, squeezing himself in among other petrified demonstrators. After a short wait, he took off and reached the Hôtel d'Europe, where he entered a ground floor with extinguished lights and deserted hallways. He stayed in the hotel until the wild, erratic shooting died away. Full of curiosity, he went back to the Nevsky, where he saw soldiers everywhere without any officers to control them. They needed leadership, and Lenin's order to Bolshevik leaders not to engage in revolutionary tactics seemed apparent on the streets. Golder observed soldiers moving aimlessly about the Nevksy, without purpose. He did not know what would happen. After midnight, he

Street Fighting during the July Days

returned home and lay down on his bed, but sleep eluded him. Outside, demonstrations consumed the night with clamorous sounds. He wrote, "It is all so fascinating and all so dreadful." [60]

This descent toward revolution changed rapidly as the Provisional Government embarked on yet another assertive effort. For the next several days, Golder watched demonstrators disappear from the streets as soon as loyal troops arrived from the front in response to orders from the Provisional Government. The Provisional Government also arrested famous revolutionary figures, such as Leon Trotsky, Lenin's comrade in revolution. Lenin himself fled to Finland, hiding there after being accused (rightly so) of committing treason by taking money from the German government for subversive purposes. By 28 July, loyal troops had restored order in Petrograd and patriotic sentiment re–emerged after the exploitation of the Bolsheviks' German connections.

After the restoration of order, Golder noted that thousands of Russians flocked to the funeral of Cossacks who had been allegedly ambushed by Bolsheviks during the demonstrations, better known as the July Days. He attended this spectacular funeral, which occurred at St. Isaac's Cathedral, where he observed standing conspicuously above the crowd for everyone to see—Kerensky, Miliukov, and Rodzianko, a loyal monarchist, as if they represented duty, honor, order, and security. [61] Golder thought this external display of confidence a charade, for, in reality, the war was still being waged, the army's morale low and discipline shaky, inflation rampant, and the food shortage ever present. In Golder's view, the tempest would soon return.

Unfortunately for Golder, he would not be in Petrograd to witness the Provisional Government's collapse. By November 1917, Lenin's Bolsheviks achieved a majority in the Petrograd Soviet, the support of the Petrograd garrison, and many sympathizers in the army, in the workers' ranks, and among the peasants. On the night of 6–7 November, Lenin ignited the Bolsheviks into action, and they took control of the city after they captured the telephone exchanges, railway stations, and electric lighting plants. A warship fired its guns on the Winter Palace, the Tsar's former palace, where the members of the Provisional Government held their meetings, and they had to flee the city since no one would defend them; Kerensky escaped in an open Pierce–Arrow touring car accompanied by another car flying an American flag. A Congress of Soviets then pronounced the Provisional Government a defunct body. [62]

Thus would be accomplished the November Revolution. But Golder's academic friends, as he prepared to leave Russia because of teaching obligations at Washington State, thought such a drastic event would not happen. When they accompanied him to the Nicholas station on 14 August, they laughed at his pessimistic omens and called his attention to the crowded shops, the busy factories, and well-attended churches. And the Bolsheviks were still weak from their defeat during the July Days. His friend Vernadsky later wrote, "We had all hoped Russia would avoid the final crash while holding herself on the brink of the abyss. I saw Golder again on the side of that abyss."[63]

Golder boarded the train. He would be traveling to Vladivostok on the Trans–Siberian in a special train car, which had been attached to the train's rear, with two Stevens Mission members, George Gibbs and John Greiner; they were returning to the United States since the Stevens Mission neared the completion of its work. After Golder's train departed the station, he traveled south through European Russia, west of the Ural mountains. From his compartment window, he observed women and children scattered in the fields harvesting grain with sickles because so many male peasants fought at the front or had died doing so. He also noted an abundance of crops in the fertile fields.[64] But this harvest would not be distributed to the front or to cities in adequate proportions because of Russia's chaotic and disabled railway network. As Golder realized, the distribution of food might have eased the soldiers' restiveness and the civilians' bitter protest. Such a pastoral scene made Golder keenly aware of the irony of history.[65]

Then, as Golder continued his trip, he came into contact with a thousand years of Russia's Imperial past. On the second day of his trip, he learned that the Tsar, Nicholas II, his wife, four daughters, and son were traveling on a train close by. In late July, Kerensky, now the Provisional Government's Prime Minister after Prince Lvov had resigned following the offensive's failure, decided to relocate the Tsar because of agitation from reactionaries pressing for the Tsar's release and death threats from vengeful leftists. Moreover, the discipline of the garrison at Tsarskoe Selo, where the Imperial family was under house arrest, could not be trusted. If new disturbances broke out, a violent mob might easily slaughter the family. Kerensky chose to move the Tsar and his family to Tobolsk, north of the Trans–Siberian main line in Siberia, as the place for the Tsar's isolated captivity.[66]

The following day, 17 August, the locomotive of Golder's train ran short of water. It detoured off the main rails to make a special stop to refill a water tank, leaving behind the Tsar's train. But that night, around nine o'clock, Golder's train caught up with the Tsar's train, following this train which moved slowly on the tracks. Close to midnight, the Tsar's train, near Tyumen, where the Imperial family would transfer to a boat on the Tura River, pulled into a siding to let Golder's faster train pass by. Golder, as his train paralleled the Tsar's, saw with fascination two sets of trains—one housing the Imperial family disguised with Japanese flags and placards reading *Japanese Red Cross Mission* and the other one spilling over with 330 soldiers. No matter where Golder traveled, history seemed to be following him.[67]

After two more days of traveling, Golder forgot about the Tsar. The third morning, however, Golder received a shocking surprise. Just after he had awakened, a porter informed him that Russian authorities did not know about the Tsar's escort but believed that he had escaped from his captivity at Tsarskoe Selo and had hidden himself in Golder's special car. Soldiers had been posted on the train to guard the car. At nine o'clock the same morning, the train rolled into the station at Krasnoyarsk, a Siberian city with a large Bolshevik contingency. As soon as the train stopped, officers placed several companies of soldiers around the suspected train. In a short time, an officer entered Golder's car, demanding to see his papers in the name of the Krasnoyarsk Soviet. While the officer inspected Golder's papers, three soldiers searched the car. Golder, perhaps close to terror, wrote, "Fortunately for us we had with us the Petrograd papers which showed that the Emperor was being sent to Siberia. This seems to be the first time these people have heard of the move."[68]

The knowledge that the Tsar had not escaped sobered the officer. He explained to Golder that the Krasnoyarsk Soviet had received a telegram from the Soviet at Ekaterinburg which stated that the Tsar was traveling through Siberia, probably with an American mission. Golder's special car, with its two members of the Stevens Mission aboard, had drawn the officer's suspicion. He also said that the local Soviet had placed a guard at a bridge across the Yenisey River just outside the city with instructions to blow it up if Golder's train had failed to stop. Golder had indeed been fortunate that the train's chief engineer had stopped the train.

Even though the Russian officer released Golder, he still did not completely trust him. Golder wrote, "One of the Krasnoiarsk 'commissars' kept his eyes on us as far as Irkutsk [a day's ride], occasionally examined our papers, although not always sober."[69] At Irkutsk, the "commissar" disappeared, but authorities there, having heard the rumor of the Tsar's escape, conducted another search for him. By this time, the Imperial family had reached Tobolsk, where they would live unharmed until the emotions of the Soviet Civil War led to their murder by Bolsheviks. After the futile search, Golder traveled past

Lake Baikal, then through Manchuria, China, Korea, and by ship to Japan, where he boarded the steamship, *Empress of Russia*, whose name now belonged to history, and sailed for the United States.[70]

Chapter IV

From the Inquiry to the Hoover War Collection

When Golder returned to the United States in September 1917, the American public regarded the Provisional Government as representative of the Russian people struggling for victory in the Great War for the cause of democracy. Most Americans did not suspect the Provisional Government's weakness and Russia's exhaustion and that the Bolshevik Party moved closer to victory. President Wilson, along with numerous newspapers that spread a pro–Provisional Government sentiment, inspired this false impression, hailing the March Revolution as a victory for democracy and the Provisional Government as a suitable partner in the Allied coalition against the Kaiser of Germany rather than autocratic, Tsarist Russia. Wilson's view emanated from his moralistic crusade to rid the world of German autocracy, imperialism, and militarism (to replace them with American globalism). But Golder, having just returned from Russia, knew that most Russians wanted peace and that the Provisional Government could not endure much longer because it had alienated the support of the soldiers, the workers, and the peasants.[1]

Golder not only had direct experience with Russia's revolutionary aspirations, but he also had a personal archive regarding the March Revolution.[2] While at Petrograd, he had shipped out of Russia his collection of books, pamphlets, newspapers, and other documents related to the revolution. In October 1917, he began organizing these documents with the idea of writing a history of the March Revolution. But a new assignment cut short this ambition that represented one of the earliest attempts to treat the March Revolution in a scholarly fashion.[3]

In November, Golder became involved in the preparations for the peace that might follow World War I. What Wilson wanted concerned a righteous peace to morally justify having brought the United States into a war on such a high principle as "saving the world for democracy." To achieve this purpose, Wilson wished to establish an independent research organization for collecting documents, writing reports, and presenting cartographic and statistical information in preparation for the United States' case at the peace conference.

In September, Wilson had assigned his personal diplomatic advisor, Colonel Edward House, to select historians, economists, political scientists, and geographers as members of this research organization called the Inquiry.[4]

Wilson hoped to keep the Inquiry a secret, but in September an Inquiry underling leaked the story to the press that a special diplomatic organization was being put together. Metropolitan newspapers across the country printed the story on the front page. Golder, reading his newspaper in tiny Pullman, Washington, learned about the Inquiry, and decided that he would like to participate; scores of other intellectuals responded similarly. Golder's interest reflected fundamental patriotism, but scholarly considerations and his recent experience in Russia prompted him to think he might be able to assist the Inquiry. Furthermore, as a young man, he had flirted with the idea of becoming a career diplomat. And lastly, he was not timid about enhancing his own reputation.

In quest of an Inquiry assignment, Golder wrote a friend, John F. Jameson, Director of Historical Research for the Carnegie Institution, "that he would be delighted to be of service to our government."[5] Jameson had founded the National Board for Historical Service (NBHS), whose chairman, James T. Shotwell, was an Inquiry leader. Shotwell enlisted NBHS's assistance in the Inquiry's work, and Jameson informed Shotwell of Golder's interest in working for the Inquiry. Jameson, a leading historian, wrote Shotwell that:

> Golder speaks and writes Russian with facility, has a very exceptional familiarity with the history of the diplomatic relations between the U. S. and Russia, and has had excellent opportunities of observation during several of the earlier and several of the most recent months of the war. But what I should emphasize most, is, that he is an observer of extraordinary intelligence, insight, and good judgment, and that, being a man of catholic sympathies, he has put himself in contact with quite an unusual variety of people in Russia, so that he is exceptionally able to estimate the opinions and tendencies of different classes there.[6]

Shotwell, impressed by Jameson's opinion of Golder, sent Golder a telegram, asking him to join the Inquiry.[7]

After accepting this assignment, Golder secured a two month leave of absence from Washington State and left on the train for New York City in late November. When he arrived at New York, Golder visited Shotwell at the Inquiry's headquarters located in the building of the American Geographical Society on upper Broadway. There

Golder discussed with Shotwell the Inquiry's organization, various planned assignments, and overall goals. Golder also found out that he would be working for $240 a month. He stayed in New York for a week, and then traveled to Harvard University, where he joined the other fifteen members of the Inquiry's Eastern European Division under the supervision of Archibald Cary Coolidge, Golder's mentor at Harvard.[8] After moving into his living quarters at the Colonial Club, Golder began his sundry Inquiry assignments at Harvard's Widener Library, which had been established by Coolidge.

The Inquiry hired over 100 scholars to fill positions in fifteen different divisions. The Eastern European Division had some of the best qualified Inquiry members, a tribute to Coolidge, who had a wide knowledge of Eastern European studies and a facility with Slavic and Middle Eastern languages. In other divisions, however, many of the members were not experts in the fields relating to their particular assignments; some members had been selected because of scholarly reputation or connections with an eastern university rather than acquaintance with world politics. The reason for this dearth of talent lay mostly at the door of American universities which had trained few historians in the fields of contemporary history. The Inquiry's leaders had to rely on historians of ancient history and early American history, archaeologists, medievalists, and experts in other fields that did not relate to contemporary European problems. Golder, though, contrasted sharply with this general academic trend. His background of multi-linguistic skills and practical European experience, especially in revolutionary Russia, qualified him above scholars of more brilliance but unfamiliar with contemporary Europe. Coolidge wrote, "I have not thought of any man better than Golder for Russia."[9]

At first, the Inquiry hired Golder for two months. On 17 December, he wrote Shotwell, asking if the Inquiry planned to extend his membership after January 1918 so that he could make arrangements with Washington State College. Shotwell sent Golder a contract that involved securing a leave of absence for six months, devoting all his time to research for the Inquiry, and taking a monthly salary of $245. Golder signed the contract, but Washington State would not allow him a leave of absence with academic salary. E. Holland, President of Washington State, informed the Inquiry that the college had already committed its funds to special agricultural projects and could not pay Golder a salary while not teaching. As a result, Golder complained to Shotwell that he needed an increase in salary from the Inquiry to compensate for the loss of income from the college as well as from public lectures he had planned to give. Shotwell wrote back to Golder, stressing that one ought to place patriotism above financial reward. He stated, "May I point out that so far as I know every worker in this Inquiry is engaged upon it at some sacrifice to himself. It is not to be regarded as a purely business proposition."[10] Despite the financial loss, Golder accepted the salary arrangement and still viewed his role for the Inquiry optimistically, a role which seemed to offer him the opportunity to engage in original research, to influence diplomatic policy, and to attend the actual peace conference in some capacity.

The Inquiry had chosen Golder as an expert on Russia. Its leaders, Sidney Mezes, a philosopher of religion and ethics, James T. Shotwell, a historian of contemporary history, Isaiah Bowman, director of the American Geographical Society, Walter Lippmann, a writer, and David Hunter Miller, a lawyer, did not directly charge the Eastern European Division with assignments regarding the new Bolshevik regime. In fact, no Inquiry member was given such an assignment. The Inquiry leaders considered the Bolshevik regime a transitory event; upon its collapse, Russia would develop democratic institutions.

The Inquiry might have assigned Golder to explore the themes of diplomatic, economic, and cultural cooperation with Soviet Russia. But Wilson, with the aid of the State Department, arrogated Russian matters to himself. Wilson and Robert Lansing, the Secretary of State, although aware of the appeal and challenge of Bolshevism, lacked the knowledge of Russian life and politics to face the reality of cooperation.[11] Instead the Wilson administration refused to recognize the Bolshevik government for a host of reasons: the Bolsheviks had withdrawn from the war in December 1917 and negotiated a separate peace at Brest–Litovsk in March 1918 (treasonous acts according to the Wilson administration), divided landlord estates, nationalized land, banks, and factories (threats to capitalism), repudiated the Provisional Government's national debts (act of international theft), and confiscated church property (signs of a heathen world). Wilson and Lansing viewed the Bolsheviks as the bitter foes of capitalism, morality, democracy, and international law, a new enemy, as threatening to world stability as German autocracy, imperialism, and militarism. Their ignorance of Soviet Russia spawned the United States ideological opposition to the Soviets, which prepared the way for global confrontations between these two countries.

Golder, although conservative, had an independent mind, and could have undertaken topics related to the new Bolshevik regime. Instead, he received assignments that dealt with former Tsarist provinces, such as Lithuania and the Ukraine.[12] Wilson, in January 1918, had announced in his Fourteen Points speech the principle of self–determination as the inherent right of all nations in a new world order of international cooperation. This speech established its mark on the Inquiry's assignments; the Eastern European Division dealt with, as Coolidge called the unit, Questions of Nationalities. Golder therefore researched territorial boundaries, and linguistic, ethnic, and cultural differences between Russia and its borderlands. His reports tended to be factual, concise in style, and illustrated with maps. He wrote approximately thirteen reports, and they varied in length, from over 100 pages to only a few pages.

From his analysis, Golder recommended the independence of Finland, Lithuania, and Poland while viewing, for example, the Ukraine and Estonia in *realpolitik* terms. He thought that Estonia could not govern itself because of its political inexperience from seven centuries of Russian domination, and that Russia needed an outlet through Estonia to the Baltic Sea. The Ukraine, he believed, had ethnic, linguistic, and cultural similarities with Russia, as well as coal and agricultural resources indispensable to Russia's economy. Golder therefore recommended that Estonia and the Ukraine be included in a federation with Russia. As matters turned out, the Inquiry did not accept Golder's suggestion for Russian unification, recommending to Wilson the independence of Estonia and the Ukraine, along with every former Tsarist province, recommendations which fit neatly into Wilson's conception of the fulfillment of national aspirations. Golder's recommendations, however, reflected his awareness of the problem of being too idealistic in a very complex world.[13]

Golder did not protest the fact that the Inquiry failed to assign him topics that directly dealt with the issue of the new Bolshevik regime, although in his reports on the Ukraine he cryptically indicated that Russia should be allowed to pursue its own destiny. What he did complain about involved lack of information. Golder, being a thorough, careful and thoughtful researcher, wanted the latest information, for example, from the State Department for his report on Siberia, since American observers had been sending data to the State Department. Walter Lippmann, the Inquiry's secretary, would not give him permission to use the State Department's files. Golder failed to receive permission because of friction between the Inquiry and the State Department over the Inquiry's independent function. Moreover, Lansing and Wilson were considering the possibility of intervening in Siberia as an anti–Bolshevik measure, bringing self–determination to Russia through the victory of Russian reactionary armies. After finishing his report on Siberia, Golder wrote Lippmann,

> It is longer than it should be and not as good as it might
> be. The last part of it is incomplete owing to the difficulty

of getting accurate information about the present situation in Siberia.[14]

In researching his other reports, Golder also sought out information beyond Harvard's Widener Library. This library, although rich in sources on western Europe, had few contemporary sources involving eastern Europe, the Baltic region, and Russia. As Golder found out in his determination to secure information, there did not exist a single archival center in the United States for the study of modern eastern Europe and Russia. Golder's difficulty in finding source materials brought him not only frustration but also irritation with an Inquiry member who critiqued his long report on Lithuania. Golder wrote Lippmann:

> The critic says there "must be somewhere in existence" better material, better judgment, etc. Perhaps there is but I have tried hard, but in vain, to locate it. He says, "there are many studies in Russian of special aspects on the Lithuanian question: economic, linguistic, social, historical." If the critic would give us such a list and tell us where they may be obtained we should be very grateful to him.
>
> I have no controversy with the critic, but I wish you to know that I use the best data available and if it is a little old, it is because I cannot get anything more recent.[15]

In spite of this conflict over source materials, Golder remained a loyal historian for the Inquiry. In March 1918, he received a letter asking him to accept a commission with the American Red Cross in France, a request which would place him in one of the countries that had suffered the most devastation during World War I; the German army had fought on French territory for the entire war and continued to do so. Golder informed Lippmann of this request (exciting to Golder), asking if the Inquiry would require his services beyond the first of June 1918. Lippmann responded:

> We are unanimous in wanting you to stay with us after June first. . . . Your very special qualifications and ability make you practically indispensable to us. We feel that there are few opportunities that might be offered you in which you could be of more immediate service to the cause.[16]

Golder decided to stay with the Inquiry.

For the next several months, Golder labored over his reports in order to meet time schedules. Then, on 11 November 1918, Germany signed an Armistice with the Allies, bringing to an end the war that had brought about two revolutions in Russia, driven Germany's

Kaiser into exile, slaughtered millions of young men, and turned democratic governments into instruments for encouraging sacrifice, hatred, amorality, and passion to win the war. Just before Golder had departed from Russia in August 1917, he wrote, "The thing to do now is to finish with this war and then let us all go to work to make this world a better place to live."[17] The Armistice meant to Golder the next stage of his role in the Inquiry–his participation at the peace conference in Europe's reconstruction.

The Secretary of State, Lansing, established mechanisms for selecting the American personnel, from plenipotentiaries to advisors to clerks to go to the international gathering. By late November, ten Inquiry members had been chosen as part of the United States delegation for the voyage to Europe with President Wilson for the peace conference. At that time, Golder learned that the Inquiry had omitted his name. Having expected to take the trip as the logical conclusion to his tenure with the Inquiry, he was stunned by the sudden realization that he would be left behind in the United States. He considered himself the most qualified among the Inquiry's personnel, except Coolidge, to represent Russia. In a letter to Isaiah Bowman, an Inquiry leader, Golder wrote:

> Not that it will do any good . . . but in justice to myself I must protest at the way I am being treated. For a year I have given the Inquiry all my time and all my strength. It was done at a financial loss and an impairment of health, but it was done willingly.[18]

Golder also noted that he had decided not to take the assignment in France because of Lippmann's characterization that the Inquiry believed his work to be "indispensable," and mentioned that he should have negotiated a trip to the peace conference for his continued service with the Inquiry; (Robert Kerner, a historian of eastern Europe, had negotiated such a deal). Golder ended his letter, stating: "I trusted the committee to do the right thing and as a result I have before me the humiliating position of having to answer the question—'Why are you not in Paris with the others?"[19]

Golder had suddenly found himself the victim of a bureaucratic purge. Lansing, who considered the Inquiry a competing diplomatic agency, had insisted that Wilson reduce its membership for the peace conference. Wilson gave in to Lansing's recommendation, since only the State Department could handle the administrative, organizational, and personnel responsibilities for an entire delegation. In conformity with the State Department's wishes, the Inquiry leadership whittled down a total membership of 123 to 80 and then to 10 representatives bound for the peace conference.[20] Robert Lord, aged 32 (Golder was 41), who had replaced Coolidge as head of the Eastern European Division after Coolidge had departed for Europe as a special assistant to the State Department, represented Russia and Poland. Lord, a highly regarded expert on Polish history, was not a specialist on Russian history, even though he had studied in Moscow. Such an ill-qualified selection for Russia reflected the Wilson administration's determination to settle diplomatic questions regarding Poland and unwillingness to negotiate with and develop an understanding of the new Soviet regime.[21]

What did happen between the United States government, the Allied governments, and Soviet Russia from 1918 to 1920 involved an unofficial war against the Bolshevik regime. In 1918, Wilson, a wavering moralist, let his predilection for anti-Bolshevik sentiment compel him to participate with France and Britain in surrounding Soviet Russia in an effort to gain territory, to get revenge for Russia's withdrawal from the war and separate peace, to stop the spread of Bolshevism, and to help Russian reactionaries in the overthrow of the Bolshevik regime. The British established a blockade in the Baltic Sea, closing off ports with shipments for Soviet Russia. British, French, and American troops came to Archangel, where they closed the Arctic Sea to the Bolsheviks and offered soldiers, war materials, food, and money to assist the reactionary armies (Whites) in fighting against the Bolshevik army (Reds) in the Soviet Civil War that had begun in November–December 1917. The French who had an interest in Ukrainian coal and iron, occupied southern Russia, where they supported the White armies there and cut off Ukrainian resources to the Bolsheviks. The British also had an interest in the oil fields of the Caucasus, where they supported the Whites and closed off the Black Sea. Contingents of British, French, Japanese, and American soldiers landed at Vladivostok, thus cutting off the Pacific to the Bolsheviks. This unofficial declaration of war, a war the Bolsheviks would rally to win, compelled the Soviet regime to impose on Russia repression, administrative centralization, and forced requisitions in the countryside. The price of this war in human life and economic devastation, like any war, was high.

In conjunction with American intervention, Wilson did try a diplomatic solution to the Soviet question. He attempted to bring about a conference at Prinkipo or Prince's Islands in the Sea of Marmora close to Constantinople between the United States, the Allied governments, the de facto White Russian governments, and the Bolsheviks, who had not been invited to the Paris Peace Conference. Wilson decided to consider a conference for a variety of reasons:

Bolshevik Russia's Isolation during the Soviet
Civil War

Allied intervention was proving ineffective, the Russian people were rallying to the Bolshevik cause, congressional opposition was growing, and troop morale was low and conscription out of the question with World War I over. Wilson also thought that a peaceful settlement might place Siberian territory in the hands of a de facto White government favorable to United States interests—an anti–Bolshevik state in opposition to the Soviets and hostile to the spread of Japanese imperialism in the Far East. The United States had not only joined the Allied governments in intervening in Soviet Russia as an anti–Bolshevik measure but also as a measure to prevent Japanese imperialism in Siberia, Manchuria, and China so that the United States could dominate China and Manchuria under the guise of an Open Door policy.

From the outset, though, Wilson's diplomatic solution with a conference at Prinkipo ran into difficulties. It was accepted by the Bolsheviks, but rejected by the Whites, and vociferously opposed by the French government, which, under the illusion of eventually crushing the Bolsheviks, advocated a military solution. After the failure to carry out the Prinkipo conference, Wilson and House sent William Bullitt, a United States diplomatic agent, on a special diplomatic mission to Soviet Russia which might lead to a conference. Bullitt, who favored a cooperative view toward the Soviets, returned with negotiable diplomatic terms from Russia. Wilson was not interested in a rapprochement with the Soviets, only in a fact–finding mission. He therefore withdrew active support for a conference, and in March 1919 decided to continue the intervention policy, aiding Admiral Kolchak, the White leader in Siberia, assisting the counterrevolution in southern Russia, and maintaining an economic embargo against the Soviets. Wilson had certain qualms about supporting Kolchak, a fanatical reactionary, but Wilson thought Kolchak the best alternative because of his anti–Bolshevik rigidity, willingness to pay Russia's old debts, and opposition to the Japanese. In the end, the Bolsheviks forced the United States to withdraw from Siberia in January 1920, and captured and executed Kolchak.[22]

While the Allied military intervention took place in Soviet Russia, Golder, in December 1918, returned to Pullman with resentment and bitterness toward the Inquiry. Years later, when he was in a more satirical than bitter mood, he wrote:

> The warring armies did not fight half as bitterly [during World War I] over the frontier lines as did the peace experts. I had the best plan, which, I am grieved to say, aroused the jealousy of both Lansing and House, and they refused to take me to Paris. Had I been there to guide Wilson, I am certain

we would have made a better treaty than we did. After this fling in world politics, I returned to the mountains and prairies of the wild west and busied myself in criticizing the American and European statesmen.[23]

In spite of Golder's seeming exile from world politics, he always looked forward to new challenges. Little did he know that in 1920 he would embark on the greatest challenge of his life.

In the summer of 1920, Ephraim D. Adams, a professor of American diplomatic history at Stanford University, invited Golder to take over a departing faculty member's summer classes in history. Golder accepted the invitation, and during July 1920 traveled to Stanford, where he taught classes on modern European history. At this time, Adams introduced Golder to a new archival center, independent of Stanford University, called the Hoover War History Collection (a title soon shortened to Hoover War Collection),[24] which had been founded by Herbert Hoover in 1919.

In 1915, Adams had written Hoover suggesting that he should preserve the records of the Commission for Belgian Relief (CBR) at Stanford. Hoover, a wealthy mining engineer, who had graduated from Stanford University, had been the director of the CBR, which had shipped food for Belgians trapped behind the British blockade during World War I; the CBR's records included diplomatic correspondence with governments, the reports of field workers, shipping, accounting, and administrative records, and general reports on conditions in Belgium and northern France. When the CBR finished its operations in 1919, Hoover acted on Adam's suggestion, giving the CBR's records to Adams. More importantly, Hoover asked Adams to broaden this archive to one involving a general European collection on the Great War and offered $50,000 for establishing such an archival center at Stanford. Adams eagerly accepted Hoover's suggestion.

Within a year of its inception, the Hoover War Collection developed strong archival sections on western and central Europe, but lacked extensive documentary materials on eastern Europe, especially Russia. Adams thought Golder would be the logical choice to galvanize a large eastern European collection at Stanford because of his knowledge of foreign languages, travel, scholarship, and personality. That summer of 1920, while Golder taught summer school at Stanford, Adams recruited him to be the Hoover Collection's curator of the eastern European collection and offered him a position on Stanford's history faculty.[25]

In spite of Golder's deep attachment for Washington State College, he considered working for the Hoover Collection, with its scope of the economic, political, military, diplomatic, and social aspects of

World War I, an irresistible temptation—not to mention a history professorship. Being at Stanford offered him adventure, travel, new friends, a stimulating academic environment, and research possibilities beyond his imagination. Not surprisingly, he agreed to be a curator for the Hoover Collection and to take a position in Stanford's history department.

As early as August, Adams scheduled Golder for a major collecting trip to Europe. He would thus become the Hoover's third historical sleuth, joining Adams, who, with a professional background in American–British relations, developed the western European section, and Ralph H. Lutz, a professor of German history, who handled the central European section. In 1919, Adams had traveled to Paris, where he had collected materials on the Paris Peace Conference. During the same year, Lutz had traveled throughout central Europe, laying the foundations for the central European collections, especially Germany. Before Golder's departure to Europe, Adams and Lutz gave him encouragement, advice, and a general collecting plan.[26]

Adams charged Golder with an immense task. Adams wanted him to collect as many documents as possible throughout Europe, with an emphasis on Russia, the Balkans, eastern Europe, and the Baltic region, documents which included European involvement in World War I—diplomatic records, legislative proceedings, military reports, diaries, private papers, pamphlets, leaflets, proclamations, and posters. To collect such a mass of information, Golder needed the cooperation of individuals, institutions, and governments.

There were opportunities for gaining this cooperation. Wartime censorship and restrictions had ended in many countries. Certain governments hoped to receive aid from the United States since Wilson had appointed Herbert Hoover as chairman of the American Relief Administration (ARA), an organization designed to feed starving Europeans following the economic dislocations of World War I. The ARA and the American Red Cross (ARC), which had offices throughout Europe, could provide Golder with transportation, storage and mailing privileges, and introductions to key governmental authorities. And certain governments with a grievance against another government (individuals, too) might offer archival materials for a reasonable price.

On the other hand, there still loomed a particularly sticky problem. This concerned governments either hostile to the United States, such as Romania, or having diplomatic controversies with the United States, such as Soviet Russia. Golder, at the outset of this trip, did not know if he would be able to enter Russia. The Soviets had little trust of Americans because of their involvement in the Soviet Civil War and because of the State Department's ideological and economic opposition to the Soviets. During this trip, Golder would have to personally negotiate with the Soviets for permission to enter Russia.[27]

Golder left Stanford on 20 August. After his train arrived at New York City, he booked passage on the steamship, *Imperator*. He then sought out information on his chances of entering Russia from Ludwig Martens, the Russian Soviet Federated Socialist Republics' (RSFSR) representative in the United States, who had an office in New York. The Soviets had sent Martens to the United States in order to obtain status as an official Soviet diplomat and to establish Soviet–American commercial ties. The State Department, however, refused to recognize Martens as an accredited diplomat and claimed that he disseminated anti–American propaganda. After the United States government had pulled its troops out of Siberia in 1920, the government's revulsion for Bolshevism turned into a domestic Red Scare, a witch hunt against so–called domestic and foreign subversives. Golder, who had a tolerance for varying views, , had no qualms about speaking with Martens. Martens acted friendly towards Golder and promised to contact the Soviet representative in London regarding Golder's request to enter Russia. This response satisfied Golder, since he realized that getting into Russia would not be easy.[28]

After this meeting, Golder boarded the *Imperator* and looked over the passenger list for anyone who might be able to contribute to the Hoover Collection. Not spotting any possible contributors, he settled into the leisurely pace of a ship passenger. During the voyage's second day, however, he unexpectedly met a Russian in the ship's smoking room. This Russian turned out to be Nicholas Golovin, who had been a Tsarist general during World War I and had recently been a military leader for the White army in Siberia, although not a fanatical White commander such as Generals Yudenitch, A. Deniken, Peter Wrangel, and Admiral Kolchak.[29]

The curious Golder spoke with Golovin until late at night, and he found out that the General had been wounded in battle while in Siberia, had escaped to Japan just before the defeat of the White military forces there, and then had traveled to the United States with the idea of publishing a book on World War I. Now an émigré, like thousands of other Russians who fled Russia because of Bolshevik Revolution, Golovin had to face many uncertainties with a wife, two children, and enough money for only two months. Golder considered Golovin an intelligent man who had a light–hearted sense of humor and seemed prepared to face the unknown future stoically. Golder also thought that Golovin could be potentially helpful to the Hoover

Collection, since he had many connections with Russian military and diplomatic émigrés in Europe.

That night, Golder told Golovin about the Hoover Collection and that Hoover hoped the books resulting from this Collection might enlighten the leaders of nations so that another international war might not happen again. Of course, this view was idealistic, and not lost on Golovin, who had no illusions about the shortcomings of statesmen. But he thought highly of the concept of an archival center devoted to the Great War and Russia's involvement in the war. As a result, he volunteered to assist the Hoover as a roving acquisition agent in Europe and accepted this role without pay.[30] Golovin's commitment impressed Golder, a commitment he had secured even before reaching London.

When Golder did arrive in Great Britain, he rode the train to London. While in London, he continued to contact Russian émigrés and visited one of the more famous Russian émigrés in western Europe, Paul Miliukov, whom Golder had defended during Miliukov's controversial train ride with the Stevens Mission. After the Bolshevik Revolution, Miliukov, to escape capture, had fled northern Russia and joined the White armies of Generals Kornilov and Deniken in southern Russia before deciding on permanent exile in western Europe in 1918. Golder had lunch with Miliukov, and the Russian, in response to the knowledge of Golder's collecting enterprise, said that he had lost archival collections at Rostov and Kiev because of the Soviet Civil War, but that he still had a large collection of papers and rare books which he had hidden at a village in Finland. He offered to let Golder buy the collection if he wished to take the trouble of securing it in Finland. Golder accepted the challenge, as well as a book by Miliukov, *Bolshevism: An International Danger*.[31]

During his stay in London, Golder continued to probe the possibility of entering Russia. He made an appointment to see Leonid Krassin, who chaired the Russian trade delegation which was in London to negotiate trade agreements with the British government; unlike the United States government, the British government proved to be responsive to trade with the Soviets after the failure of British interventionist policy in 1919.[32] Golder called on Krassin on the morning of 24 September. After some initial difficulty with secretaries over the appointment, Golder gained access to Krassin and gave him an introductory letter from Walter Brown, director of the ARA office in London. This letter stated that Golder wished to collect documents in Soviet Russia covering the Bolshevik Revolution as well as write a report on food conditions in Russia for Hoover's evaluation. Krassin said that the Soviet government discouraged Americans from entering Russia because of the State Department's hostility to Soviet Russia. Golder, well aware of the State Department's economic and diplomatic boycott of Soviet Russia, tried to portray his document and food investigative mission as strictly non-political, as a purely humanitarian matter. In response, Krassin stated that he would communicate Golder's request to the Soviet government, informing the ARA office in London of the result. Golder wrote, "I have some hope that Krassin's efforts will not be in vain."[33]

That evening, Golder had dinner with Count G. Benningson and his wife. Count Benningson worked at the former Provisional Government's consulate in London, which still kept its doors open as an information center. The Count told Golder that he and his wife had suffered many privations in Russia and abroad after the Bolshevik Revolution. Golder wrote in his diary, "Unlike other refugees, they have little bitterness towards the new order, and give their enemies credit for their good points."[34] He also found out that the Benningsons had no consistent source of income except the generosity of Russians who came to the consulate for assistance. The Count's wife, who spoke several languages, asked Golder if he would find her work as a translator. He said that such jobs were scarce, and that unfortunately he could not help her. The Count appreciated Golder's honesty and company, and, as a token of good-will, gave him a large package of rare Bolshevik and White Russian propaganda which he had collected in northern Russian in 1918.

A few days later, Golder left London, traveling to Paris, which he had not seen since 1907. After his arrival, he reacquainted himself with the city. He soon found that Paris had changed greatly. He encountered hundreds of American expatriots, discharged soldiers, and disillusioned Europeans. The war had uprooted many of them, and now they floundered in a world of political uncertainty, economic chaos, social alienation, and cultural confusion. These young people had crowded most of the hotels in Paris so that Golder returned to a familiar one at 7 rue des Feuillantes. Here, Golder had lived during his student days, in an unshattered, pre-war world, living a carefree, contemplative life, unconcerned with the world's state.[35]

The following day, Golder contacted James Logan, who headed the ARA branch in Paris. He arranged with Logan to receive documents from other countries which he would be collecting, just in case circumstances eliminated regular mailing channels. After making this arrangement and with Logan's approval, he toured the ARA's maze of bureaus, discovering neglected statistical and economic reports about contemporary Europe in the aftermath of war. As Golder noted, these reports had pertinent historical information, but there they were collecting dust and destined for obliteration. He spoke with several of the ARA's bureaucrats about preserving their records for historical investigation at Stanford. They agreed to do so. He also persuaded them to ship copies of new reports to the Hoover. In less than a few weeks, Golder had become a discerning collector of documents.[36]

Golder then visited a number of diplomatic delegations which had represented their countries at the Paris Peace Conference. As Adams had done a year earlier, Golder secured a large quantity of pamphlets and propaganda material from such delegations. While collecting materials from diplomatic delegations, he went to the Provisional Government's Embassy in Paris. At this embassy, he asked its staff for their diplomatic records. The staff, bearing a grievance against the Bolsheviks, gave him more than he bargained for—documents dealing with Russia in World War I, the March Revolution, and the November Revolution. This acquisition overwhelmed Golder. They also agreed to send additional documents to Stanford. He realized, though, that after the memory of his visit faded, the embassy staff might forget their promise. Golder therefore gave one high ranking embassy official some money to encourage further collecting activity.[37]

On 3 October, Golder departed Paris. He took the train through terrain ravaged by the war and stopped at Coblenz, Germany, a city located close to the French border in the Rhineland. During the Paris Peace Conference, French diplomats, demanding security against another invasion from Germany, had secured a demilitarized zone stretching thirty–one miles east of the Rhine, which encompassed Coblenz, with French, British, and American troops occupying the zone for fifteen years. Golder had chosen an ideal place for collecting documents; the American section of the Inter–Allied High Command at Coblenz had reports depicting military, economic, social, and political conditions in Germany, as well as reports of its own activities.[38]

To acquire a hotel room at Coblenz, Golder had to go to the Billeting Department of the American Army. After securing a hotel room and dropping off his luggage, he visited Colonel David Stone, the deputy to Major General Henry T. Allen, who headed the American section of the commission. During their conversations, Golder and Stone discussed the controversy surrounding the French in the Rhineland, and Stone told Golder that the French insisted on crushing Germany. Indeed, the Treaty of Versailles, largely inspired by French diplomacy, had saddled Germany with a war guilt clause, had given Lorraine and Alsace to France, had permitted French control of the Saar coal mines, had stripped Germany of its colonies, and had burdened Germany with fantastic reparations. Golder then broached Stone about offering the United States commission's reports to the

Hoover for preservation. Stone liked the idea of an archival center that included the study of Germany, and agreed to assist Golder in extending the Hoover Collection's repositories.[39]

After finishing with Coblenz, Golder moved on. He boarded a train, passed through central Germany, and stopped at Berlin on 5 October. In newspaper accounts, he had read of the Germans' pitiful state. The British naval blockade of Germany for nine months after the Armistice and the economic deprivation resulting from the Treaty of Versailles had demoralized a substantial part of the city's population. Golder noted from his travel by train to Berlin that the German railways had deteriorated severely and suffered from overcrowded conditions. In Berlin, he noted that Berliners could not expect coal, stood in bread lines, and had little money to buy items. Golder wrote, "The German is crushed, humbled, and humilitated."[40] He also discovered that many Germans had a thirst for revenge against France. He wrote Adams:

> The porter of the sleeping car, with whom I talked, said he had nothing against England and America, but he added, "I am forty–eight years old, am wounded, but if the time ever comes, so help me God, I will take up arms against France."[41]

In 1917, Golder had observed such hate and demoralization in Russia, and how these grievances could be channeled into extremist movements, completely altering a nation's social, economic, cultural, and political fabric.

While making such observations, Golder went to the Russian Red Cross in Berlin, which assisted Russian émigrés there, and he arranged to have dinner with its leaders, Madame and Baron Wrangel, cousin of General Peter Wrangel, a monarchist who was still fighting against the Bolsheviks with a White army in southern Russia. During his dinner with the Wrangels, they told Golder that they thought the Bolsheviks would fall in another month or two, and they believed that they would be able to return to Russia, establishing the old Tsarist traditions. They had reason to be hopeful.

As the Soviet Civil War came to an end and the Polish–Soviet War neared a negotiated settlement, Soviet Russia had to confront internal problems—the hostility aroused against forced requisitions, long, taxing hours in the factories, strict military discipline, demobilizing an army with a limited employment market, and continuing economic deprivation in the countryside and in the large cities because of the Allied government's boycott of Soviet Russia and the destruction during the Soviet Civil War. Even Golder wrote, "The situation in Russia is quite disturbing and I do not wish to be far away should the Bolshevik government be overthrown."[42]

While Golder awaited developments regarding Russia, he knew that the Wrangels had connections with many White army officers who might have personal papers. Consequently, he interested the Wrangels in the Hoover Collection, and they consented to solicit materials from Russians who came to the Red Cross.

After his visit to Germany, Golder next planned to collect documents in Lithuania, Estonia, and Finland. On 8 October, his train pulled into the station at Kovno, Lithuania. At this time, the Polish army, intoxicated by its moderate success against the Bolsheviks as the Polish–Soviet War wound down, proceeded to take the city of Vilna, just east of Kovno, as a result of a boundary dispute with Lithuania. At Kovno, Golder saw scores of ragged, dirty, and famished refugees streaming into the city, fleeing Vilna in order to escape the ferocity of the Polish army. He wrote Adams:

> The people of Lithuania fear the Poles more than they do the Bolsheviks—by the way, they are called Bolos here— and this is especially true of the Jews. The majority of inhabitants [at Vilna] are neither Poles nor Lithuanians, but Jews. However, the Jews prefer Lithuania to Poland. In Lithuania they are treated decently and as equals. In Poland they are not. An honest plebiscite would give the city to Lithuania, but no such animal exists.[43]

Golder stayed at Kovno four days conducting Hoover work against the discouraging background, nevertheless succeeding in securing some worthwhile materials. He wrote a short note to Adams, "I have collected a lot of documents which are being sent out. More to come later."[44] On this trip (and later) he acquired such materials as the acts of the Lithuanian Constituent Assembly, files of the first issues of the late Lithuanian newspaper *Lietuvos Aidas*, and other records that illuminated the economic, cultural, and political life of the new Lithuanian republic—a state created by the Paris Peace Conference as part of the French–inspired plan to establish a *cordon sanitaire* against Soviet Russia, a string of states from the Baltic to the Black Sea which served as a bulwark against the spread of Bolshevism.[45]

After Golder departed Kovno, his traveling path took him through lands scarred by war, since the Baltic region had been the scene of many battles during the Soviet Civil War. Golder's train took him first to Shavly in Lithuania, where he had arranged with the ARC to secure an automobile for traveling to Riga because a railway did not connect Shavly with Riga. Several ARC members met Golder at the station, and they drove him to their headquarters where an automobile and driver awaited him.

The same day, Golder departed Shavly in the automobile, which moved slowly on the rutted and dusty roads of the countryside. Along the way, he viewed the ghastly pitted and scorched fields of battle which had been the fighting ground between the Red army and anti-Bolshevik forces—White Russians, Balts, and German reactionaries. Almost every town and village that Golder's automobile passed through had demolished structures and half of its population killed in the frequent artillery exchanges. When Golder neared Riga, the capital of Latvia, he saw twisted trenches, exposed dugouts, and burned barbed wire. The madness of the post-war era seemed to be everywhere.[46]

After Golder's automobile reached Riga on 11 October, he got in touch with Evan Young, the American Commissioner of the Baltic states. Young, as the State Department's representative, had the duties of investigating trade opportunities in the Baltic region (to keep the British from securing a monopoly there), promoting American political influence, collecting information on Soviet Russia, and providing counteractivity against Russia. Because of Young's multi-faceted purpose in the Baltic, Golder believed that Young could assist him in finding potential contributors to the Hoover Collection.[47]

Young secured Golder an invitation to meet Karlis Ulmanis, Latvia's Prime Minister, who owed his power in office to Herbert Hoover. Hoover, as chairman of the ARA, used this organization for political purposes rather than purely humanitarian ones in order to establish republican governments in Europe as a counterbalance to Bolshevism. Hoover had helped to stabilize Ulmanis' government in Riga. During the Soviet Civil War, the Red army had occupied Riga, and in May 1919 Hoover, as a countermeasure, had been instrumental in sending against the Red army the German army of General Count Rudger von der Goltz (literally a private army following the war), and, in conjunction with White forces, they successfully drove out the Red army of occupation. Hoover was embarrassed by the bloody White Terror in Riga that followed after the Red army's retreat, forcing him to compel von der Goltz's army to depart. Ulmanis, who had taken flight when the Red army had occupied Riga, returned there. With the economy in disarray, the ARA had sent in food supplies to draw support to Ulmanis, who established a democratic and anti-Bolshevik state.[48]

When Golder met with Ulmanis, he found the Prime Minister eager to assist him in his collecting endeavors. But Riga's occupation by the Bolsheviks, their expulsion, and the transition to a Latvian nationalist government had prevented the accumulation and organization of any archival centers. In spite of this fact, Ulmanis promised Golder to do what he could, and, as a gesture of friendship, gave the historian an invitation to sit as a spectator at the signing of the preliminary treaty between Soviet Russia, Poland, and the Ukraine following the end of the Polish–Soviet War.[49]

After this meeting with Ulmanis, Golder went to the building in which the treaty would be signed by the designated plenipotentiaries. He walked into a rectangular hall, observing portraits of Latvia's former rulers, the Tsars of Russia, hanging on the walls. He then sat down among the Polish delegates, since Ulmanis had assigned him to be their guest. Taking note of the Bolshevik delegation, Golder wrote in his diary, "The Bolsheviks had about a dozen secretaries, the majority being women, none of them pretty, and all have cigarettes."[50] After a long wait in the crowded, noisy, and smoky hall, the plenipotentiaries came in. When they read the treaty, the representative of each country did so in his native language. Golder wrote, "Every one of the delegates knew Russian and yet they went through the farce of not understanding and wasted many hours."[51]

After Golder had left the stuffy hall and tedious proceedings, he came across a member of the Polish foreign office whom he had met on one of his earlier trips to Russia. This Polish friend gave him a copy of the treaty in English which had just been signed by Soviet Russia, Poland, and the Ukraine, and promised him a copy of the map illustrating this settlement. Knowing so many people provided Golder with some amazing coincidences.[52]

While in Riga, Golder attempted to see Adolf Yoffe, head of the Soviet delegation at the peace conference, about getting into Russia, because he had not received word of Krassin's efforts from the ARA office in London. But a secretary would not let Golder see Yoffe. Then Hoover backed off his original support of Golder entering Russia. In Riga, Golder received a telegram from the ARA London office at the ARC: "Hoover considers entirely unsafe for Golder to enter Bolshevik Russia."[53] During the previous year, the Soviets had imprisoned several Americans in Russia and Hoover thought that Golder might be arrested if he entered Soviet Russia. Golder, though, was willing to undertake the risk. Recently, he had spoken to various people about their personal experiences in Soviet Russia, and they informed him of the desperate situation there; he heard tales of Russians burning books and tearing down wood structures for fuel in order to keep from freezing, and the occurrence of famine in the countryside, bread riots in the cities, and the shooting of dissidents. Such information gave Golder a greater sense of urgency for crossing into Russia, to help

Russians if he could do so.[54]

In lieu of Russia, Hoover telegraphed Golder to collect documents regarding the Bolsheviks in the Baltic states. He tried to conform to this advice, but he soon found out the difficulty of finding such documents. The German army that had invaded Riga had destroyed pro–Bolshevik materials, and the retreating Red army had destroyed anti–Bolshevik materials. Presently, the Latvian nationalists prohibited the sale of any book, newspaper, or pamphlet concerning the Bolsheviks. Several times, Golder had witnessed policemen searching bookstores for Bolshevik paraphernalia. Because of this prohibition, he decided to circumvent the law. One night, he had a rendezvous with a book dealer who slipped him a file of newspapers, *Die Rote Fahne* (The Red Flag), which the Bolsheviks had published during their occupation of Riga. Golder then stored this illegal newspaper at the headquarters of the American Commission for the Baltic States. While at the Commission's headquarters, Golder induced its Commissioner, Young, to assist him in acquiring Bolshevik documents, and Young offered miscellaneous items involving local and Russian Bolshevik activity in the Baltic states collected by the American Commission's officers. Young also agreed to ship everything through his organization. Golder particularly enjoyed this adventure in collecting Bolshevik documents, having outsmarted local authorities.[55]

While searching for Bolshevik materials, Golder also came across book collections that were selling inexpensively. During his European travels, he had discovered a number of inexpensive book collections as well. He wrote Adams, "Collections are being disposed of right and left in order to buy bread. It is not fair to take advantage of such miseries, but after all we are in a position to pay better than the Jew merchant who squeezes the needy as hard as he can."[56] He also found out that several academic institutions in the Baltic had duplicates, even whole sections of libraries, for sale at low prices because of the depressed economy. He wrote Adams that he would like $2,000 from Stanford University to spend for special book collections and the authorization to do so, adding, "Stanford University must make a special effort to buy now, while buying is cheap and collections are thrown on the market. It is the opportunity of the century."[57]

In response, Adams conferred with Stanford's President, Ray Lyman Wilbur, regarding Golder's request for funds, and Wilbur helped secure $2,000 from the main library's trustees for the purchase of book collections. Adams, though, had reservations about such purchases, although he sent Golder the money. The books fell outside the Hoover's scope; many of them involved pre–World War I history, archaeology, commerce, economics, and literature. And they would go to the main library, which Adams, quite rightly, viewed as a threat to the Hoover Collection's independence, creativity, and uniqueness. Even the main librarian, George Clark, who resented the Hoover's holdings in his building, did not sympathize with Golder's buying scheme. But Golder had a vision of Stanford University one day becoming a world–renowned institution. He wrote Adams, "This is a great opportunity to make the Stanford Library not only the best on the [west] coast, but one of the best in the world."[58]

After receiving the money, Golder began purchasing a few book collections. But, with time running short, he decided to put off buying books momentarily and to track down Miliukov's hidden archive. At Riga, he boarded the train for a trip to Finland and traveled in a train that had neither heat nor lighting as he headed toward Estonia; passengers carried candles in order to provide themselves with light. Golder sat huddled in an overcoat, with wraps around his feet. About two in the morning, the train made an unexpected stop and Golder, along with the passengers in his car, had to exit. He did not know that the railway tracks had been severed because of a disputed boundary line between Latvia and Estonia. This situation forced Golder to hire a *droshsky* in order to reach the next train station. In cold weather, he rode for an hour until he reached the frontier posts, an ominous setting with the area surrounded by barbed wire. The frontier guard would not let anyone pass unless he was a diplomat. Golder, to get across, relied on subterfuge. He wrote, "I waved my passport full of seals and visas which he could not read and he let me pass."[59] Golder traveled on in an automobile, reaching an Estonian railway station a half hour later. There he looked forward to acquiring a room from the ARC headquarters, but they gave him one with dirty floors and a "not very clean bed." To Golder, this traveling experience did not seem the auspicious beginning of a successful collecting trip.

Two days later, Golder arrived at Helsingfors, Finland's capital. He met with Rudoft Holsti, Finland's Foreign Minister, who enthusiastically assisted him in securing Miliukov's collection. Holsti did so because of his indebtedness to Herbert Hoover.[60] Hoover, as food administrator of the Supreme Economic Council in 1919, had ordered food shipments to Finland and had been instrumental in bringing about Finland's independence at the Paris Peace Conference, measures designed to prevent the rise of Bolshevism in Finland. Holsti, whom Miliukov had contacted regarding his collection, arranged to have an army officer accompany Golder to Terijoki, a town near the collection's location, and wired to inform the Commandant at Terijoki of Golder's plan.

That evening, Golder and the officer took the train to Terijoki.

After they arrived there the following morning, Golder discovered that the town's Commandant was away on an assignment. He waited, staying two days at the ARC. When the Commandant returned to Terijoki, he told Golder that the caretaker of Miliukov's collection had threatened to sell the collection because Miliukov had not paid the storage fees. Golder could hardly wait to find the collection.

Golder, the officer, and the Commandant slid into an automobile and drove to a secluded area in a forest. They parked the automobile, and the Commandant led Golder to a barn, where the collection had been stored. The caretaker, a German farmer, then appeared on the scene, and greeted Golder affably. After discovering the purpose of Golder's visit, the caretaker stressed that he would not release the collection until someone had paid the storage fees. Golder entered the barn in order to determine if the collection had suffered extensive weather damage, but the darkness of evening prevented him from doing so. In spite of the risk of weather damage, Golder decided to go ahead and pay the storage fees. He also persuaded the caretaker to strengthen the boxes and haul them to the railway station, leaving him with a small sum of money.[61]

In a few days, Golder located the collection at a Helsingfors railway station. He counted the number of boxes, which came to 34. This number surprised him because Miliukov had mentioned only 18 boxes. He opened one box and saw for himself that there was no weather damage; he was also surprised by the contents, which revealed something greater than rare books and personal papers. In fact, Golder had in his possession a fabulous collection: in addition to rare books and personal papers, there were government documents, manuscripts, periodicals, pamphlets, leaflets, and broadsides, some 4,000 titles in all, excluding the leaflets and broadsides.[62] He wrote Adams, "Miliukov's collection is a beginning and [in time] I may say with certainty that Stanford will have the best collection west of the Atlantic.[63]

Chapter V

Voyage through South Eastern and Eastern Europe

After Golder returned to Helsingfors, he enjoyed himself socially in the Finnish capital. He wrote, "These weeks have been the most exciting of anything I have had since coming to Europe. I do not mean they were gay with banquets, and so on, but I have had many opportunities to meet men worthwhile."[1] As Golder enjoyed his social life, he also experienced more collecting success in Finland. While there, he secured a number of books on Russian history to supplement the Miliukov collection, three boxes of books and pamphlets related to Finland from a Russian library, 1,000 titles of pamphlets on Germany, France, and Russia, a gift from the Finnish government of private Russian collections which had come into its possession as a spoil of war during the Soviet Civil War, and another collection of Bolshevik materials which had been gathered by the Finnish secret police. Golder wrote Adams concerning the acquisition of the secret police, "The State Department is acquiring a great deal of this material; whereas that Department spends from 10 to 20 thousand a year for this purpose, we have spent about $20.00."[2]

Despite this success, Golder lacked the time to fully complete his collecting itinerary in Finland. On the recommendation of Professor Yyjo Hirn, Golder arranged that a Dr. Henning Soderhjelm, under Hirn's guidance, collect materials that met Adams' collecting objectives in Finland. Subsequently, Hirn became Golder's first area curator, a task which involved coordinating the exchange of duplicates regarding books,[3] inspecting and purchasing valuable collections, and advertising the Hoover War Collection.

After setting up this special arrangement, Golder left Finland on 19 November, crossing the Baltic Sea in a ferry. He disembarked at Riga, and then continued to collect documents in Latvia, Estonia, and Lithuania. During his travels throughout these states, (and on a return trip in the summer of 1921), Golder collected numerous documents, such as the minutes of the Estonian Constituent Assembly and State Assembly, the minutes of the Latvian Constituent Assembly, the official gazettes of the German forces of occupation in the Baltic States, a few German language newspapers from Latvia and Lithuania, the Latvian government's official newspaper *Validibas Vestnesis,* certain serials, the record of the ARC, ARA, and the Baltic Commissions, and a number of personal papers and archives, such as those of General Paul M. Bermondt–Avolov, a maverick reactionary who had a small German army in the Baltic, whose documents help explain the German Republic's Russian and Baltic policies after the Armistice. Golder thus established the foundation of the Hoover's Baltic Collection, bringing to historical scholarship an awareness of the significance of the Baltic States in world politics.[4]

While collecting these documents, Golder again experienced a number of difficulties. He had to deal not only with chaotic governmental archives but also with the petty annoyances of officials, especially in Estonia. Golder blamed the rudeness on the fact that the Wilson administration that summer had refused to recognize the independence of the Baltic States.[5] Other problems, as well, made Golder's overall collecting experience less than pleasant: long train stops, irregular passport checks, bureaucratic misunderstandings, and unforgettable scenes of poverty. Golder wrote:

> Last week I visited Narva (in Estonia) and saw much suffering. The wars of the last six years have killed off many of the men, typhus has destroyed many of the women, and orphan children, homeless, fatherless and motherless, are everywhere. Some lived in holes, begged, stole and did everything else to make a living. There are still hundreds and perhaps thousands of them.[6]

When Golder returned to Riga, he wrote Adams on 9 December, "There is so much poverty and so much suffering that it makes the heart ache and disturbs one's rest."[7] Golder hoped that a brief stopover at Riga, before traveling on to Paris, would cast off his gloom. He tried to stay indoors, relaxing. Typically, he became restless and walked the streets. From time to time, he lingered at shop windows and noticed frequent displays of expensive items. He knew that this frequency of displayed luxury indicated a desperate population rather than one enjoying prosperity. Hoover's food assistance to the Baltic region could not transform a depressed economy into a viable one; there were too many forces at play. The depressed economy in the Baltic region had driven Balts to sell their possessions, such as diamonds, gold rings, and other valuables at very low prices so that they could buy food and other items. Golder thought that if these fragile Baltic States failed to recover soon from six years of turmoil and depression thousands would perish because of food shortages.

One day, Golder went to visit an old German Baron in Riga, who had devoted many years of his life to historical investigation. During their conversation, the Baron, too, pessimistically viewed the Baltic States' economic situation. He foresaw nothing but deprivation for the Balts, and he felt completely helpless to struggle against this view. He confessed to Golder that suicide was a preferable alternative to starvation's agony. Golder wrote Adams, "The queerest thing and the saddest was that I [could not] discourage him, not a word of consolation."[8] Sharing the Baron's bleak outlook, Golder believed he would destroy himself if he had to face starvation. He wrote Adams, "[World War I] has settled nothing . . . "[9] Neither Wilson nor Lenin had created the new world order as they had envisioned it, ending nationalism, economic disjuncture, national hatreds, social cleavages, and diplomatic chaos.

Before long, Golder thought that if he stayed any longer in Riga he would only suffer more distress. He completed last minute business and climbed aboard the train, departing Riga in mid–December for Paris. On the way to Paris, he stopped at Berlin, where he had several Hoover matters to attend to. At the Russian Red Cross, he found a handful of manuscripts which the Wrangels had collected for him. He also secured manuscripts from other people, and commissioned Alexander Tobien to copy a number of documents belonging to various Baltic Barons, since Tobien, as their former secretary, had access to the documents. Next, Golder purchased from a private dealer a collection of German war materials, paying $150. Lastly, he prodded a Dr. Bertling, director of the Amerika Institut and one of Lutz's contacts, to continue urging the German government to send its publications to the Hoover.

While Golder collected documents in Berlin, he longed to be in Paris, to be away from suffering, which he again came across in Berlin and which reminded him of the destitute in the Baltic region.[10] But he still had to make a stopover at Coblenz. From Berlin, he traveled on to Coblenz, and checked on the American Section of the Inter–Allied Commission's efforts for the Hoover. Then he reached Paris on 20 December, and felt relieved to be there. After being in Paris for a while, he wrote, "The few days here have cheered me up wonderfully and it does not seem that I was ever depressed."[11]

Then Golder received a letter from Adams which did not provide him with much encouragement. Adams criticized Golder for neglecting to collect war materials, stating that he spent too much time collecting books unrelated to World War I. In response, Golder wrote, "I must confess . . . I have been carried away somewhat by the wonderful possibilities that I saw for making Stanford University a great institution."[12] He mentioned, though, that he had only spent

$200 of the $2,000 on Baltica and Rossica. Golder agreed to stop buying books of a general nature, although he had planned to do so in many European countries. Discouraged, he wrote Adams that he would keep the Hoover Collection as his primary objective.[13]

In spite of Adam's criticism, Golder kept busy. There had recently arrived at Paris a large shipment of Baltic materials, and a post office employee had disorganized everything when he had inspected the shipment. Golder had to check the shipment's contents, rearrange its order, and properly label each package. Next, he encouraged the staff at the Tsarist Embassy to stay alert for interesting documents. He then visited Miliukov, who lived in Paris, and told him about the caretaker's threat to sell his collection to pay the storage fee. Lastly, Golder sent off reminder notes to his new European contacts. For example, he wrote to Dr. Bertling of the Amerika Institut in Berlin:

> When I saw you last, you mentioned the fact that you could get us some war literature—posters, newspapers, etc.—for nothing. Will you please see what you can do . . . , and try and [leave] this material in your office. When I come by I will take it off your hands.[14]

Golder, now ready for new collecting adventures, left Paris on 14 January 1921 on the Orient Express, traveling to Constantinople. When he arrived there, he secured a room at the ARC headquarters. During the next few days, he mingled with ARC members, and through them he met Admiral Mark Bristol, the American Commissioner of the Near East. Golder wrote:

> Here as elsewhere the name of Hoover carries everything before it. Admiral Bristol has placed his destroyers at my service and I can go on any of them to any part of the Black Sea and Mediterranean wherever I think I can find material.[15]

Golder decided to take advantage of this unusual offer, and gained permission to travel on a destroyer to the little country of Georgia in Asia Minor, a country whose border ran along the Black Sea. Once in Tiflis, Georgia's capital, Golder planned to collect documents from this former Tsarist province. After the Bolshevik Revolution, Georgia had declared its independence and had established a Menshevik government, a party in opposition to Russian Bolshevik elitism and expansionism. Before long, intense controversy had developed between the two governments over Georgia's refusal to transfer the defeated General Wrangel's ships (considered Russian property) to Soviet Russia, the failure to let Soviet trains pass through Georgia to Armenia for helping famine victims of the Armeno–Turkish War of 1920, the suppression of the Bolshevik Party in Georgia, and the conflicts surrounding frontier disputes. Such controversies had brought Soviet Russia and Georgia close to war. In this unpredictable part of the world, Golder would seek documents regarding the relations between Soviet Russia and Georgia, as well as documents regarding German and British involvement in Georgia during and after World War I and documents regarding the Armeno–Turkish War.[16]

Golder boarded the *USS Barker* with Major C. L. Davis of the ARC on 21 January. For the next several days, the voyage passed pleasantly, but on the 25th Golder noted that the ship's barometer indicated stormy weather. Soon, a howling storm forced him to remain confined to his couch in the dining room—the destroyer's only sleeping accommodations for passengers. When the destroyer reached Batum, a Georgian port–city, stormy weather still harassed the ship. The Captain, unable to see either the city or the harbor in the darkness, had the destroyer anchored at a safe distance from land juttings and floating mines left over from World War I. During the following forty–eight hours, the storm continuously rocked the destroyer; Golder later wrote: "I have been seasick before, I have been pitched and rolled before, but never like this."[17] One time, the destroyer pitched so sharply that Golder's couch skidded across the dining room and flung him into a wall. Perhaps he wondered if the preservation of historical documents might be accomplished with less sacrifice.

After two days, the storm subsided. A crew rowed Golder and Davis, exhilarated by the sight of dry land, to the shore. By the time Golder and Davis came ashore, a crowd of Asians had gathered and they became unruly as they begged for the privilege of carrying the newcomers' luggage. Golder, fearing this volatile crowd, looked for an escape route. The din, though, paralyzed him and Davis; they could neither run nor choose someone to carry their luggage. Then, William Richards, director of the Near East Relief (NER), responding to a radio message to pick up Golder and Davis, appeared. Effortlessly, he diffused the emotional situation with a simple act: he took the luggage himself, leading Golder and Davis away to safety at the NER headquarters at Batum.[18]

Feeling a bit foolish after Richards had rescued him, Golder planned to travel on from Batum to Tiflis, Georgia that evening. However, the locomotive scheduled to take the train to Tiflis had stalled in the mountains. Golder and Davis, forced to spend the night at Batum, decided to paint the town with Richards. They exchanged five dollars for 28,000 rubles in this city with a very depressed economy, and took off. Golder wrote, "What Batum was like before the war I do not know, but today it looked like a wild west town of one of Bret Hart's novels."[19] Visiting the cafes, Golder came across flamboyant ladies, sporty gents, disbanded soldiers, and dissipated officers with revolvers, daggers, and swords. In this western–like town, Golder and Davis celebrated their release from the sea's discontent and their rescue from the over–friendly Asians until three in the morning.

At eleven the following morning, Richards burst into Golder's and Davis' room, abruptly awakening them with the announcement that the train for Tiflis would be leaving shortly. Scrambling, Golder and Davis managed to arrive at the railway station just in time, and they shoved their way through a crowded, malodorous car and into a small, dirty, dark, and cold compartment reserved for them. The train had no diner, no sleeper, and no heaters. Having rushed to the station, Golder had neglected to bring food and warm clothing. After the train left the station, Golder bought a cooked half–turkey, a few loaves of bread, a bottle of liquor, a few blankets, and candles from vendors at different stopping points. Golder and Davis ate part of the turkey and fortified themselves against the cold with cognac. They then prepared for sleeping, wrapping their feet in blankets, buttoning their overcoats, and sitting on the floor with their backs to the wall, since the compartment did not have any seats. Golder now waited for sleep to overtake him.

Golder's preparations for warmth proved ineffective as the train, climbing higher and higher in the snowy mountains, became very cold. Unable to sleep, he and Davis let every candle they had brought from vendors in an attempt to provide themselves with a little heat. This measure soon turned into a less than welcomed alternative. The flickering candles attracted the passengers, who were mostly peasants, in the car's aisle, and every few minutes someone would slide open the compartment's door to light a cigarette from the candles' flame, letting in an unbearable stench. Golder wrote, "The most unpleasant part of traveling in these cars is the stench of the toilets which penetrates everywhere."[20]

Golder then received another surprise. At about eight–thirty that evening the train came to an unexpected stop in the middle of nowhere. Wondering what had happened, he located the conductor, who told him the train's locomotive had been unhitched so that it could return to Batum; a locomotive from the opposite direction, Tiflis, would be arriving soon. Golder patiently waited for the locomotive which came in around midnight. Quite naturally, he expected the trip's resumption. The chief engineer, however, informed Golder that he could not operate the train because of exhaustion from lack of sleep; the train would be delayed until morning. Golder returned to the compartment with the idea of catching some sleep, but all night long his fellow passengers kept him awake by opening and closing the compartment door to light cigarettes. Finally, around eight in the morning, "the engineer," wrote Golder, "[after] his nap and his breakfast, . . . bumped the engine into the train in a way which made us all jump."[21] Tired, bemused, and relieved, Golder rode on toward Tiflis.

After passing through several mountain ranges, the train descended into a valley and traveled across a flat plain. In the valley the warm temperature melted some of the ice on the window. To fill the compartment with fresh air, Golder and Davis forced open the window, and scraped off the remaining ice. Looking out, Golder saw that the surrounding countryside seemed very poor, as if economic deprivation did not discriminate anywhere. In this valley, he observed rickety shacks on platforms standing several feet off the ground, and in the fields he saw undersized horses and cattle. The train sped on and Golder finally reached Tiflis that night. He and Davis went to the NER headquarters, where its director made the two weary travelers comfortable after their unusual trip.[22]

Soon, the NER staff arranged a meeting for Golder with the President of Georgia, Noah Zhordania. Golder called on him, stating his case, as Golder said, "in a way that would appeal to him,"[23] playing up the importance of Georgia's history, even though a small country, and the necessity of preserving its recorded past for historical study. On this occasion he hit the jackpot. Zhordania issued a memorandum to every government department, every public institution, and every learned society to be as flexible and as responsive as possible to Golder's want lists. When Golder visited the ministers of state, they reacted friendly and were very generous; they gave him everything he requested. He wrote that they considered themselves flattered that "a great man like Hoover, a great institution like Stanford, and a great country like the United States should be interested in Georgia and its ministers."[24]

Golder also visited several newspaper editors. One particular editor hestitated about giving him a file of newspapers covering the war years. Golder carefully praised the quality of the editor's newspaper, and this flattery let loose an avalanche of favors; the editor offered Golder the Russian edition of his paper, editions in two other languages, pamphlets, maps, and finally a photograph of himself. Golder wrote:

> At times I am really ashamed of myself, not because I do anything underhanded, for I treat the Georgians as I do Frenchmen and Germans, but because they concede so eas-

ily and lay themselves open to childish flattery (a Georgian character trait) [that] it makes me feel somehow guilty.[25]

After a week of collecting materials in Tiflis, Golder prepared for his departure. He wrote, "It seemed to me that we were to come in possession of a rare collection of literature which could not be duplicated."[26] He also believed that his large Georgian collection would require two months of on-the-spot supervision to have everything collected, organized, and prepared for shipment. The entire task involved too much time, and Golder wished to embark on a collecting trip to eastern Europe. As a result, he hired Woldemar Elsner, a young scholar, to finish all of the necessary details, leaving him $60.00 for his labor and another $70.00 to buy periodicals and books. Furthermore, while in Tiflis, Golder had met a number of former Tsarist generals, Russian scholars, and other Russians in exile, and he secured the help of a young Georgian professor to obtain copies of their memoirs, letters, and diaries. Golder left the young professor $40.00 for this work. Lastly, Golder arranged that the Georgian collection be shipped through the American Consulate at Tiflis by courier to Colonel Logan's ARA office in Paris.[27]

His Georgian quest over, Golder arranged to travel with C. Moser, head of the American Consulate at Tiflis, on his return trip to Constantinople. For the trip to Batum, Moser tried to reserve an ordinary train car for himself, Golder, and seven other Americans. But transportation problems in Georgia prevented the reservation of an entire train car. The Soviet Red army had occupied Baku, Azerbaijan, an oil rich region neighboring Georgia, and the Bolsheviks refused to give the Georgians any oil, crippling railway service. The few remaining train cars were overcrowded with travelers, refugees, and Georgian soldiers. Moser then suggested to Georgian authorities that the Americans be allowed to occupy an unused special coach that had once belonged to Tsar Nicholas II. The Georgians objected to coupling the coach to a passenger train, claiming that it weighed too much. But after Moser's insistence, they agreed to couple the car to a freight train.

Golder then climbed aboard with seven men and one woman. He wrote, "Our coach had sleeping accommodations for four persons; consequently five of us had to sleep on the floor and for three days and nights none of us had a chance to take off our clothing."[28] Golder, who slept on the floor, deferring the sleeping accommodations to the Consul, Vice-Consul, and a newspaper man and his wife, played bridge during the night with the other travelers to compensate for the lack of comfort. Golder recalled that the game always started pleasantly enough but degenerated into quarreling late in the morning, keeping everyone awake. Trying to be philosophical about the experience, he wrote, "At least we had the car to ourselves and did not suffer from the stench of the ordinary cars."[29]

When the train arrived at Batum, Golder, Moser, and the other travelers boarded the *USS Barker.* Golder, preoccupied with not wasting time, wanted to proceed directly to Constantinople. But the Consul, Moser, had previously planned to go to Poti and to Sukham, two Georgian ports, regarding official business. The *Barker* traveled first to Poti and then to Sukham, where Moser would be staying while the remaining party traveled on.

While waiting for the *Barker* to leave the port of Sukham, Golder visited the city, which he thought a beautiful resort, populated with charming Georgians. Then he heard a rumor that placed the city's coziness in the background: the Red army was invading Georgia. He had expected the Bolsheviks to invade Georgia, but not so soon.[30] Moser discounted the rumor as a false alarm (there had been many such rumors) and preferred to remain at Sukham, while Golder, showing concern, returned to Batum with the *USS Barker* to find out what was actually happening. At Batum, he discovered that the invasion had taken place. He wrote, "alarming reports reached us of the Bolo (Bolshevik) invasion, of the flight of the diplomatic missions, and of the removal of the Georgian government."[31] As the reality of the rumor spread, Moser, no longer dismissing the rumor, telegraphed an order for the *USS Barker* to bring him back to Batum. The following day, Golder boarded the *USS Tracy*, a ship bound for Constantinople.

Once safely located at Constantinople, Golder wrote to the campus newspapers at Washington State:

> Had I remained another ten days in [Tiflis, the Bolsheviks] would have been attacking me. [Luckily, I escaped just in time]. This explains why I am here writing to you instead of feeding the small animals which infest the Bolshevik prisons. Though the Reds did not make a home run in my case, they got a hit and spoiled all my efforts of a month and have secured some [documents] to which I had better right than they. C'est la guerre. The first round between us ended in a draw and I look forward to more decisive fights in the future. . . .[32]

Writing to Adams, though, Golder showed tentative optimism regarding the Georgian collection. He wrote,

> The men whom I engaged are connected with learned institutions and the Bolos have usually respected libraries and universities and I wish to believe that they will let our men

work and save up the material for us and some bright day we will get it.[33]

In spite of this optimism, Golder had one misgiving:

My great regret is that I did not have another week there, for in that time I could have brought out much valuable material. The week I needed was wasted in traveling of a useless sort.[34]

Golder then put this Georgian episode in the back of his mind as he tackled the problem of uncovering documents in Constantinople. While doing so, he developed certain impressions of the city. His living quarters had a window view that he thought quite spectacular. He wrote, "I am sitting here in Europe and looking across the Bosphorous into Asia."[35] He imagined that a Spokane real estate dealer could be very eloquent over Constantinople's land–selling advantages: wonderful climate, location, and scenery. And what a heroic past, too—the meeting ground of East and West. Golder noted that the sites of many famous battles could be pointed out from his window.

Golder reflected, "Those were glorious days and all that is left to us now are stone windows and beautiful monuments."[36] He saw for himself that, in reality, these monuments disappeared amid crowds of various nationalities and the ugly physical configuration of the city's newer structures. He wrote, "Its streets are dirty and crooked, its sanitary conditions are very primitive, its shambling houses and frail shacks are regular fire traps."[37] What he disliked most of all, though concerned the intangible element—values, the lack of community spirit, of human involvement and pride. He observed thousands of individuals who belonged to all sorts of ethnic groups and to many religious sects, each with its own church and school. Golder wrote, "There is not a common school system in this large city, but each group teaching to its children its own particular prejudices and dogma and hatred of the others."[38] Constantinople seemed to be a microcosm of the post–war world.

While avoiding Constantinople's "clever businessmen, painted women, religious hatred, racial quarrels, and all that is disagreeable to me,"[39] Golder collected a number of documents on Turkey's participation in World War I, a country which had fought on the side of Germany and Austria. He succeeded where the less bold may have fallen short: The Minister of Public Instruction appointed someone to help him in the collection of public documents, the Secretary of the Minister of Finance assisted him with his requests, and the Minister of War appointed two high–ranking officers to aid him in securing documents.

Golder's biggest conquest came through the Minister of Education, Rahid Bey. Golder had lunch with Rahid at his home and his family treated Golder as a celebrity. With Rahid, Golder arranged to have two scholars during a two-month period copy archival documents on Turkey's diplomacy regarding the war, or as Golder wrote, "all the secret papers and intrigues of the last twenty years insofar as the Turkish government has any written or verbal record of it will be laid bare."[40] This agreement, plus his other acquisitions in Constantinople,[41] pleased Golder, especially in consideration of the disorganized state of the Turkish government's archives. He wrote Adams:

> The result of my efforts with the Turks has not been wholly in vain. We will not get much material but we can have the satisfaction that we will get all there is. You cannot imagine how little organization this government has and how little continuity of policy. Yesterday I had a talk with the Minister of Education, [Rahid Bey], who was Minister of Agriculture, and three months or so before that he held the post of Minister of Commerce or some such ministry. No attempt is made to preserve even departmental documents, even for the use of the department itself.[42]

After collecting documents in Turkey, Golder thought of traveling to Beirut. But he decided to venture into eastern Europe, fearing that the Soviet Red Army might invade Romania. Romania had incorporated Bessarabia, a former Russian territory, and this aggrandizement had brought about Soviet threats of war. In light of his experience in Georgia, Golder wrote, "The ghost of Bolshevism is ever nearer and no one knows when it will strike."[43] He also wanted to collect documents in eastern European countries because many of them had accessible archives, while France, Great Britain, and Italy, the victors in the Great War, had closed their archives to collectors and researchers in order to hide their less than glorious deeds.[44]

When Golder departed Constantinople, he had few regrets. He wrote, "I pray that this may be my last Sunday in this city for some months."[45] From Constantinople, Golder traveled to Sofia, the capital of Bulgaria, which had fought with the Central Powers against the Allied governments during World War I. After reaching Sofia on 12 March, he searched for a capable Bulgarian assistant because of his unfamiliarity with the language, the city, and the archival centers. He asked Constantine Stephanov, a graduate of Yale and a professor at the University of Sofia, who had an acquaintance with Bulgarian professors, archivists, and politicians there, to help him. Stephanov agreed to do so, and indicated that he would like in payment for his assistance only a small reward—eleven books in the United States which he needed for a research project. Golder wrote Adams to order the books and write Stephanov a complimentary letter for his assistance, believing that such small touches often worked wonders on one's cooperation.[46]

Golder and Stephanov called on several leading scholars, directors of museums and libraries, the president of the University of Sofia, and the Minister of Foreign Affairs. With these luminaries, Golder used a ploy that he had sometimes found successful in other countries. He showed them the list of materials which the Finnish government had prepared for him as an example of how favorably some governments considered Hoover's collecting scheme. When Golder noted that this ploy brought about a certain enthusiasm among the Bulgarians, he followed through with a series of compliments regarding Bulgaria. He said that Hoover would like to have a Bulgarian collection, that every phase of recent Bulgarian history should be represented, that Stanford University hoped to give courses in Bulgarian history and culture, that some day Stanford may invite Bulgarian scholars to come and lecture, and that Stanford might be able to offer an annual scholarship to Bulgarian students chosen by the Bulgarian government. Such flattery appealed to Bulgarian nationalism and pride, and Golder soon became a popular man with the Bulgarians as well as a successful collector of Bulgarian documents.

Golder did not view his suggestions to the Bulgarians as mere expressions of flattery, either. He wrote, "I am not exaggerating and I am sure all these statements may come true."[47] Many of them, in fact, did occur, with a large Bulgarian collection at the Hoover, with Golder later teaching one of the first American university courses on contemporary Balkan history, and with invitations to Bulgarian students and scholars to come to Stanford University.

As Golder continued collecting documents in Bulgaria, he and Stephanov had an unanticipated experience with the Minister of Public Instruction. While waiting in the outer office of the ministry, Golder heard the minister's harsh–sounding voice speaking into the telephone to a teacher, informing him that if discipline failed to improve at his school he would be sent to prison. When this minister appeared in the outer office, Golder observed a man who looked like an uncouth peasant, unshaven and disheveled, with a strong, domineering face. Golder knew that an Agrarian party had come to power in Bulgaria in 1920, and that this party had legislated peasant land reform and let peasants enter the administraion to create support in the countryside as a campaign against the aristrocracy, which had followed a pro–German policy in the war and had controlled the government. In spite of this knowledge, Golder still found the minister's appearance intimidating. But as soon as the minister engaged Golder in conversation, he proved to be quite friendly, much to Golder's relief.[48]

The minister had previously heard of Golder's mission and the idea of establishing a Bulgarian section in the Hoover Collection deeply appealed to him. The minister, though, had another motive besides the expansion of Bulgarian scholarship. No doubt, he hoped that Bulgaria would be able to benefit from extensive trade and loans from the United States, since Hoover had become the Secretary of Commerce in the Warren Harding administration in 1921. Reflecting on Golder's connection with Hoover, the minister said, "the Bulgarians' only hope is that the United States and the two countries must live in friendship. Then to demonstrate his government's friendliness toward Herbert Hoover, the minister "gave orders at once that every public institution in the state should contribute" to the Hoover Collection. Golder added, "He is also head of the government printing office and orders have been sent there to select two copies of every publication for us."[49] After this meeting with the Minister of Public Instruction, Golder thought Stephahov's assistance in selecting potential donators exemplary.

While collecting in Sofia, Golder received word on the afternoon of 17 March that Prime Minister, Alexander Stamboliski, wished to see him. At 6:30 p.m., Golder, along with Stephanov, met Stamboliski, a national hero who had been imprisoned during the war because of his opposition to Bulgaria's pro–German policy. Golder related to Stamboliski the purpose of his collecting activities, and this led to a discussion of World War I's origins, the flight of the Bulgarian King Ferdinand after his abdication in 1918 over his pro–German policy, and the fact, according to Stamboliski, that the King had taken all the secret documents regarding German–Bulgarian relations with him. Golder was stimulated by the discussion, although the news of vanishing secret documents was an unhappy revelation.

Apparently impressed with Golder's collecting goals and opinions of the war, Stamboliski asked Golder if he would like to visit the King, Boris III, who had succeeded to the throne after his father's abdication. Golder replied, "I would be highly honored but I do not wish to take up his Majesty's time." Stamboliski, who had a reputation for being iron–fisted, shot back, "His Majesty has more time than I." Stamboliski then telephoned Boris' secretary and asked him to arrange an early appointment for Golder because he would be leaving Bulgaria soon. The secretary said that Boris had a busy schedule and had left orders not to be disturbed. Stamboliski, Golder noted, roared defiantly, "You do as I say and tell the King that I sent you."[50] Stamboliski's assertiveness made an impression on Golder—a popular leader bullying a King. Shortly a reply came that the King would receive Golder.

The evening on the following day, Golder met with King Boris III, a young man of twenty–seven, at his palace. They spoke in English, interspersed with French, and Golder thought the King refined, intelligent, inquisitive, and well read. Boris, though, had less interest in Golder's Hoover work than in contemporary world history. While discussing the Russian question, Boris said, "What a pity people do not read history to better advantage,"[51] referring to the historical dictum that reactionaries will always try to overthrow a new regime and try to re–establish the old order, which happened in the French Revolution and now in Soviet Russia. Little did Golder know that Boris III, in 1923, would participate in overthrowing and killing Stamboliski.

During his travels, Golder had many opportunities to discuss intellectual topics with men of action, politicians and military leaders, and intellectuals. While speaking with Golder, Boris brought up a rather unexpected topic—camping. Golder seemed delighted by Boris' boyish enthusiasm for camping, and no doubt agreed with him that being in the mountains gave one unparalleled happiness. And when Boris revealed a knowledge of plants and trout in California, Golder probably became homesick. He wrote, "I remained with the King for about forty minutes and enjoyed them all."[52]

After two busy days with Hoover matters following his visit with Boris, Golder was ready to leave Sofia. He was overjoyed with his Bulgarian collection of books, pamphlets, newspapers, and war materials. On top of this, he had become something of a celebrity. He wrote:

> I leave this afternoon for Bucharest [Romania]. This morning I have been busy leaving thank you cards for the ministers and others. I have been honored far above my merits, thanks to the name of Hoover. (Hoover had sent food relief to Bulgaria in 1919.) This morning I have been received by the leading men of the Holy Synod and my opinion and advice were asked on a number of important questions. Yesterday I had committees of one kind and another come to see me to consult me and get my opinion. Sometimes I wonder where I am and who I am; it seems like a dream.[53]

Golder left Sofia on 21 March, traveling to Bucharest, Romania.

Arriving there after a relatively pleasant train ride, he went to the American legation and asked for a room; they had none available. A clerk at the legation then found Golder a room in a private house, but it turned out to be cold and cheerless. This room's unattractiveness put a damper on Golder's spirits, a mood which failed to improve during his initial collection rounds in Bucharest.[54]

As Golder already knew, Romanians were strongly anti–American, even though their country had fought with the Allies during the war. In particular, Romanians resented Hoover's interference with their conquest of Hungary. After the fall of Bela Kun's communist regime in Hungary in 1919, which Hoover had been instrumental in bringing about through an economic blockade of Hungary, the Romanian army had invaded Hungary (an act of vengeance against Hungary's plundering of Romania in the war), occupying Budapest and looting railway rolling stock, industrial machinery, farm animals, banks, art galleries, homes, and even hospitals. Hoover, as chairman of the food section of the Supreme Economic Council, had urged the Supreme War Council to adopt a policy of economic blockade against Romania to stop, as Hoover said in his memoirs, this "setback to the evolution of self–government in Hungary."[55] The Council had followed Hoover's advice, voting to impose an economic blockade on Romania, which then forced the Romanian army to withdraw.

No wonder when Golder asked American diplomatic officials in Bucharest to help him with his collecting efforts, he found that they had little influence to do so. However, the American chargé d'affaires did manage to arrange a meeting for Golder with Take Ionescu, the Minister of Foreign Affairs. When Golder met with Ionescu, he stated how enthusiastically other countries had responded to his collecting requests, mentioning his success in Bulgaria. "Oh, yes," Ionescu remarked, "the conquered nations have more reason for talking than those that conquered."[56] Ionescu's incisive statement jolted Golder, but he kept prodding Ionescu. Reluctantly, Ionescu did half–heartedly promise to appoint someone to collect what Golder wanted for the Hoover. Two days later, Golder heard nothing of the appointed man's efforts, a non–communication which made him impatient, since he could not stay in Bucharest very long.

Golder's next step involved a familiar one. He wrote, "to get anything done, one must keep on the good side of the less conspicuous figures."[57] While in Paris, he had become acquainted with Professor Nicolae Iorga, a historian popular among Romanian scholars and politicians. Iorga set the wheels rolling in the right direction, showing a resourcefulness equal to the task. Together, Iorga and Golder secured materials from the Minister of War, the Minister of Food, the

Romanian Academy, the Geographical Society, endowed institutions, and other archival centers.[58] Although Golder had experienced considerable success, he still had received nothing from Ionescu. Golder wrote Adams:

> When I went to Bucharest, I had hoped that it would not be necessary for me to go there again, but I am not so sure now. Please list everything as it comes, and later in the summer, send me a copy so that when I return to Bucharest, I can check up.[59]

Golder, however, underrated his achievement. Adams had expected far fewer, if any, documents from Romania because of the Romanian government's resentment toward Hoover.[60]

In fact, after Adams' initial criticism, he had developed considerable respect for Golder's collecting ability and so had Hoover, who read copies of Golder's correspondence to Adams. Adams cabled Golder that he should stay in Europe for an extra year to collect documents. The stern, sometimes inflexible Adams now honored Golder with an encouraging compliment. Golder, though, acknowledged the strain, loneliness, and apprehensions that played a part of his assignment. He wrote Adams from Bucharest:

> My work is exceedingly interesting and profitable, yet it is very tiring. I so often long for green grass and rushing water and a bit of quiet academic life. However, I am going to stay with the job as long as there is something to be done.

Then he touched upon Russia:

> I must be there as soon as possible, and "make a killing" if I can. I shall not feel that our work is finished until we have a good collection from Russia.[61]

Finished, for the moment, with Romania, Golder next headed for the Kingdom of Serbs, Croats, and Slovenes which had sprung forth after the collapse of the Habsburg Empire of Austria–Hungary. The Kingdom, created in 1918, with its name changed to Yugoslavia in 1929, failed to achieve any real unity during the post–war period— the Slovene and Croat leaders, for example, western in culture and Catholic in religion, viewed the Orthodox Serbs with disgust, considering them an uncivilized people. This loosely knit Balkan Kingdom intrigued Golder because the region's history had been crucial for World War I's origins: tensions between Austria and Russia over Serbia's independence, the two Balkan wars in 1912–1913, and the international commercial rivalry in the Balkans. And World War I had been ignited when Serbian nationalists, resentful of Austria's

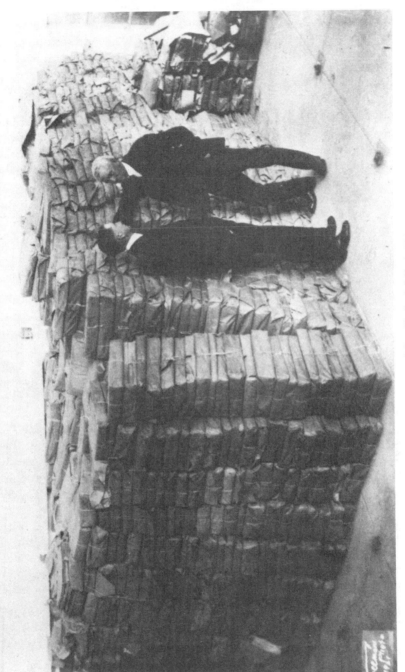

Shipment of Documents Collected by Frank Golder in 1921

geo–political strategy in the Balkans, had assassinated the Austrian, Archduke Ferdinand, at Sarajevo, Bosnia in August 1914.

Golder chose to first stop at Belgrade in Serbia, and arrived there on 4 April 1921.[62] He went to the American legation, where he visited his chargé d'affaires, Henry Dodge. Dodge, who had prior knowledge of the Hoover Collection, had sent a number of books to the Hoover. Dodge had also tried to collect government documents, but complained to Golder about the lack of cooperation he had received from the various ministries. Golder decided to try his luck. At the Ministry of Foreign Affairs, he approached several Serbian officials, and he found them uncooperative. Not to be discouraged, he continued his efforts, using a combination of persistence, humor, flattery, and affability, and finally succeeded in gaining the Foreign Ministry's support. Its staff gave him considerable latitude in acquiring documents involving diplomatic and propaganda publications housed in the Foreign Ministry's library and storeroom. Golder visited these two archival centers, selected pertinent materials for the Hoover Collection, and befriended the ministry's librarian, Ivan Subbotitch, who promised to collect additional materials for the future.[63]

Golder then added other materials to the Serbian collection— legislative acts, newspapers, and war books. He also wanted a set of war maps, and to accomplish this goal he sought out Colonel S. P. Boskovic, the director of the Geographic Section of the General Staff, at his home one afternoon. Boskovic's daughter, eighteen years old, invited Golder into the Colonel's house. When the young woman found out that Golder had an interest in Russia, she said that she had just returned from Soviet Russia, commenting how actively the Soviets encouraged the development of art. Golder remarked that he greatly admired Russian ballet. After he said this, the woman jumped up, clapped her hands, and exclaimed, "Do you really?" As Golder learned, she had danced with a ballet company during her recent trip to Russia. The woman then scurried away, and returned with her father, mother, and sister to meet Golder. He soon discovered that Colonel Boskovic also admired Russian ballet, and this common interest helped Golder in his quest. From Boskovic, he secured an excellent set of war maps, as well as a personal collecting commitment. Golder wrote:

> In all these countries, I find that these personal elements, these little things that decide the success or failure of an undertaking, are most vital. I suppose my failures may be explained on the same grounds—failure to make the proper contacts.[64]

When Golder came to the end of his collecting in Belgrade, he traveled to Croatia, reaching Zagreb on 11 April, and he fell in love with the city. In traveling through Bulgaria, Romania, and Serbia, he thought that these countries had been influenced in a negative way by Eastern cultures, especially Turkey, or as he said, "the hand of the orient, and occasionally the smell," an influence which revealed itself through an absence of civic spirit, literacy, culture, and efficiency. Golder thought Zagreb, influenced by Western Europe, devoid of such a characterization. He noted with admiration the city's flowering culture, intelligent citizenry, and, above all, its "public–spirited body of citizens," who had created many fine museums, a professional opera, a learned academy, a stimulating university "with a library building that is greatly superior to ours," efficient hospitals, clean streets, and beautiful parks. Golder wrote, "I do not know of another city of its size (100,000) that has so much in the way of the spiritual things of life as Zagreb." [65]

This cultured city, so delightful to Golder, helped him to cope with illness while there. He wrote Lutz, "I suppose I will reach Paris next week sometime and rest for a few days. I am tired and have a bad cold which has settled in my lungs and causes me pain, but it will pass." [66] Persistently, Golder pursued his Hoover work at Zagreb, visiting the American legation, various governmental offices, the Academy of Arts and Sciences, newspaper editors, and an Austrian officer with a personal collection regarding Sarajevo from 1914 to 1918.

After finishing with Zagreb, Golder traveled to Ljubjana, Slovenia. Although still ill, he completed more Hoover work in order to round out his Balkan collection. [67] From Ljubjana, Golder traveled to Paris, which he reached on 21 April. He stayed there until he had recuperated on 30 April. Rejuvenated, he boarded the train again to begin further archival solicitations in Europe. His train took him to Vienna, Berlin, Budapest, Coblenz, Paris, the Hague, Vienna again, Prague, Warsaw, Reval (Estonia), and Helsingfors. Besides collecting documents in Helsingfors, in late June he set in motion a scheme for getting into Soviet Russia, since the State Department and Hoover had restricted him from personally negotiating with the Soviets. Golder contacted Holsti, Finland's Foreign Minister, who agreed to act an an intermediary between the historian and the Soviet government. Before long, Holsti successfully negotiated permission for Golder to enter Russia unofficially, without representing any United States organization, to report on famine conditions in Russia to Hoover. But Golder, not wishing to gain Hoover's and the ARA's enmity by circumventing them, let the ARA know of Holsti's successful negotiations. In July, Golder learned that the ARA disapproved of the unauthorized procedure.[68]

Even though Golder's scheme failed to work out, he continued collecting documents in Europe.[69] On 8 August, his train rolled into Vienna, and there he found out that he might be able to officially enter Soviet Russia because of recent new developments. In July, Maxim Gorky, the Russian novelist, had appealed to Europeans and Americans to provide food and medicine for Soviet Russia because starvation threatened millions of Russians. Destruction during World War I and the Soviet Civil War, forced requisition of food from the countryside because of the Allied blockade, and a recent drought had brought about widespread famine in Soviet Russia. Hoover's ARA representatives began negotiations in August with the Soviets at Riga about sending the ARA into Russia. Hoover, as Secretary of Commerce, had to present the ARA as a private, humanitarian organization during the negotiations, but he had strong political motives, too, in sending the ARA to Soviet Russia: to support capitalist sentiment, to bring about opposition to the Soviets, and to etch in the minds of Russians the beneficence of Americanism.[70]

Golder, though, had little interest in Hoover's political motives regarding the ARA in Russia at this time. Golder's motives involved being able to collect documents and to play a humantarian role in Russia. But, having been stopped by Hoover previously from entering Russia, he feared that he still might encounter difficulties in the realization of his goal. He wrote Lutz from Vienna:

> I am anxiously waiting to hear from Brown (ARA director for Europe) that I am to go to Russia. I assume that I will go, for that was the purpose of Hoover in sending me over here. However, you cannot tell what these wise-heads are going to do; the fact that I belong to the tribe of professors is against me.[71]

While Golder waited to hear from Brown, another problem beset him. He wrote Lutz:

> Tomorrow are holy days and everything is closed. As I am unable to do anything I have bought a couple of books and I am going to have an operation on my breathing apparatus this afternoon and I am looking forward to two enjoyable days in bed.[72]

Golder did not specify what ailment required this operation or how dangerous it would be. After the operation took place, he stayed at a Vienna hospital a few days recuperating and then returned to his hotel room. On 18 August, five days after the operation, Golder wrote, "I am able to be about again, though a bit wobbly."[73]

In spite of illness, Golder was still obsessed with entering Russia. Brown had not yet responded to Golder's inquiries about joining the ARA. He wrote Lutz on 18 August, "I wish that d _ _ _ ARA director would act. It is getting on my nerves and in addition it is wasting valuable time for me.[74] That same day, Golder wrote Brown, "Better than any of the ARA men do I realize the hardship before us . . . ,"[75] and emphasized that he wished to be a part of the Russian ARA unit. In the meantime, he received a number of callers who had read about his historical mission in an interview he had recently given to an Austrian newspaper. The free publicity had prompted his callers to donate a variety of documents which were unavailable on the open market.

This unique opportunity to collect documents at his bedside, though, failed to change Golder's somber mood.[76] On 20 August, he viewed his collecting journey to Europe, with the primary goal of obtaining a Russian collection, in a less than satisfying perspective: "A year ago today I left Palo Alto for the Great Journey and here I am waiting, idly, sickly, and impatiently."[77] Two days later, he learned that the ARA and the Soviet government had signed the so-called Riga Agreement on 20 August, permitting the ARA to operate in Soviet Russia. This news compelled Golder to leave Vienna the next day on the train for Riga.

After he arrived in Riga on 26 August, Golder negotiated with ARA personnel permission to enter Soviet Russia with the next party of ARA members. But, in a letter to Adams, he bitterly complained that he had already missed traveling in with the first ARA party, and stated that the ARA viewed him as a nuisance since he had not been involved in any ARA field work. Still, his persistence had paid off. Suddenly, Golder, who had not been in Russia in four years, faced a great challenge.[78]

Chapter VI

Back to Russia: The Famine

Golder left Riga for Soviet Russia on 29 August 1921. Two days later, his slow–moving train reached the outskirts of Moscow, the new capital of Soviet Russia. During the civil war, Lenin had changed the capital from Petrograd to Moscow, a safer location. As Golder's train rolled into a station at Moscow, he stared out his compartment window at the worn–out locomotives and the many broken down cars on the railway sidings. He now saw up close that Russia's railway system had not recovered from the strains of World War I and had deteriorated even further. Kerensky had been able to buy rolling stock and spare parts from the United States.[1] Lenin had to struggle against White armies, backed by the West, and economic isolation.[2]

In spite of Hoover's political motives in sending the ARA into Soviet Russia, this introduction of Americans to Russia at least encouraged contact between two different ideologies. Americans on the local scene might gain a better understanding of Soviet Russia. Golder's first impression of the human condition in Russia, though, put politics in the back of his mind. As his anxious eyes looked over the railway yard, he saw starving Russians searching, like animals, for scraps of food.

When the train stopped at the station, Golder got off. He walked around the station's loading platform in a state of complete curiosity and saw large numbers of sickly, ragged, and famished refugees. Looking at their faces, he saw in them the tragic expression of despair and incipient thoughts of death. Golder moved on through the station, passing the lethargic flow of refugees. A special ARA automobile had come to pick him up, and he searched for it outside the station. After finding the automobile, he climbed inside and headed for the ARA headquarters. The automobile kicked up palls of dust as the driver steered it on a zig–zagging route to avoid the many potholes in the street. Golder noted the road's pitiful condition, as well as the heaps of refuse rotting in the streets, the houses stripped of their doors and woodwork for fuel, and the listless Moscovites who walked on the sidewalks like shadowy ghosts. Life in the city had the appearance of death. But, in actuality, the famine existed primarily in the countryside, a reality which would soon personally touch Golder.[3]

When Golder reached the ARA headquarters, Soviet officials assigned him and other ARA members to their quarters. Golder wrote:

> The quarters set aside for us, a huge building, formerly the palace of an oil king, is full of dirt and empty of furniture. It has not even running water or the ordinary conveniences. Fortunately, we have brought cots and blankets, so that we can keep off the floor and make ourselves comfortable for the night. Two of us started out in search of food and walked ourselves tired before, by mistake, we found a place and persuaded the woman in charge to give us a simple meal. . . .[4]

The following day, Golder learned that the ARA wanted him to be a special representative of this organization destined to alleviate the Soviet famine. The ARA needed someone like Golder who had traveled in Russia, had a knowledge of its history, and, above all, could speak the language, a qualification the other ARA members did not have. Golder's selection as a special representative placed him among the ARA Russian unit's five highest leaders.

Golder, who had a profound love for the Russian people, eagerly anticipated his role in the disbursement of food in Soviet Russia. In a few days, the ARA gave him an investigative assignment. Phil Carroll, temporary director of the ARA Russian unit, asked Golder to accompany John Gregg and Bill Shafroth on a lengthy mission along the Volga River, a region where the famine appeared to be devastating. Carroll charged this ARA party with determining crop damage, food resources, medical needs, and population health.

At eight o'clock in the evening on the first of September, Golder, Gregg, and Shafroth left their quarters, driving to the train station. There Russian officials had assigned them a train car and a flat car to haul their Ford *camionnette*. At the station, Golder saw that the assigned car had been coupled to the train, but that railway workers had not attached the flat car. In addition, Soviet authorities had chosen a Russian chauffeur to drive the Ford, but he had not yet arrived on the scene. Golder blamed this set of circumstances on Soviet inefficiency in a period of economic chaos. Little did he know that Soviet officials had set in motion a last minute scheme of locating a Russian driver who could understand English in order to spy on the ARA party. As yet, Golder had no awareness that Soviet spying would be typical during ARA operations in Russia as a counterbalance to American investigations of the RSFSR's economy.

While the ARA party waited for the driver, Golder had the station's superintendent attach the flat car and stow the party's luggage in their train car. Then the Russian chauffeur, who knew little, if anything, mechanically about automobiles, showed up. Finally, at midnight, two hours behind schedule, the ARA party, the chauffeur, two porters, and a Russian liaison officer (also a spy), boarded the special train car to begin the trip.

Golder, Gregg, and Shafroth slept little that night because of the trip's late and somewhat anxious beginnings. In the morning, rain pelted the countryside in a year when the Volga region had received only slight rainfall. After the rain let up, Golder observed what seemed to be endless tracts of fertile land that lay untilled, without crops to feed Russia's numerous population. He placed the majority of blame for this untilled land on the civil war's destruction—the uprooted peasants, the many killings, the damaged crops, the lack of seed, and the death of farm animals. As Golder's train traveled on, he spotted a few scattered patches of cultivated land. He noted, though, that this cultivated land had received extra care. The land's cultivators knew that their very lives depended on its preservation.

After traveling for two days, Golder reached his first stop along the Volga River, whose length stretches 2,300 miles from northern Russia to the Caspian Sea. His train pulled into Kazan, the capital of the Tartar Soviet Republic.[5] After the train halted, the liaison officer went in search of Kazan's ruling authorities so that the ARA party could begin gathering information.

In the meantime, Golder walked around the station, where he saw thousands of refugees from the villages around Kazan. He thought that many of the refugees would remain at the station because damaged railway lines, broken down cars, and unserviceable locomotives hindered railway transportation. He believed that if the refugees did stay there and did not receive any aid, they would die of starvation. The refugees he saw were without shelter, forced to live a daily existence exposed to rain, wind, and cold. They had no money for buying even the crudest forms of food. He observed that even the "most fortunate refugees," those who had a small measure of protection as they huddled together in the station's corridors, looked pale and skeletal. Most distressful for Golder, though, concerned the many orphans, whose parents had either died or abandoned them in order to search for food. The children's gaunt faces, spindly legs, and fluttering, tattered clothes saddened him. They were, he realized, on the ragged edge of death. Only a meager ration of bread and soup had saved them from such a tragic end. However, as Golder learned, this supply of food was steadily declining.

After the liaison officer returned from his mission of locating the city's governing body, Golder, Gregg, and Shafroth walked into Kazan, a city which sprawled over a vast, flat plain. While they walked through the city, Golder saw many damaged buildings, streets littered with debris, and rusted, dangling street car wires. This city, once teeming with human activity, shops and theaters, now closed and in a ruined state, again stirred Golder. He concluded that the civil war had executed its destructive work to perfection. The Reds and the Whites had occupied the city many times, with each army bent on recrimination and the struggle for survival against the enemy.

The ARA party had to walk a long distance in the gloomy city before they reached a house—the improvised headquarters of the local government authorities. Moscow had forewarned them of the ARA party's arrival, and the Tartar officials regarded the strangers with suspicion. Golder eased his way into their favor after he found out that before the civil war they had taught school. He mentioned that he was a teacher, and this revelation prompted the Tartars to ask him a number of inquisitive questions about the United States school system.

Golder then asked the Tartars to give the ARA party a tour of the local hospitals and public eating places. The Tartars agreed to do so. They guided the ARA party to several hospitals where doctors informed Golder that they had a severe shortage of medicine for treating the sick and those wounded during the civil war. The ARA party next inspected several public eating places, learning that thousands of people ate their only meal there each day. The Soviet government could not supply more food because of distribution problems. Golder foresaw that the lack of nourishment would eventually lead to many deaths at Kazan, unless a massive ARA food and medical shipment came there.

When the Kazan inspection ended, the Tartar authorities suggested to Golder that the ARA party travel to Bogorodsk, a refugee camp whose population particularly suffered from the famine. Golder, Gregg, and Shafroth decided to embark on this trip. So eager to go, they left Kazan at two o'clock that morning, driving the Ford six miles in the night's dangerous obscurity to secure transportation at the Volga River. Upon arriving there, the Captain of an old river boat greeted them. In view of the late hour, the ARA party hoped to catch a few hours of sleep on the boat while traveling to Bogorodsk. The Captain took them to their cabin. When they opened the cabin door, they stared aghast at the beds on which lay piles of bloody, slaughtered game. They turned away from this scene and then found sleeping accommodations on rough, wooden benches in the boat's smoking room. Understandably, Golder could not sleep, and his thoughts dwelled on the famine's anticipated grimness as well as the dreadful sights he had already seen.

After a sleepless night, Golder stood on the deck as the river boat slid into the beach at Bogorodsk, and he, Gregg, and Shafroth disembarked. Golder, as he walked on the beach, observed a very discouraging scene. He saw hundreds of families, who had gathered at Bogorodsk, without the strength to continue wandering the countryside in Russia. He noted that they had built platforms two feet above the ground as their domiciles and used discarded blankets, worn hides, and even miscellaneous socks for thatching a roof. The refugees' long stay at Bogorodsk and insufficient food had brought over them an overwhelming stupor. Golder noticed their complete indifference to the proximity of death. Everywhere he walked he saw the same indifference, until a group of women surrounded the conspicuous stranger and broke the sullenness with cries as they lamented their starving condition and their children's death.

The ARA party then moved on from the crowded beach to the town's edge. Without a guide, they wandered through Bogorodsk, until they found a hospital, which they entered to inspect. Throughout the hospital, he observed children cramped four to a cot, whose bones seemed visible through taut, transparent skin. Golder knew that they would soon perish, and left the hospital full of discouragement.

After finishing his tour of Bogorodsk, Golder learned of a Tartar settlement a short distance away. He, Gregg, and Shaforth felt compelled to visit this settlement, as if obsessed with adding further detail to the famine. The ARA party acquired an automobile and drove to the settlement, where Golder saw pale and lethargic adults walking as if in a daze. He had observed such miserable people in Kazan and Bogorodsk, but in this particular settlement he encountered something new regarding the children. The majority of them had distended stomachs—the last stage before starvation's death throes. In the midst of this bleakness, Golder wanted to bring some solace and cheerfulness to the adults, and spoke to a group of them about the ARA's intention of sending food shipments for feeding their children. The men looked on without expression, as if unaware of the ARA, although offering words of gratitude.

The ARA party then left the settlement, drove back to Bogorodsk, took the river boat down the Volga, and returned to Kazan in the Ford. Golder had experienced an exhausting two days of investigative work, but he decided to take still another side trip. The ARA party scheduled a trip to Titiushi. That evening, they drove the Ford back to the river boat, which they boarded, traveling in the darkness for two hours. Around nine o'clock, the boat docked and they disembarked to look for suitable transportation for reaching Titiushi, a town located on top of a mountain.

Soon, the ARA party found a carriage, which they squeezed into. The driver then sent the carriage in motion. It moved onto a roadway that led up the mountain's steep incline and the horses, even though powerful, struggled as they climbed. During the slow ascent, Golder saw nothing because of the darkness, but he felt the roadway flatten out after the carriage rolled into Titiushi. Suddenly, something starlted the horses and they leaped into a gallop, racing through the dark, narrow street. As the carriage careened, Golder thought he would crash, injuring himself. The driver, tugging relentlessly at the reins, fortunately gained control of the horses, and they slowed, becoming manageable again. Golder felt immensely relieved to be moving along safely again.

The carriage stopped on the street after Golder spotted a nearby hospital. The ARA party went directly to this hospital, a small building, where the staff cordially greeted them. Golder then conducted a rapid but thoughtful inspection, noting the scarcity of hospital beds which had prevented the staff from accommodating the town's sick who suffered from disease and lack of nourishment. The delivery of hospital beds, however, could not take place because of the hospital's remote location. On the other hand, Golder stated that the hospital would receive medicine, which gave the staff encouragement in this period of despair.

The ARA party returned to the carriage after this inspection. They got in, and the driver carefully guided the unpredictable horses out of the town. The carriage had just begun its descent down the mountain, when its brakes broke, locking tightly around the wheels. The carriage continued downward because of its weight and the locked brakes caused it to sway. Golder froze as the carriage occasionally slid close to the road's edge, beyond which opened a deep chasm. The driver struggled desperately to keep the horses on the road as he yanked and slapped the reins, shouting, and he somehow managed to guide the carriage to the mountain's base without anyone being hurt. With undisguised gladness, Golder hurriedly got out of the carriage. He had achieved an investigative goal, but the incident forced him to realize that he would be facing life threatening situations. The ARA party then walked to the river boat that would take them back to Kazan. Even though they had worked a long and exhausting day, they could not sleep, since they had to try to do so on the same uncomfortable wooden benches.

When Golder reached Kazan, he stayed there two days completing his Kazan investigations.[6] On 7 September, the ARA party boarded the train at 11:35 p.m. Golder wrote, "The rest of the night until six in the morning was spent in preparing a report for the Moscow office which we sent by one of our porters."[7] Inspired by a sense of urgency, Golder never complained of the exhaustion surrounding his ARA work in the field. He, like Gregg and Shafroth, wished to stem the famine's tide, and in their report they emphasized the staggering number of ill people and the harsh deprivation, especially among the children, recommending large shipments of food rations and medical supplies. The report stated, "Speed is the essence of our problem. . . . Food must be gotten out into the country with the least delay possible."[8]

Two days later, Golder awoke one morning and discovered that the train he was riding in to his next destination, Simbirsk, had stopped on the tracks for no apparent reason. Puzzled, he looked out the window. After having seen so many demoralizing scenes at Kazan, he now saw peaceful meadows and woodland pastures with a layer of frost which glistened in the bright sunlight. He then left the car to discover why the train had stopped. As he walked alongside the train, whose cars stretched throughout the meadow, he saw a group of ostensibly dispossessed peasants. Most of them were women, who had climbed onto the flat car carrying the Ford *camionnette* for a free ride to Simbirsk. Golder went over to speak with these peasants, and inquired about the crops around Simbirsk. The peasants replied bluntly: the crops had withered away and all the people in Simbirsk and in the vicinity would die in the winter cold. Golder noted that they spoke of death with an insouciance, as if they had resigned themselves to their fate.[9]

When Golder mentioned the Soviet government, the peasants showed no emotion. One peasant said succinctly, "Russia is without a master and therefore everything is bad."[10] They all accused Soviet officials of stealing in the times of scarcity, instead of making sacrifices. Golder reminded the peasants that the officials under Tsar Nicholas II had committed the same abuse. "Yes," one peasant said, "they did, but then we had so much that we did not notice it, and they always left us enough to live on."[11] The statement had a kernel of truth. The peasant, though, pushed aside any historical perspective regarding the famine: the cumulative effect of World War I, two revolutions, and a civil war on Russia's disrupted contemporary history.[12] But, as Golder noted, the peasants' complaining constituted "a cry for food and not for a change of government."[13] Golder then gave pieces of chocolate to the women and handed out American cigarettes to the men. (Russian cigarettes at that time were made of a grass substance.) This small kindness brought the peasants a few moments of joy.

As Golder continued to speak with the peasants, the train lunged forward and began its accelerating roll. Golder leapt onto the flat car, directly behind the locomotive, and stood precariously among the peasant passengers. As the train gathered speed, the locomotive, a wood burning one, sprayed hot sparks that fell on everyone, "setting fire to the clothes and sacks of the poor people."[14] The famine victims seemed to suffer harassment no matter where they traveled in Russia, and Golder seemed determined to share some of their bizarre experiences.

That day, the train came to a stop at a station in Simbirsk. Golder jumped off the flat car and rejoined Gregg and Shafroth. At Simbirsk, they planned a trip to a small town named Sengiley before traveling on to Samara. There was no gasoline in the Ford's tank, but they managed to acquire a few scarce gallons. They poured the gasoline into the tank, and drove off in the automobile that proved very dependable in spite of the rough road conditions. The roads around Simbirsk were in an especially deplorable state, and Golder had to travel on dirt trails that other cars had turned into provisional roadways alongside the direction of telephone poles. When this roadway came to an end, the ARA party crossed plowed fields and experienced a jolting ride, which brought laughter to them. They could not repress the hilarity of their rugged course of travel.

When the ARA party reached Sengiley, the Russian chauffeur stopped the dust–covered automobile in front of a theater building that served local Soviet officials as their headquarters. Golder went in, and saw a band playing to attract people to a current lottery. The prizes, Golder noted ironically, consisted of huge pumpkins and heads of cabbage. The ARA party then met with Soviet officials, and the presiding officer told Golder that the crops had failed and that the hungry population would kill their sheep, cows, and horses in order to delay starvation. The officer next guided Golder, Gregg, and Shafroth through the town to show them in physical terms the famine's destructive force. As Golder moved along, he saw examples of squalor and discouragement everywhere—rotting houses, crumbling buildings, ragged and skeletal adults and children with pitiful despair in their eyes. Golder found out that death among infants had been particularly high. He wrote, "the war and the famine, bringing in their wake typhus, cholera, and other diseases, have [decimated the population of children]."[15] Golder hoped that ARA food shipments would prevent a local disaster of greater proportions. Within a week, limited food shipments would be sent out to different parts of Soviet

Russia, beginning an ARA program that would touch the lives of one million children.[16]

From Sengiley, Golder returned to Simbirsk on 12 September. In the evening, he, Gregg, and Shafroth went for a walk in the freight yard near a number of warehouses. As they proceeded, they passed several peasants, who asked them who they were and why they had come to Simbirsk. Golder said that they had come to bring food to starving Russians. The peasant expressed appreciation for this humanitarian act and bemoaned Soviet Russia' deplorable state—the one time granary of Europe. This led them to charge that the Bolsheviks had mercilessly plundered the peasants during the civil war, bringing on their present woes. Golder wrote:

> Before I realized it I was defending the Soviet and pointing out that the suffering of the Russian people is due to the "German" and especially to the "civil" wars; that the Soviet is distributing grain for seeding; and that as soon as that is done it will take up the question of feeding the people.[17]

This argument failed to convince these peasants; someone said, "The Soviet knows how to take but not to give." Golder asked them, "Would you like to go back to the Nikolai regime?"[18] Golder observed that most of them remained silent.

The following day, the ARA party transferred from the train to a steamboat—the most efficient mode of travel to Samara. For one day, Golder had the good fortune of enjoying a comfortable voyage. And when he saw the city of Samara in the distance and its magnificent towering churches and glittering mosques against the horizon, he thought that life there might not be so horribly depressing as in other cities. After the steamboat came closer, he saw that, in fact, the city radiated a dull, ashen gray; the famine had not spared this city either.

When the steamboat docked, Golder noted that the city's gloomy background fused with the dreary image of peasants swarming the beach. He then departed the boat. As he customarily did, Golder walked around the beach, observing the dazed refugees, who, like so many others, had little to eat, subsisting on a soup mixture of watermelon, pumpkin rind, and potato peelings. They, too, lived under the open sky and spent much of their time sleeping in order to forget their misery. Golder discovered that these refugees were waiting for a steamboat to take them to the Ukraine or Turkestan, where they thought they would find abundant food. He knew that the arrival of this transportation would never happen; experience had taught the Bolsheviks that, if they permitted refugees to go elsewhere, millions more would gravitate to the railway stations, spreading even greater chaos in Russia.

After Golder, Gregg, and Shafroth threaded their way through the masses of refugees, they entered Samara. Wearily, depressingly, they plodded down the torn up streets littered with mounds of rubbish and dead animals. Finally, after a long, searching walk, the ARA party contacted the ruling authorities of Samara, from whom they received a room at the Red Army Hotel. They walked to the hotel, entered it, and moved along the hallway, which reeked of a foul stench. When they came to their room, they opened the door and found the room bare of furniture, except cots made of hard planks on which they would be sleeping. But, as Golder learned, the hotel personnel considered the cots a luxury. Everyone else in the Red Army Hotel had to sleep on the floor.

During the next few days, the ARA party inspected the famine conditions at Samara. They walked into one home established for children and discovered the building overcrowded beyond anything imaginable. The home had a capacity for sixty children, but over six hundred children, who had been abandoned by their parents, lived there. Golder saw some children, under the age of ten, sitting huddled on wood cots, their emaciated legs dangling over the edge, and he thought their pale, morbid expressions resembled those of people in old age. As Golder continued his tour, he walked with trepidation because he feared that he might accidentally step on a child in the unlighted corridors. Soon, he further discovered that the children's ward for the sick had no partition, exposing all the children to communicable diseases. Lastly, he learned that at least one child died every day in the home. In light of this tragedy, Golder wanted to report the famine's severity in Samara as quickly as possible to the ARA office at Moscow.[19]

However, telegraphic problems hindered Golder from communicating with the ARA office in Moscow. He wrote, "it takes longer for a telegram to reach destination than a train."[20] Impatiently, the ARA party waited several days before they received a message from Moscow. When the message did arrive, ARA headquarters ordered Gregg to return to Moscow so that he could present ARA authorities with facts, observations, and conclusions regarding the Volga famine.[21]

Golder and Shafroth then had a meeting with the *Gubispolkom*, the Provisional Soviet Executive Committee, in Samara. Golder presented the ARA's feeding agreement with the Soviet government to this committee, explaining that according to the agreement the ARA intended to use Soviet transportation, storage facilities, and Russian

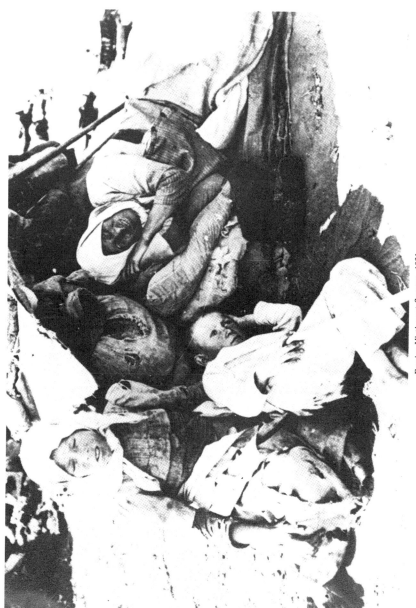

Famine Victims at Samara, 1921

personnel. In addition, he said that trains, warehouses, and Russians connected with the ARA would be directly responsible to American ARA employees. Further, the ARA staff would select the Russian ARA personnel. Such autonomy reflected Hoover's ARA methods in other European countries for gaining popularity for the U. S. and for stopping the spread of Bolshevism.[22] Suspicious, the Soviet representatives at Samara were not supportive of Golder's explanation of the ARA's role; they viewed the ARA's independence as a threat to their internal security as well as their sovereignty.[23] Because of this conflict, Golder's and Shafroth's first meeting with the Soviet representatives ended inconclusively. As Shafroth wrote in his report,

> [The *Gubispolkom*] was uncertain as to whether we had come in for purely relief purposes, and feared to give us the free hand we wished to have in building an organization which they thought might be used as we saw fit.[24]

At a second meeting, a Soviet official stated that the ARA could not select Russians for the storage, paper work, and distribution of food, insisting that only Soviet officials in Samara could do so. This decision brought the meeting to an end. In response, Golder and Shafroth sent a telegraphic message to the ARA office in Moscow, informing headquarters of the controversy with Soviet officials. The ARA office took action, compelling the Soviet government to inform the Soviets at Samara of the ARA's power to control the selection of its personnel; a sharp telegraphic communication from Moscow reprimanded the Samara officials. While this reprimand had an effect, the controversy over the ARA's autonomy persisted regionally as well as in Moscow.[25]

On 27 September, the first shipment of supplies of food and medicine arrived at Samara. Another one arrived the following day, accompanied by ARA representatives, who would help run local operations. Golder and Shafroth then began choosing Russian personnel to assist in running the ARA station at Samara—a doctor, a lawyer, a woman "belonging to the oldest and richest families of Samara," students, and other Russians. The ARA favored the Russian intelligentsia and other Russians who did not believe in communism.[26] Golder, whether he liked it or not, had confronted and served the political side of the ARA. On 28 September, a Samaran, whom Golder had spoken with several times in the city, visited him and stated, "The coming of charitable organizations from bourgeois countries will compel people to ask the question: Why are countries living under another economic system better off than Russia?"[27] Golder had no idea if this economic comparison would inspire a revolt against the established political order, leading to a capitalist Russia. He wrote, "The Russian situation is full of interest, but it is not easy to understand it."[28]

After the selection of ARA personnel in Samara, Golder returned to Moscow on 2 October, having experienced one of the saddest months of his life. He wrote, "'The famine is bad beyond all imagination. It is the most heartbreaking situation that I have ever seen. To see Russia makes one wish that he were dead."[29]

In Moscow, though, Golder had to divorce himself from this harsh reality and concentrate on the Hoover War Collection. The night of his arrival at Moscow, he had a conversation with his mentor Archibald Cary Coolidge, also an ARA member, who planned to collect materials for the Widener Library at Harvard. Speaking with Golder, Coolidge found out the wide magnitude of Golder's collecting success in Europe over the past year. Golder wrote Adams the following day, "I was talking with Coolidge last night, and he admits that Stanford is going to be the place for the study of history since 1914."[30]

To begin collecting in Russia, on 6 October, Golder visited Professor Mikhail Pokrovsky, the Commissar of Education, who was a trained historian. Pokrovsky received Golder warmly, and after learning of Golder's mission, he devulged that he had control of all government publications. Golder wrote Lutz, "everything of importance since 1917 was published by the government, and he at once gave orders that two copies of every book and pamphlet should be set aside for us."[31] In addition, Pokrovsky gave him a circular letter that would permit him to go through the confusing commissariat maze to finish the job. Thus, in a single meeting, Golder had increased the Hoover's documentary depth and range. Golder's connection with the ARA as well as the Soviet wish for greater contact with the United States—not to mention the Soviet interest in scholarship—had perhaps motivated Pokrovksy to be so compliant.

As Golder continued to collect materials, he moved to new living quarters. He soon found himself living in a museum, closed to the public, which the ARA called the Pink House (other living quarters being called Blue, Brown, etc.), and this museum provided the ARA with living quarters and headquarters. Golder wrote that the museum had once been the house of a wealthy Russian merchant who had spent around a million dollars on rare treasures of art—ivories, porcelain, and paintings. After the November Revolution, the Bolsheviks had confiscated the merchant's art collection and put him in jail. Later, the Bolsheviks assigned him a room on the upper floor of his former house, and the Commissar of Fine Arts, Olga Trotsky, converted the

house into a museum, permitting the merchant to be its custodian.
Golder noted, however, that the proletariat, showing more interest in
opera, ballet, and movies than in works of art, had prompted Soviet
officials to close the museum so that the ARA could use the building.
In Golder's room hung paintings by such world–famous artists as
Rubens and Van Dyck. But Golder wrote, "Unfortunately, I cannot
remain here long enough to enjoy all the beauty. Tomorrow, I go
again down the Volga."[32]

Golder had accepted another ARA mission, which involved a trip
to Astrakhan in the lower Volga region along the Caspian Sea. His
traveling companion, as far as Samara, would be James P. Goodrich,
a former governor of Indiana and a special ARA investigator whom
Hoover had dispatched to Russia.[33]

On 8 October, Golder and Goodrich departed the Pink House.
When they arrived at a railway station, they boarded a train a little
before one o'clock. They expected to find George Repp, an ARA
worker, who would be traveling with them, but he was not there. His
absence concerned Golder, because Repp had promised to bring the
supply of food. Golder had in his possession only two small packages
of chocolate and half a box of raisins. As Golder and Goodrich waited
for Repp, the train suddenly moved forward, departing the station a
half hour early. There was no food on the train. Later, for their first
meal, Golder and Goodrich drank tea, which was always available,
in typical Russian fashion: they sucked the tea through pieces of
Golder's chocolate.[34]

Golder ended up buying something to eat along the way as he
traveled to Tarbelovo, Syzran, and Samara. In spite of the famine,
he discovered that if one had money, which most Russians did not
have, he could buy food. At Samara, Goodrich, who began a lifelong friendship with Golder during this trip, departed the train to
begin a study of the famine there, and another top ARA investigator
and economist, Lincoln Hutchinson, joined Golder. On 17 October,
Golder and Hutchinson arrived at Baskunchak, and, as a gesture of
good will, they invited the station's superintendent to have tea with
them. When the superintendent walked into Golder's car, he saw the
two ARA investigators playing cards to pass the time. Golder observed that as soon as the superintendent spied the cards he asked
Golder and Hutchinson if they would like to play poker. They agreed
to do so, and began playing. The game continued for only a short
time, though; the superintendent suddenly claimed that he had some
unfinished business to attend to. On his way out of the car, he said
that he would return if the train happened to be delayed for some
unforeseen reason.

In half an hour, the superintendent appeared at the car. Quite calmly, he informed Golder that some technical problems would postpone the train's departure. In view of this delay, the superintendent wished to resume the poker game. With pleasure, the three gamblers played until twelve–thirty that evening, when Golder and Hutchinson managed to clean out the superintendent. They had used paper chips for money, and the superintendent scratched out an IOU note payable at Astrakhan. He also offered to continue the game there and then left the car without showing any sign of dejection or anger over losing. Shortly afterwards, the train jerked forward and its wheels screeched under the car. And then it dawned on Golder that the superintendent's obsession for poker had compelled him to purposely delay the train so that he could indulge in this pastime. The experience affirmed Golder's belief that no political system could change human nature.[35]

Two days later, Golder and Hutchinson reached Astrakhan in the evening. They disembarked the train and quickly became frightened of this city laden with a lugubrious darkness; they knew that beyond its gates stood a city scarred by the civil war's turmoil, a city with an unforgotten past. They decided to stay that night in the train car, but were not left in undisturbed peace. That night, the chairman of the local Soviet government and another Soviet official paid a special call on the two investigators. During this meeting, the Soviet dignitaries acted as though they wanted to expedite an ARA investigation of Astrakhan, promising to send out an automobile at ten the next morning.

Hopeful of a smooth investigative experience, Golder appeared at ten in front of the train, but the special car failed to arrive. Disappointed but not surprised, Golder and Hutchinson then decided to strike out on their own and headed for the city that had unnerved them the previous evening. They had not proceeded very far, when two young men stopped them. Golder learned that they were Cheka agents, the Soviet government's security police, legendary for its harassment, arrest, and execution of counterrevolutionaries during the civil war. The Cheka agents announced to Golder and Hutchinson that they would accompany them in order to be of useful assistance. Golder wrote, "We needed the special attention as much as scarlet fever."[36]

Previously, whenever the Cheka came around, Golder felt very uncomfortable. When one knew he was being watched, he was at a disadvantage: it put a restraint on conversation with civilian officials. Golder had noticed Russians stop or change their conversations as soon as his liaison officer came near. He also objected to spying because Russians in general spoke against the Soviet government as a way of venting their frustrations rather than posing a threat. He wrote, "Here as elsewhere, people are against the government, a little more so here because of the hunger and because of the need of a scapegoat."[37]

As matters turned out, these Cheka agents did prove to be useful, taking Golder and Hutchinson to the *Gubispolkom*. And then they disappeared as Golder conducted an investigation of the famine at Astrakhan. Before long, he found out that the food situation here was less critical than at Samara. If thousands of refugees had not traveled on the Volga River to Astrakhan as a point of departure for other parts of Russia or as a resting place, he thought the community could almost take care of itself because of its fishing and salt industries. The high number of refugees, however, compelled Golder and Hutchinson to ask the ARA to extend its operations to the Caspian Sea.[38]

When Golder and Hutchinson completed their investigation, they departed Astrakhan on the train on 3 November. On the way back to Moscow, Golder thought through his experiences regarding the famine and wrote Adams:

> During the last two months, I have been up and down the Volga, from Kazan to Astrakhan, that is to say, the whole famine area, and I have had the opportunity to study it a bit carefully. The result of our investigation is rather interesting. The famine is quite local, in spots. It is true that thousands will die of hunger this winter, [unless ARA rations can alleviate this tragedy]. Yet it is equally true that right alongside of them, at their very door, there is an abundance of food, but lack of money and poor distribution.[39]

After Golder arrived in Moscow, he wanted to pursue his Hoover Collection obligations. He had traveled over more territory in Russia since his arrival there than any other ARA worker. When a letter came to Moscow from the ARA London office which requested that Golder and Hutchinson conduct an investigation of the Ukraine, Golder declined the request. He informed the ARA headquarters in Moscow that he would like to devote all his time to the Hoover Collection. But pressure from the ARA to accept the assignment became so great that he consented to take the trip.[40]

However, Alexander Eiduk, the Representative Plenipotentiary of the RSFSR with All–Foreign Relief Organizaions, would not give Golder and Hutchinson travel papers to the Ukraine. Eiduk, for political reasons, objected to the ARA Russian unit splitting its forces by feeding both Russians and Ukrainian populations; he thought the

ARA should concentrate its efforts in the Volga region. In December 1920, the Ukraine had signed a treaty with the Soviet government which permitted the RSFSR to take over every Ukrainian commissariat except that of foreign affairs. Through this office, the Ukrainian government had declared the Ukraine an independent and sovereign state. The Soviet government, which needed Ukrainian agricultural resources, would not accept this declaration.[41]

While the ARA and the Soviet government haggled over an ARA investigative trip to the Ukraine, Golder undertook Hoover Collection matters and trekked to Soviet departments of government with his circular letter from Pokrovsky, asking for their publications since 1917. He also began collecting newspaper files. In a few days, after Golder looked over his collected mass of publications and newspapers, he wrote Adams, "It looks now as if our Russian collection will probably be the largest of our collections and it will be the only collection of its kind in America."[42]

Then the travel papers for the Ukraine came through. Before leaving, Golder decided to attend a Thanksgiving party, which would take place at the Pink House. For the occasion, ARA members invited a number of ballet dancers and Bohemian artists and purchased copious amounts of liquor and abundant food. During the party, Golder listened to the phonograph play somber, melancholy music and watched the unconventional dancer, Isadora Duncan, as she danced in strange but graceful movements for the smiling assembled male crowd; she wore the flimsiest clothing and begged her audience to remove what remained of it. Golder wondered if the party would evolve into a wild orgy as he spied Coolidge and Hutchinson slipping away secretively into a room with a group of ballet dancers carrying cognac.[43]

After the festive night, Golder and Hutchinson departed Moscow, no doubt sleepy-eyed and with a hangover. Two days later, on 26 November, they arrived at Kiev, Russia's ancient capital, in the Ukraine. After arriving at Kiev, they sought out the chairman of the *Gubispolkom,* and asked for his cooperation regarding the distribution of food packages in Kiev. In October 1921, the ARA had negotiated the Food Draft Agreement to supplement the Riga Agreement with the Soviet government, and this agreement provided for the distribution of food from American and European donors to specific beneficiaries. At first, the chairman hesitated to permit any food packages to be delivered to Kiev because of tense Soviet–Ukrainian diplomatic relations. But he soon agreed to do so and promised cordial assistance, assuring Golder that arrangements would be made to establish residences, offices, and warehouses for ARA representatives. This assurance eased Golder's fear that he might have trouble in negotiating with Ukrainian officials in the capital, Kharkov, over extensive ARA operations.[44]

Golder and Hutchinson arrived at Kharkov on 30 November. They contacted officials of the Ukrainian central government, and they received a cool welcome. Despite the unfriendly initial meeting, Golder went ahead and arranged a formal meeting with Nikolai Skrypnik, the Vice President of the Ukrainian government. On the first of December, Golder and Hutchinson met with Skrypnik, and Golder explained to him that the ARA wished to secure the Ukrainian government's consent to carry out relief work in the Ukraine in conformity to the agreements signed between the ARA and the Soviet government. Golder wrote:

> We were given to understand . . . that the Ukrainian Socialist Soviet Republic is not a party to the said agreements and consequently not bound by them. Nevertheless, the [Ukrainian government] would be glad to let the ARA work in its territory, but on condition that agreements be concluded with it similar to those made with [Russia]. We pointed out that, in the first place, the agreements already made by the ARA with [Russia] are sufficient for our purposes. At least that was the understanding of the contracting parties. He remarked, good–naturedly, that we were poorly informed, that the Ukraine and Russia are different states, and that, though federated, the union between them is not of such a character as to make agreements concluded by one binding on the other, that each state has its own diplomatic agents and power to negotiate treaties.[45]

Golder did not want to debate with Skrypnik and asked him a direct question: Would the Ukrainian government permit the ARA to carry its work to the Ukraine? Skrypnik declined to commit his government until after consultation with his colleagues.

The next day, Skrypnik admitted to Golder and Hutchinson that there existed unexpectedly severe famine conditions in southern Ukraine. For this reason, he said the ARA's aid would be welcomed. Still, he attached a prerequisite to any final relief transaction: an agreement had to be concluded between the ARA and the Ukrainian government that took account of the Ukraine's independent status, laws, and institutions. Golder said, "Such questions are not a part of our business. We have come to the Ukraine not to discuss politics, but to feed the hungry." "But you are mixing in politics," exclaimed Skrypnik, "when you differentiate between the two Republics; when you treat one, and refuse do do so with the other; when you regard one as a sovereign state, and the other as a subject state."[46] This discussion continued for some time, as Skrypnik strove for a temporary agreement to be drawn up immediately. Golder stated his lack of diplomatic authority and then requested that he and Hutchinson be allowed to conduct their investigation. Skrypnik's response proved threatening. Golder wrote:

> To the question whether Prof. Hutchinson and I should go on investigating the food conditions in the Ukraine, Skrypnik said that he would be [happy] to have us proceed but in view of the fact that we would require police protection and other such guarantees it would be advisable to conclude an agreement on that subject before we went anywhere.[47]

In spite of this threat, Golder acquired agricultural information from Kharkov's Central Statistical Bureau. Golder and Hutchinson then left Kharkov, arriving at Moscow on 7 December, and filed a report with Colonel William Haskell, the ARA's new director in Soviet Russia. The report concluded:

> Whatever may be the real facts as to the food production of the Ukraine as a whole, there seems to be no question that a serious shortage exists in certain parts of it. All reports agree in this respect. The trouble there appears to be exactly similar to that in Russia proper; there is enough food for all the people but under present conditions it does not flow from the regions of surplus to the region of scarcity. This was frankly admitted by the official statistician of the government.[48]

As Golder had already predetermined, the thorny Ukrainian question would delay ARA relief operations to the Ukraine. Finally, in January 1922, Colonel Haskell negotiated an agreement that admitted the Ukraine's independence with Dr. Christian Rakovsky, chairman of the Council of People's Commissars of the Ukraine. While Golder himself did not believe in the Ukraine's independence since he thought the Ukraine and Russia were too similar in language and culture and that Russia depended too greatly on Ukrainian agriculture to justify a separation between the two countries, he had risen above the tanglement of political considerations, becoming instrumental in bringing about ARA aid to the Ukraine.[49]

After finishing with his mission to the Ukraine, Golder resumed his Hoover Collection work. This time, he sought a large collection of books which documented Russia's transformation from Tsardom to the Provisional Government and the Soviet regime. Such a task involved Golder in considerable physical movement throughout the sprawling city. This bustling about failed to bother him, since he felt optimistic about acquiring large numbers of books. He based this assumption on current Soviet economic policy. War Communism and nationalization had disrupted traditional buying and selling patterns during the civil war. In 1921, Lenin introduced the New Economic Policy (NEP), a plan to improve the collapsed Soviet economy, a so-called retreat from communism, which allowed small businesses to flourish and permitted peasants to sell on the open market, while the government operated major industries. All of a sudden, a proliferation of books began to fill the bookstores, and these books could be bought inexpensively, since the Soviet ruble was not worth much in relation to the American dollar.[50] Golder wrote Lutz:

> I have been watching the book market, and it makes my intellectual mouth water. Rare editions, beautiful bindings, heirlooms of great value are thrown on the market. I have decided to cast prudence aside, and spend a part of the two thousand on purchases here. Tell . . . Adams . . . and all the others they might as well begin abusing me and get done with it for they cannot stop me. In a century from now, when I am dead of a broken heart caused by their reproaches, the scholars of 2,000 will thank me.[51]

Golder went ahead and purchased thousands of books which cost only a fraction of their list price. He believed that if the New Economic Policy did succeed, which turned out to be the case, prices would go up substantially. In a short time, Golder achieved his goal of having an outstanding book collection on Russian history. As a result of his book purchases, Soviet publications, newspapers, and other materials—diaries, letters, personal papers, periodicals, pamphlets, posters, even paintings, that he had collected since he entered Russia, Golder boasted to Adams, "I am glad that I got in here, for we are making a clean-up which those who follow after us cannot duplicate."[52]

Despite Golder's seemingly effortless success at collecting in Soviet Russia (he never could have duplicated such success in Tsarist or Kerensky's Russia), he experienced his share of apprehensions. The Cheka, perhaps thinking Golder a curious anomaly because of his dual role of collecting documents and investigating the famine, shadowed him everywhere he went in Moscow. He wrote, "My great crime is that I understand the language and talk with the people, something that most ARA men cannot do."[53] The Cheka even claimed that he had condemned the Soviet government; certainly, in an emotional moment, he could utter critical statements. The Cheka also stated that he had fought with Admiral Alexander Kolchak's White army in Siberia during the civil war. Perhaps this charge resulted from Golder's involvement with the Stevens Mission in 1917, a mission which had been the harbinger of American intervention in Siberia. Golder, of course, did not take the charges seriously, and the Cheka never dared to arrest a high–ranking ARA representative. Nevertheless, he wrote that while collecting documents "[he] walk[ed] around as if a sword hung over [him]."[54]

After Golder had collected a bountiful Russian collection by December, he wanted to ship it to the United States. In this endeavor, he sought out his loyal supporter Pokrovsky. Pokrovsky assured Golder that he had authority to issue a train shipment permit for the unusual cargo. But when Golder went to the Soviet transportation department to complete details regarding the shipment, officials there informed him that Pokrovsky had exceeded his powers. He concluded that the Cheka had perhaps brought about this critical snag, which distressed him considerably. He had a keen sensitivity for relevant historical documents, placing his Moscow bonanza above any of his eastern European collections. Documents concerning the Bolshevik Revolution, one of the most stirring historical events since the French Revolution, had to be made available to scholars. He wrote Adams, "I shall be [exceedingly] happy when I . . . have the Russian collection outside of Russia."[55] All through December, Golder tried to acquire a shipment permit, but without success. Just prior to Christmas a sense of futility struck him. He decided to postpone the idea of acquiring a permit because "the Bolos are having their big pow-wow (Ninth All–Russian Congress of Soviets), and it is difficult to get them to pay attention to anything practical."[56]

With shipment plans in abeyance and Christmas approaching, Golder thought of his Russian friends in Moscow. That Christmas, he wished to help out friends who had suffered during the Soviet Civil War. He knew of one family in particular, the Ivanovs, who, before World War I, had been known for their wealth, culture, and hospitality. War Communism, a euphemism for confiscation, had deprived the Ivanovs of their wealth during the civil war, and they had to move into a small apartment in a poor section of Moscow. There they lived precariously while periodically selling a few personal belongings in order to survive.

To help unfortunate Russians they knew, Golder and Coolidge decided to play Santa Claus in authentic folklore tradition. At the ARA general store, they bought a number of food packages. On Christmas morning, they trudged many miles through the winter snow, dropping off the food packages at different residences. They also stopped at the Ivanov residence, and later a servant asked one of the Ivanov daughters to come down to see "God's blessing." Excited, she followed the servant to the doorway where she saw a sack full of flour, sugar, milk, rice, tea, and other assortments of food. She asked where these items had come from; the servant could only identify the benevolent deliverers as two mysterious men whose backs were covered with white powder. Little did Golder know that the night before, Madame Anna Dimitrovna Ivanov had called her large family together, explaining that the family had only a meager amount of black flour for the holiday and that she had nothing else to sell so that family could buy food.[57]

After Christmas, Golder learned, on 30 December, that Congress had appropriated 20 million to buy United States grain and seed for shipment to Soviet Russia.[58] For the past three months, he had believed that the famine could not be averted without great tragedy. On 3 October, he had written, "The situation is desperate—millions will perish this winter. (One to two million Russians died during the famine.) It is a very pathetic scene, and my heart bleeds for poor Russia, as much for the living as for the dead."[59] Early ARA food shipments had brought sustenance to only a small portion of Russia's population; the shipments had been limited since Congress, as yet, had not appropriated any funds for ARA purchases. On 30 December, a new feeding agreement was reached, in the light of the famine's severity, which included funds for adults as well as children.[60] Now, in spite of the Congressional appropriation of funds, Golder foresaw major problems in the process of distributing the food. He wondered if the Russians could unload, transport, and sack the grain in view of Russia's severe transportation disjunctures. He also worried that lack of coordination between the Soviet government and the ARA would intensity distribution problems. Golder wrote, "In a thousand and one ways [the Soviets] worry us, they arrest the Russians who work for us, they block us here and sidetrack us there."[61]

After Golder learned of the new appropriation, he decided to travel to Petrograd regarding the Russian collection.[62] He arrived at the former capital on 31 December. That evening, he wanted to see an opera. He noted that the ARA representatives in Petrograd "had been afraid to go near anything red" because of the particular Soviet hostility toward the ARA there. (Petrograd, the city of the Bolshevik Revolution, had a workers' population strongly committed to communism.) But Golder managed to persuade Dr. Herschel Walker, the ARA District Supervisor for Petrograd, to go to an opera. Walker notified a Russian liaison officer, and he secured tickets for the two Americans. Golder had not been in this specific opera house since 1914, and noted the guards at the door were dressed in uniforms of the old Imperial Guard, but looked slovenly and were smoking cigarettes. He wrote, "I suppose the reason for presenting this relic of tsarism is the lack of other clothing."[63] Inside, he discovered that he had an extraordinary view of the stage. He wrote:

> Formerly, I used to look into the box where royalty sat, and now I look out of it. We were at first put in the box of the Grand Dukes, but a little later were transferred to the loge of the Tsar itself.[64]

As Golder sat in the Tsar's loge, he wanted to see how this audience, composed mostly of proletarians who had been let in free, would react to the opera. He thought that in general the Soviet government had broadened the scope of culture among its citizens, especially the working class. What he saw this night did not impress him. He noted that the audience had no conception of how to behave. The men kept their hats and coats on, others read newspapers, some talked, and still others walked around, and he found such behavior distracting him from a performance of high quality. Golder wrote, "I concluded it was a vaudeville audience, rather than an opera crowd, dressed in proletariat clothes and thinking how much superior they are to the rest of the world."[65] He then wrote, "I am afraid I am becoming pessimistic and sour, and that is not a good way to start the new year."[66]

The city of Petrograd itself, too, contributed to Golder's sour mood. The following morning, he walked to the Nevsky Prospect, the boulevard which had been the scene of vociferous protest against the Tsarist government and then Kerensky's. Curious to see how the city had changed since 1917, he saw only a few signs of human activity on the Nevsky, while other streets revealed only desolation. Then he tried to find old friends. He wrote, "I knocked on a number of doors and received in reply a hollow, dead sound, no one there."[67] After some difficulty, he located the family with whom he had lived while working in the archives in 1917. He noted that before 1914 they had had a beautiful home and considerable wealth, but that the war and the Bolshevik Revolution had completely disoriented their lives. Husband and wife had separated, one daughter had married a dissipated fellow, leaving the mother and two sons living together. They occupied two small, dark, and overcrowded rooms near a building's roof. In one room, they had bunk beds and in the other a kitchen, dining room, and laundry. The mother worked in a bureau, the older son, who had been arrested several times, for the Red army, and the younger one at odd jobs. Golder wrote, "But the efforts of the three are clearly not enough to feed and clothe them, for they look gaunt and ragged."[68] Such a scene of tragic ruin made Golder nostalgic for the gaiety, the flowering culture, and the prosperity of pre–war Tsarist Russia in 1914.

While Golder went on to visit other Russians, he carefully collected documents for the Hoover Collection. He visited Petrograd's Revolutionary Museum, and received free of cost nearly a complete set of revolutionary newspapers from 1917 to 1918, which supplemented his Moscow newspaper collection from 1919 to 1922. The Museum staff also selected a very large collection of posters and pamphlets, which also supplemented his Moscow collection. Golder wrote, "Our poster collection of the revolution will be large and unique."[69] After this acquisition, the Soviet printing office, established before the capital was moved to Moscow, gave Golder a carte blanche to its stacks. He next proceeded to the Academy of Sciences and other learned institutions which offered him their publications. Golder attributed his success in part to recent favorable reviews in Soviet Russia regarding two of his publications. He wrote:

> I am fairly well known, and just this week there has come out a review of the *Guide to the Russian Archives*. It happens to be favorable and it has given me quite a boost. I also discovered that the article, "The March Russian Revolution," I wrote for a publication house in 1917 was translated into Russian and published as a pamphlet and has had quite a success. All these things help.[70]

He also saw friends at various Petrograd archival centers, who, wrote Golder, "loaded me down with sets of publications until I was ashamed to take them, but I took."[71] Lastly, Golder invaded the book market, finding books in Petrograd cheaper than in Moscow. He selected books (50 boxes) with high quality bindings in a market of rare books. Golder wrote, "We are getting now what cannot again be had."[72]

After this month–long visit to Petrograd, Golder returned to Moscow on 30 January 1922, and seemed very satisfied with his collecting acquisitions at Petrograd. In Moscow, Golder received another ARA mission that involved a trip to the Transcaucasian Soviet Republics—Georgia, Azerbaijan, and Armenia, because the new Congressional appropriations made ARA relief there possible. He wrote, "It is Hoover's special request that a certain investigation take place and the work falls on [myself] and Hutchinson because there seems to be no one else to do it."[73]

Golder soon learned that the Soviet government, fearing a repetition of the Ukrainian separate agreement, had tried to discourage the ARA from penetrating Transcaucasia. Soviet authorities informed the ARA party that they could not proceed by train beyond the Russian border of Transcaucasia, a circumstance which would force the investigators to secure a U. S. Revenue cutter in the Black Sea and enter the region through Batum, Georgia. Golder wrote, "It is a long way to Tiflis and our troubles have already begun."[74]

Other incidents then occurred to discourage the investigators. On 1 February, Golder and Hutchinson went to the Kazan station in order to locate Car 85, which Soviet officials had assured them would be there, prepared for traveling. At the station, no one knew about this assigned car. Golder and Hutchinson then searched for the car themselves, and they found it on a siding—locked and smashed. Golder wrote, "Last night, in switching, it was forced to run on two switches, with the usual result."[75] They returned to ARA headquarters, fussed about this mishap, and received a telephone call from Soviet officials at five; they announced that Car 1021 had been assigned to them at Bryansk station. Golder hurried to the station. After a long search, he found the right car. He wrote, "[The] car had been used until recently for transporting typhus patients, and ,. . . it had not been fumigated, cleaned or aired since."[76] The sight horrified Golder.

At the ARA headquarters the next day, Golder learned that Car 2522 awaited him. Skeptical, he again returned to Bryansk station, where he found a large wagon–lit (sleeping car) cleaned and ready. After returning to headquarters, he stated that the unconventional car was adequate enough. Then a new problem confronted Golder. His traveling papers, signed by Colonel Haskell and sent to a Soviet agency for authorization, had been tampered with. Two of the three Caucasian states, Georgia and Armenia, had been crossed out by a Soviet official, invalidating travel to these countries. The ARA submitted a strong protest, and before long new travel papers appeared without a blemish.

After securing the papers, Golder and Hutchinson rushed to the station, having only twenty minutes before departure time. When they arrived at the station, they discovered that no one had coupled the wagon–lit to the train. Golder raced to the technical engineer and handed him three packages of Lucky Strike cigarettes, hoping this small bribe would be effective. By the time Golder returned to the wagon–lit, railway workers hooked it on just as the final bell for the train's departure rang out. He wrote, "We threw on our stuff, crawled in after it, paid the porters two or three times what they usually receive . . ., crossed ourselves in the Orthodox and Catholic

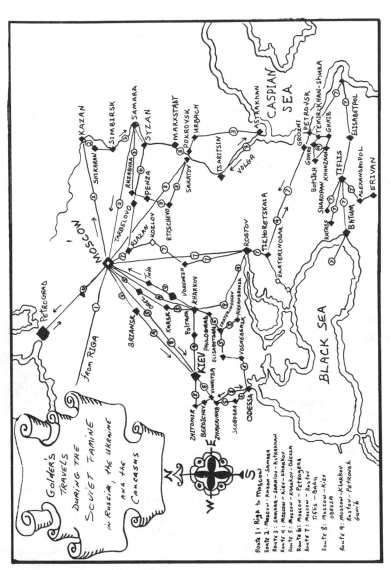

Golder's Path of Travel during the Soviet Famine

fashion, and got way."[77] On board, he noticed with relief, "for some reason, there is no representative of the government with us, to look after us and to watch us."[78] Exploiting this situation, Golder invited several passengers who had been riding on box cars and on bumpers while a blizzard raged around them into the wagon–lit. He wrote, "We should like to take in more but do not dare for fear of the typhus."[79]

After traveling two days, the porter awakened Golder at 5:30 a.m. at Voronezh, informing him that a Cheka officer wished to speak with him. Golder thought that the Cheka officer wanted to see his papers and invited him in. The officer explained that he had been ordered to southern Russia, where he would be responsible for a company of soldiers in fighting against bandits roaming the countryside. He asked for permission to ride, along with his two adjutants, in Golder's car. Golder consulted with Hutchinson, and they, not wishing to cause any trouble, agreed to let them in. Golder then crawled back into bed because of the bitter cold weather. Fifteen minutes later, another porter rushed in, saying, "They are taking off our car for inspection."[80]

Golder strode off with the Cheka officer and his two adjutants to complain to the railway superintendent. At his office, the superintendent stated that a cumbersome wagon–lit had no place on his line. Golder did not argue with him, but pleaded on pragmatic grounds— technicalities should not stand in the ARA's way. The plea somewhat embarrassed the superintendent, who asked whether or not the ARA party could ride in the coupé of another car. Golder said he could not because he had too much baggage and other ARA supplies. The superintendent then asked to look over Golder's and Hutchinson's papers. Golder hurried off to the train, leaving behind the Cheka officer, who, he noted, had taken a personal interest in the wagon–lit's fate.

Returning with the papers, Golder saw the Cheka officer coming toward him. The officer shouted, "We are going." Right behind him, the superintendent called out, "It's all right, the car is going through."[81] Golder then spoke with the Cheka officer, who boasted how he had telephoned a top railway official and received orders that the wagon–lit had to proceed on its way. He also remarked, "One good turn deserves another,"[82] to acknowledge his gratefulness for the ride. In light of the Cheka officer's success in freeing the wagon–lit, Golder asked him to find fuel for heating the wagon–lit. Before long, two workmen brought to the wagon–lit six pieces of wood. The Cheka officer said, "If they had not brought it we should have arrested the whole gang."[83] Golder noted that the Cheka officers had a fondness for such threatening words as "arrest" and "shoot," but that they had become far less effective after the civil war.

Golder again started to return to bed, when he learned that railway officials were taking off the wagon–lit. Rushing outside, he found out that no one had countermanded the original order. The Cheka officer straightened out this matter, too. Finally, the train departed the station, and the Cheka officer said, "the railway [officials] tried to get the car for their own joy–riding, and had it not been for us they would have succeeded. . . . They ought to be arrested and shot."[84] As much as Golder despised the Cheka, this officer had proven useful to him, while the Soviet authorities in Moscow had tried to discourage Golder's mission to Transcaucasia. Golder seemed to be living in a topsy–turvy world.

Golder reached Novorossisk in southern Russia on 8 February. He and Hutchinson transferred to a U. S. destroyer that took them to Batum. They then took the Batum–Tiflis line to Tiflis, and there Golder recovered a portion of the Georgian collection he had lost a year ago to the day, 11 February 1921, to the Soviet Red Army. Then, he traveled on to Zestafoni, in Georgia, to conduct a famine investigation of the villages in the area. At one point during this investigation, Golder wrote about the fun–living Georgians:

> Our hosts invited us to a banquet, but we, knowing how short they were of food and long on drinks, declined on the plea that we were busy writing reports. Imagine our astonishment when a few hours later [our hosts] came with the banquet to the train, in order, they said, to save us time. The dinner consisted of delicious native dishes. The great object of the [headman, however,] was to get us drunk, and he concentrated all his energies on Hutchinson and me. He drank toasts and made long speeches; his associates drank toasts and made long speeches. Consequently, we talked much and drank not a little, but neither Hutchinson nor I crawled under the table, which was a great disappointment to the Georgians. After that our host insisted on having a little poker, a game which he said he once played. We agreed to it as the lesser of two evils, but we were saved by the approaching train time.[85]

From 17 February to 6 March, Golder and Hutchinson traveled in Georgia, Armenia, and Azerbaijan. During his investigation of the famine in these countries, Golder discovered that political causes rather than natural ones had brought about deprivation in Transcaucasia. The fighting between Deniken's White army and the Red army, and the struggles of the Menshevik governments in Georgia and Azerbaijan against both the White and Red armies had disrupted crop production; the fear of requisition by the Whites had also reduced planting. In Armenia, the Turks, who had massacred thousands in conquest of that country, had carried off everything they could as the Red army drove them out, leaving behind barren valleys. These events had reduced the planting in Georgia by 23 percent, in Azerbaijan by 32 percent, and in Armenia by 56 percent. Moreover, other factors contributed to the famine. A large number of refugees from the Volga region had drifted to the Caucasus and they needed food. The Red army of occupation, numbering 20 to 30 thousand, also needed food. Still, Golder wrote, "[The Transcaucasian famine is] so much less serious than in Russia or the Ukraine that [this famine is] hardly worth mentioning in the same connection."[86] In spite of this comparison, Golder's and Hutchinson's reports lead to the ARA allocating 6,000 tons of corn and 5,000 tons of rye to the region. Golder had again helped in the preservation of life.

After his expedition to Transcaucasia, Golder arrived back at Moscow on 13 March, where he planned to concentrate on shipping his Moscow collection out of Russia. New circumstances favored this goal. In March, the ARA flooded Russian ports with relief supplies because of the Congressional appropriation, and Colonel Haskell and ARA members, along with the new Commissar of Transportation, Feliks Dzerzhinsky,[87] (he was also head of the secret police) worked together to loosen railway traffic jams, so that relief supplies could be speedily sent to famine districts. This close working relationship, a joint American–Soviet cooperative effort, which proved to be effective in solving the transportation quagmire for ARA shipments, encouraged Golder to be hopeful of acquiring shipment permits.[88]

What Golder needed in this direction was a little forceful help from the ARA hierarchy. Apparently, Colonel Haskell, who at first had distrusted Soviet officials, had not showed much interest in assisting Golder. But, after he had workedin cooperation with them on a day to day basis solving distribution problems, Haskell changed his tune. Golder wrote:

> Colonel Haskell and his men have [finally] taken the needed interest, [and] the Soviet officials have come through. During the last few days, I have purposely kept in the background and let the ARA do it all. Last night, [Alexander Eiduk, the Soviet plenipotentiary assigned to the ARA Russian unit], impressed upon my mind that a very special favor had been granted in letting us take out the [materials]. I thanked him that we appreciated it and let it go at that, for I could have added a word or two.[89]

The Soviets proceeded efficiently in guaranteeing the shipment's packing and safe delivery. Russian workers double–sealed the large fifty-five crates of books, newspapers, pamphlets, journals, periodicals, government publications, archival documents, memoirs, diaries, letters, and posters.[90] They loaded this cargo onto the train, and a special Russian convoy accompanied the train to the Soviet border. The train continued on to Riga, where the ARA office would transship the documents to the United States. Golder wrote Lutz, "it is a good collection and you had better tell librarian Clark to get ready to have an exhibition of Russian bindings, for, all things being equal, I took beautiful bindings."[91]

Golder's delight in his coup measured especially well against the collecting procedure of his Harvard mentor, Coolidge. Coolidge failed to buy in the low price market, because he thought the better policy would be to buy the Hoover Collection's duplicates, a less wasteful, less troublesome method of purchasing. Golder wrote, "I believe our policy is the wiser. . . . From the great abundance of material that we have, we can sift and select what we need, and with the remainder we can trade for what we do not have. Prices are going up fast, and we bought in a cheap market." Then he added, "Our regret in the future will be that we did not buy more."[92] Both Adams and Lutz acknowledged Golder's collecting ingenuity. Adams wrote, "When you return [to Stanford] University we shall, of course, expect to swing you . . . into a director's position."[93] Lutz, too, wrote,

My feeling is that you have covered the ground thoroughly.[94] I do not believe that any scholar in the U. S. could have accomplished two–thirds of the results which you have achieved since you left Stanford.[95] As for the Bolos, you will be the greatest authority in America on them when you return.[96]

Chapter VII

Diplomat and Humanist

Now that Golder had his Russian collection (at least a part of it, for he would collect thousands of other source materials while in Soviet Russia) on its way to Palo Alto, he decided to leave Russia for a temporary collecting trip in Western Europe. Since he had spent so much time on ARA assignments, he wanted to stay closer to the primary reason for his European trip—collecting documents. He also wanted to be away for a brief period, two months, from the scenes of bewildering human suffering. With relief, he left lugubrious Russia as his train took him toward Western Europe. In early April 1922, his train reached Berne, Switzerland. After he arrived there, Golder noted the temperate weather and the blooming flowers of springtime. This refreshing seasonal atmosphere, however, could not take away Golder's depressing memories of the Soviet famine.

In a gloomy mood, Golder began his Hoover work. He visited Joseph C. Grew, chargé d'affaires of the American legation, and asked him if he would help in the collection of diplomatic papers at the Swiss foreign office. Golder wrote, "Mr. Grew asked that I leave the matter in his hands and, because of his great admiration of Hoover, he desired to take a personal interest in the matter."[1] The following day, Grew set out by himself for the Swiss foreign office and induced several staff members to collect the desired diplomatic papers. He then informed Golder that he would organize and ship the collected materials. Such assistance did not reduce Golder to inactivity, though. He wanted to double check the foreign office's commitment because he realized that promises could be as easily broken as made. Golder went to see the foreign office authorities, and they assured him that the requested papers would be sent to Grew. This assurance satisfied Golder, and he left the city with a sense of accomplishment, even though his personal efforts had been minimal.[2]

From Berne, Golder traveled to Vienna and then to Coblenz. He then went on to London, arriving there with Goodrich. At London, they would discuss matters related to the ARA in Soviet Russia at the ARA London office—the main center for European operations. Although ARA discussions kept him linked to his recent Russian experience, he tried to enjoy himself. He ate kippered herring and filled his lungs with English air. He wrote Lutz, though:

> It was interesting to come through Western Europe once more and to see organized life, no one lounging on the [train] car steps, no one begging, no one in rags. [But] the shadow of the Russian experience still clings to me and makes me sad.[3]

But Golder did write Lutz about an achievement with a happy note. Golder stated that just before leaving Moscow he had bought a collection of Russian laws, from Peter the Great to the Bolshevik Revolution, a collection of 200 volumes. There were only eighty–one sets in the world and only two in the United States, one at Harvard and one at the Library of Congress. Golder failed to explain to Lutz in this letter how he had secured the collection for what he said to be the equivalent of twenty–five to thirty dollars. Lutz later recorded the circumstances of the collection's purchase:

> The story is told of a communist who was living in a house which once had belonged to a lawyer, and using the lawyer's library for fuel. Dr. Golder heard of these books and sent word that he would buy them. "Perhaps the professor will give me a box of food for them?" the communist suggested, and the bargain was closed. The books were immediately removed to a place of safety. The next day the communist appeared and asked for Professor Golder. "I have made a mistake," he said, "I must have two boxes of food." "Very well," the professor answered, "but this thing stops right here."[4]

From London, Golder traveled to Paris. He liked the idea of being in Paris again, especially the pleasant thought of attending the theater. He assumed that perhaps this city, always his favorite, might brighten his mood. In Paris, though, he wrote of his continuing depression: "The shadow of Russia follows me and it is rather difficult to laugh. I think I have almost forgotten how. It is not that I am morbid or even blue but [I am] in a kind of stupor."[5] But he did find Paris beautiful in the mid–April springtime and full of excitement, a city recovering its pre–war nonchalant spirit. One evening, he went to Notre Dame Cathedral and watched a performance of Shakespeare's *Merry Wives of Windsor*. The play enlivened Golder, and he decided to see another play the following evening. On this occasion, he saw a modern tragedy. He wrote, "[The tragedy] was wonderfully well played, indeed so well that I could hardly go to sleep after that."[6]

Golder then traveled to Denmark, to Luxemburg, and back to

Paris. He next stopped in Rome.[7] He had never before seen this center of the ancient Romans and the Italian Renaissance, with its Roman ruins, flawless sculptures, and radiant fountains. Golder toured the city, looking in awe at some of these treasures of the past, and then he pursued Hoover business. When he visited Italian officials, they treated him extremely well and promised to the skies to give him every requested document. But Golder doubted their commitment; he recalled that Lutz, when he had visited Rome in 1919, had received similar promises, but not a single Italian document had arrived at Stanford. Lacking the time to find out if the Italian officials had any serious intentions, Golder approached N. Nelson Gay, director of the Library for American Studies at Rome, who was familiar with Italian archival centers, about prodding the Italian officials.

Gay agreed to do this special assignment, as well as ship out documents, draw up lists of publications, and act as an area curator. And Golder, to assure success, contributed two hundred dollars to his library and also wrote Lutz to send him an appreciative letter as quickly as possible. At the time, Golder did not realize how prescient he had been. Gay went on to acquire a rich selection of Italian diplomatic, military, legislative, political, economic, and social documents concerning Italy's involvement in World War I, shipping them out just prior to Mussolini's takeover of power in 1922, which marked the beginning of a Fascist dictatorship over Italy.[8]

From Rome, Golder took the train to Florence, Italy. While in Florence, he wished that he could stay four weeks there, instead of four days, amid the artistic splendors of this city of the Italian Renaissance noted for its elegant buildings and subtle paintings. But he wrote again of his continuing sadness.

> I have walked the streets trying to become enthusiastic. .
> . . I seem to be dead all over. . . . It is not that I fail
> to admire the great work of these Florentines, for I do very
> much, but I lack "pep" I suppose. If I could only have a
> month in the mountains or on a farm I am sure that I could
> once more kick up my heels.[9]

After four days in Florence collecting documents, Golder traveled to Genoa and Rapallo in Italy, and on to Monte Carlo in Monaco, a small country in southern France ruled by a hereditary prince. In this city, a resort for the wealthy and a gambling paradise, Golder discovered that its relationship to reality was as distant as any fairy tale. Monaco's removal from the real world certainly did not help Golder in the collection of historical documents. He wrote Lutz:

> Strike Monaco off your list. Besides permits to the gambling

casinos, paper money, postage stamps, and the official paper, *Journal de Monaco*, which I am sending by registered mail, nothing else was published here.[10]

Even though a fantasy world, Golder found Monaco somewhat captivating. He wrote, "It was interesting to watch the crowd at the [gambling] tables, so many old women. Many of them had little pads and were writing, writing, I suppose trying to discover a method of breaking the bank."[11] Golder, too, became caught up in the preoccupation. Previously, he had restricted his gambling to train car settings; now, he played like a professional. He won and continued to gamble until fortune turned against him. He wrote, "The trouble is when one gets ahead, he does not wish to stop. I am going to Calvinistic Geneva to reform."[12]

Golder did have plans to go to Geneva, but first he traveled to Vienna, Budapest, and again to Paris. After Paris, he moved on to Geneva, Switzerland, arriving there in late May, and he looked forward to seeing George D. Herron with whom he had previously arranged a meeting. Herron had in his possession useful documentary evidence that Golder wanted to procure. Herron, who had been a self–appointed propagandist for Wilson and Wilson's foreign policy, had lived in Geneva during World War I and had attended the Peace Conference at Paris where he served as an informant for the American and British governments. During these years, 1914 to 1920, a many spokesmen, who exaggerated Herron's influence over Wilson, had besieged Herron with suggestions for war involvement and peace. Herron subsequently recorded volumes of information regarding these meetings, as well as his own views, which revealed European peace–feelers, national ambitions, and plans for a post–war settlement.[13] These documents Herron had stored away, undecided about what to do with them.

When Golder met with Herron, he persuaded Herron to give his papers to the Hoover. Herron, however, imposed certain requirements concerning their acquisition, informing Golder that the documents needed to be professionally typed under his (Herron's) direction and that he needed a guarantee that they would be protected against pilfering. Golder wrote:

> It seems that there are . . . documents in his possession which do not reflect to the honor and glory of the war diplomats, including some of our own, and Herron is afraid an attempt will be made to get rid of these papers.[14]

To reassure Herron, Golder said that Hoover would guarantee their protection. The typing request bothered Golder, though. He believed that typing volumes of materials would be time–consuming and would cost the Hoover around one thousand dollars. In spite of possible delays and the extra expense, Golder told Herron that the Hoover would provide funds for typing, and Herron agreed to this offer.[15]

While visiting Herron, Golder thought him a good observer, a careful listener and a cultured man,[16] notwithstanding his stern bargaining. After this meeting with Herron, Golder then took a long walk in the countryside and returned to his lodgings near a lake. At midnight, he wrote to Adams:

> I wish I could tell you what a joyful and restful day this has been for me. I have heard the roar of the river, the song of the wild birds, gazed on the high mountains and green meadows, filled my lungs with the fragrant air of flowers and soaked in nature. It made me so happy it almost made me cry. It has been so long since I have been close to nature. It almost drove from my mind and memory the squalid Russian scenes and pitiful cries of the begging children which haunt me. I am going to bed now to get up at 5:30, but I shall fall asleep to the sound of the waters of the lake.[17]

Golder finally regained his old enthusiasm. He later wrote, "I am glad that I have had two months in Europe . . . because I convinced myself that I can throw off the gloom when[ever] I leave [Russia]."[18]

With restored vigor, Golder headed for Riga, which he reached on 4 June. There he met with Goodrich, who had recently been in the United States, where he had conferred with Hoover over the problem of diplomatic recognition and trade with Soviet Russia. Goodrich, a lawyer, banker, former governor of a grain state, Indiana, and owner of grain elevators, farmland, and stocks in agriculture, favored trade with the Soviets in order to sell United States products to Soviet Russia.[19] In December 1921, after his special investigative famine trip to Soviet Russia, Goodrich had testified, along with Hoover, before the House Committee on Foreign Relations, urging the adoption of the 20 million for buying United States corn and seed as a relief measure for the Russians. In February 1922, in a letter to Hoover, Goodrich had asked the Secretary of Commerce to explore the possibility of recognition and trade regarding Soviet Russia, adding that, "The revolution is an accomplished fact and we might just as well recognize it and, under proper assurances, cooperate in a friendly way in the rebuilding of Russia."[20] Hoover, although he firmly believed Bolshevism to be a threat to traditional American concepts of individualism, private property, equality of opportunity, competition, and economic expansion,[21] accepted Goodrich's request to let him travel to Moscow as an unofficial diplomat and to discuss with Soviet leaders the obstacles retarding the normalization of relations.[22] As the Secretary of Commerce, he felt compelled to make a cautious investigation of United States trade with the Soviets.

When Golder met Goodrich at Riga, Goodrich asked him to help organize a meeting with Soviet leaders and to act as translator and occasional spokesman. Golder agreed to take this assignment, believing that Soviet trade with the United States would bring Russia out of its isolation and enhance its industrial and agricultural progress.[23] After accepting the new assignment, he left Riga on 5 June with Goodrich, Goodrich's wife, and Walter Duranty, a journalist favoring closer United States–Soviet ties, in a special ARA train car. When Golder arrived at Moscow, he noted that the city seemed to be unchanged, at least on the surface. While visiting friends, though, he found them worried over Lenin's fate; on 22 May 1922, he had suffered a serious stroke. Golder wrote Adams:

> The topic of greatest interest is [Lenin's health]. There is very little doubt that he is a very sick man, and though it is possible that he may pull through, it is not probable that he will in the future play a big political role. Naturally, the question is who will succeed him.[24]

Lenin's incapacitation ended for Golder any thought of contacting him about a meeting with Goodrich. And this development would not help in finding a solution to the problem of United States–Soviet relations. Lenin had favored ARA operations in Russia. No matter how dubious Hoover's motives regarding the ARA in Russia, Lenin valued the usefulness of American organizational talents and the United States vast banking, industrial, and agricultural resources.[25] He looked to the United States for economic aid, trade, and even educational training for young Russians to improve Russia's low level of competence, efficiency, and culture, all of which had suffered enormously during the calamities of the previous six years. He also looked to the United States because Western Europe could not materially aid Soviet Russia for political and economic reasons. France demanded the payment of war debts, while Soviet Russia countered with its own war debts against France for its involvement in the civil war; Japan had imperialistic interests in northeastern Asia; Britain had imperialistic interests in the Caucasus; and Germany had been ruined financially by the war.[26]

Although Lenin lay ill, there were other Soviet leaders who supported his economic views concerning the United States, and these leaders Goodrich could speak with—Leonid Krassin, the Commissar of Trade, G. Sokolnikov, the Commissar of Finance, and Georgi Chicherin, the Commissar of Foreign Affairs.[27] Yet any negotiations of a serious nature faced complications. Charles Evans Hughes, the Secretary of State, wanted to quarantine Bolshevik Russia, bringing the regime's downfall. And Hoover, like many United States financial banking and import–export groups, thought that a communist system could not be productive because of economic structural flaws. He believed that the loss of industry and trade would require the Bolsheviks to abandon their advocacy of communism. He further believed that any contact with the United States in terms of trade would strengthen the NEP bourgeoisie and capitalistic farmers (kulaks) and in alliance they would destroy social ownership and restore capitalism, with "America . . . undertak[ing] the leadership in the reconstruction of Russia . . ."[28] and taking control of the Russian market. In the meantime, he and Hughes hedged about negotiating with the "treacherous" Bolsheviks.[29]

To assist in arranging a meeting, Golder sought out Karl Radek, the Commissar of the Communist International and an ARA supporter during Politburo meetings. Radek had a reputation of friendliness toward foreigners, often speaking with them and even discussing state secrets. Golder, who had met Radek at the Pink House, had developed a rapport with him. After Golder discussed with Radek the idea of arranging a meeting between Soviet leaders and Goodrich, Radek set the wheels turning to bring about such a meeting.[30]

Goodrich, in about two weeks, received an invitation to meet with Lev Kamenev, Lenin's close confidant who acted in Lenin's place as chairman of the Council of People's Commissars, Alexey Rykov, the Commissar of Internal Affairs, Maxim Litvinov, deputy of the Commissar of Foreign Affairs, and G. Sokolinkov, the Commissar of Finance. Goodrich and Golder spoke with these Soviet leaders on 19 June at Kamenev's office in the Kremlin. During this meeting, the participants discussed Hughes' 25 March 1921 Note that the Soviet government had received six months earlier after Litvinov had made an overture to the United States government for the normalization of relations. Hughes' Note stated that safety of life, recognition of private property, the sanctity of contracts, and the right of labor had to be guaranteed before the United States would consider diplomatic ties and extensive trade with and loans to Soviet Russia.

While speaking with Goodrich, the Soviets treated the Notes' conditions with flexibility, promising to maintain an equitable court system, to end further nationalization, to admit capital and profit in certain economic areas, to honor contracts, and to support the rights of labor through trade unions.[31] This eagerness on the part of the Soviets to be flexible earned Goodrich's admiration,[32] although they had obviously responded in less than concrete terms. As Golder believed, after dealing with United States–Soviet relations for several months, the Soviets could not cease being communists, the underlying implication of Hughes' Note.[33]

At this meeting, Goodrich and the Soviets also discussed the question of war debts. The Harding administration claimed that the Soviet government owed the United States 187 million in credits to the 1917 Provisional Government.[34] Prior to this meeting, the Soviet government had maintained that all its war debts had no legal foundation since the Soviet government had repudiated the Provisional Government.[35] Subsequently, the Soviets changed this view in regards to the United States and they informed Goodrich that their government would willingly consider the debt's payment as well as compensation to American nationals for confiscated property, in exchange for credits. (The Bolsheviks, for example, had nationalized Standard Oil's property, while other American property had been simply abandoned by its owners during the Soviet Civil War.)

In response to the question of war debts, Goodrich reiterated the Harding administration's view: the debt's payment constituted a fundamental prerequisite before credits, or for that matter, diplomatic relations, loans, and extensive trade would be granted to Soviet Russia. The Soviets would not agree to this prerequisite; if they gave in, France and Britain would follow suit with similar demands, and the Soviet government was not in a financial position to make blanket war debt payments. Still, the Soviets wished to begin negotiations toward resolving this stalemate with the United States. Such a conciliatory tone further impressed Goodrich. And Golder, too, seemed to appreciate this opportunity for reconciliation. He wrote in his report to Hoover that Kamenev "hoped Governor Goodrich was convinced that the Soviet government had a real desire to come to an understanding with the United States."[36]

Soon after his meeting with Soviet leaders, Goodrich returned to the United States and attempted to bring about a method for resolving United States–Soviet relations. On 15 July, he met with Hoover and Hughes recommending that "the first thing to do is to appoint a commission of experts to go into Russia, and carefully examine the economic situation and report to our government."[37] In Goodrich's view, such a United States Commission, reaching favorable conclusions, might pave the way for United States–Soviet trade. Golder himself endorsed this approach, and had discussed it personally with Goodrich. Reluctantly, Hoover accepted the commission's idea. Hughes, although a former international lawyer for Stanford

Oil, whose property the Bolsheviks had nationalized, and an anti–
Bolshevik ideologue, also approved the proposal, while adding a qual-
ifying recommendation: Besides conducting a survey of the Soviet
economy, the United States Commission should apply pressure on
Soviet leaders to adjust their communist goals to the free market
system of capitalism.[38] What brought Hoover and Hughes around
to supporting a United States commission seems to be the fact that,
after the ARA began to slowly dismantle its operations in Soviet Russia, they believed the best way to deal with the Soviets would be on
a unilateral basis. Through this procedure, the United States could
capture the Soviet market without having to share the spoils by way
of multi–national conferences.[39]

In early August, Golder received a letter from Christian Herter,
Assistant to the Secretary of Commerce, regarding an American investigative commission. Herter wrote "The Chief (Hoover) [believes
that] you would be absolutely indispensable to such a commission."[40]
Golder, although in support of a United States commission, viewed
this offer with reservation. He wrote Herter:

> I note what you say about a possible Government Commis-
> sion to Russia and the desirability that I remain here to help
> out. My experience with the Colonel House Inquiry Com-
> mission has knocked out of me any wish to be on another
> unless I have an important and responsible part to play. I
> would rather return to Stanford and take up my work.[41]

But Golder did decide to accept the assignment if the Soviet government approved the commission plan. He believed that his connections
with Soviet leaders and knowledge of Soviet Russia through his collecting and ARA experience would probably lead to an influential
role. He also offered Herter advice about a United States commission: "It is not worthwhile to send a commission merely to show
up the shortcomings of the present regime."[42] Golder feared that a
United States commission, even if predisposed to the Soviets, might
blame Bolshevik ideology as being responsible for Soviet Russia's industrial and agricultural crisis, instead of blaming a combination of
historical factors.

Golder's fear of the problem of American bias against the Soviets
showed intuitiveness. Even before a United States commission could
be put together, Hughes guaranteed a troubled beginning for the negotiations with the Soviets to admit a United States commission into
Russia. Hughes selected for the negotiations a most inept diplomat,
Alanson B. Houghton, the United States ambassador to Germany, to
negotiate with the Soviets at Berlin. Houghton, a former congress-

man and president of Corning Glass, served on Metropolitan Life's board of directors, an insurance company associated with the National Civic Federation, one of the most strongly anti–Soviet business associations in the United States. Houghton even protested against being assigned to negotiate with the Soviets, believing that the regime would collapse shortly because of political chaos and economic instability. Goodrich, aware that Houghton might prejudice the negotiations's outcome, asked Golder in a letter to contact M. Sokolov, a foreign commissariat official, for assistance in explaining to Soviet leaders in Moscow that, "it would be in the interest of Russia [that the Soviets accept the United States commission],"[43] and in trying to resolve any diplomatic complications.

While Golder waited for developments regarding a United States commission, he undertook a new role that had been given him—reporting observations and conversations concerning Soviet foreign and domestic policies, as well as his own views, to the Department of Commerce. In June, Hoover's Commerce Department had asked Golder, perhaps the most experiences American historian of Soviet Russia, to act as an informant. He sent the reports through the ARA mail pouch to Christian Herter, who made many of them available to the State Department's Russian Division.[44]

For example, in a series of letters to Herter, Golder indicated his personal views on Soviet economic realities which had been based on his practical experiences in Russia. The Soviets, he believed, should not retreat from NEP, not pursue a course of advocating revolution in the West in order to obtain economic help. A country embroiled in revolution could not materially help its ideologically–similar neighbors because of economic disjuncture during a revolution's transitional stages. Moreover, Golder thought that the Soviet advocacy of revolution would only further isolate Russia from Western countries. Certain communists admitted this point to Golder. He therefore believed that economic necessity would force the Soviets to maintain the policy of NEP in foreign affairs in order to acquire credits, loans, and trade. The Soviets desperately needed foreign capital for industrial and agricultural development. In 1922, Soviet industry was far below the pre–war years; agriculture, although experiencing a famine, was improving but crops were so cheap on the market that farmers could not buy high priced industrial goods. Golder believed that this problem, mixed with the fact that Western countries were not ordering industrial goods and other products in Russia, conspired to give the Soviet economy a seemingly fatal stagnation. As Golder wrote to Herter, "The [Soviet] government is making a hard effort to organize the economic state, but it has not the means. Without the aid of foreign capital little can be done."[45] Golder, then, hoped that foreign aid would rescue Russia, while thinking that the Bolsheviks could not be wished away nor would return Russia to a capitalistic society if aid did come.

During the month of August (and later), Golder wrote such views to the Commerce Department. At the end of August, he embarked on another ARA mission to the Ukraine, and returned to Moscow on 10 September. That evening, he attended an opera and ran into A. L. Scheinmann, the chairman of the Soviet State Bank. He said to Golder that he eagerly wished to go to America for a week or two in order to discuss financial matters with United States bankers. Scheinmann had sounded out Golder previously regarding a visit to the United States; no doubt, through Soviet spying, Scheinmann knew of Golder's informant status. Scheinmann went on to ask whether or not it would be possible for him to secure a visa for himself and his wife to travel to America in a private capacity, without a staff and secretaries. Golder later wrote Herter that Scheinmann was not a great banker, nor a man of the world, nor a pleasing personality, but that he had "influence among many Reds who are like him,"[46] concluding:

> From this distance, it seems to me that it might be wise to let him come; he would learn many things that would do him and his fellows good, and it would please the leaders here and that may be worthwhile in view of the fact that we are just now trying to get in touch with them.[47]

Scheinmann would not receive a visa, since Herter (Hoover's spokesman) believed that he was completely untrustworthy.

Golder did not know that the suggestion of granting Scheinmann a visa would have little effect in Washington. Relations between the United States and Russia had cooled without Golder's realization, until it was too late. During Golder's trip to the Ukraine, Houghton had begun discussions with Soviet negotiators at Berlin. Golder had returned to Moscow in time to follow through on Goodrich's instruction to speak with Sokolov so that any diplomatic difficulties might be smoothed out. But Golder failed to seek out Sokolov, since he never received Goodrich's letter of instruction. Goodrich had inadvertently mailed the letter to the wrong address.[48] On 20 September, Golder did speak with one of the Soviet negotiators who had participated in the Berlin negotiations, Leonid Krassin, the Commissar of Trade—two days after Hughes had called a halt to any negotiations with the Soviets, informing the press that the Berlin meeting had fallen through because of Soviet obstinacy.

After the Berlin meeting, (held in late August, between Houghton, his party, and Soviet representatives, Krassin and Chicherin) the Soviet Politburo in Moscow, composed of seven members who decided policy by majority vote, had voted to accept the United States commission as long as the Soviets could send a comparable economic group to the United States. This offer, communicated to Hughes through Houghton, had compelled Hughes to stop these negotiations, since he viewed the commission plan as strictly a unilateral move. Krassin said to Golder that the Politburo had not intended to offend the United States government in any way. He said, though, that the Soviets had little choice in proposing a reciprocal Soviet commission, citing the matter as a question of self–respect. Golder wrote Herter that Krassin informed him that:

The question was put to [the Soviets at Berlin] in such a way that the Russians were obligated . . . to give the answer they did. It was pointed out to the Russians by our people [that] about thirty persons would be sent in, who would demand the right to go to every department of the government and demand information and make other such demands. When a slight objection was raised, the Americans pointed out that it was the Russians who were asking for money, not Americans.[49]

In spite of Houghton's lack of diplomacy and Hughes' opposition to any further negotiations with the Soviets, Krassin, in Golder's presence, revealed a conciliatory attitude toward the United States. Golder also wrote Herter:

[Krassin stated that] it is the desire of Russian government officials to draw nearer to the United States. They would rather tie up with the United States than with any other country and that was their feeling from the very beginning of the Bolshevik Revolution. At the time when all industries were nationalized, the American factories were left free.[50]

True enough, the Bolsheviks had exempted such United States firms as the Singer Sewing Machine Company, International Harvester, and Westinghouse Brake Company.

During this meeting between Golder and Krassin, the Soviet's conciliatory tone led to the question of a Soviet commission still being sent to the United States. Krassin hoped that the United States government would reconsider its rejection of the Soviet commission proposal. He said that the United States had nothing to fear from a Soviet commission: It would be composed of two or three Russians only and he, as Commissar of Trade, would probably be a delegate. Golder, too, believed that this Soviet commission would be quite harmless. His letter of this conversation to Herter, then, constituted, in essence, a Soviet feeler for renewed negotiations.[51]

Golder, though, as well as Goodrich, did believe that Hughes, and for that matter Hoover, who had backed Hughes' termination of negotiations, could not accept a reciprocal Soviet commission in light of the stringent non–recognition policy of the United States. In Golder's and Goodrich's view, the Soviets had been ill–advised to jeopardize the negotiations with such a counterproposal. And Goodrich blamed himself for not enabling Golder to perhaps intervene during the sensitive negotiations, elucidating to prominent Soviet leaders that the commission's membership might be biased in favor of the Soviets if he and Goodrich were members and what might happen in Washington if the Soviets offered a reciprocal commission.[52] Goodrich wrote Golder in December 1922:

> I am quite sure had the matter of a commission been presented to our Russian friends by someone like yourself, who thoroughly understood the situation instead of coming through Berlin, the Russian government would have accepted it.[53]

Not long after his meeting with Krassin, Golder departed Soviet Russia on 4 October for a brief trip to Western Europe. When he arrived in London regarding ARA business, he still had on his mind the Harding administration's refusal to negotiate further with the Soviets. He wrote Herter on 16 October:

> During the last two weeks I have mused over the Russian question . . . and I have come to the following conclusion: It would be best for Russia and the world to tie up with the Soviet authorities. The Bolsheviks are very human and very parvenue, and very eager to stand well in the eyes of their neighbors. If the United States should give them some form of recognition and should send to Moscow one of our big–hearted Americans, a man with plenty of good sense, a true democrat, who would invite the Bolos to his table and treat them as human beings, he would wield much influence for good. I know all the objections that will be raised but we can bury our pride and eat our words, if necessary, but we must save Russia and she is worth saving. I do not know any other way except the policy of waiting; if we wait . . . . thousands of Russians will die, and millions of others will approach the state of savagery.[54]

Golder's advice vanished into thin air; he could not, even fleetingly, hope to change the growing bureaucratization of the United

States anti–Soviet policy which affected the State Department. Moreover, the Soviets could not even hope to induce American businessmen and bankers with lucrative concessions into exerting pressure on United States governmental institutions to grant the Soviet regime diplomatic recognition since the policy of ideological opposition to the Soviets, as an institutionalized policy, gripped tighter and tighter around the State Department, thus becoming insulated from counterinfluences and functioning in a void.[55]

After his stay in London, Golder next embarked on a trip to see Herron. Golder arrived in late October at Herron's sixteenth century villa at Florence, which over looked the Arno valley. There Herron negotiated with Golder the pre–payment of secretarial work, editing, and travel expenses involved in completing his diplomatic papers. This detail taken care of, Golder turned the visit into a short but needed vacation. With one of Herron's sons, he climbed the summit of Fiesole hill, on top of which stood a Franciscan monastery. He entered the chapel and heard an organ rendition of the prelude to Parsifal, met with friars, and toured the monastery's relics and monuments. Golder was delighted by this retreat from the secular world, but not as much as by Herron's villa and what it had to offer. Golder wrote:

> The villa in which the Herron's live is a very beautiful place, with fine Florentine gardens. Along the walks are roses, lemon trees, and other semi–tropical plants. I walk through the garden and think of the wonderful history of the city, of the men and women who walked and planned and dreamed great things in that place.[56]

And the family, too, represented a certain ideal to Golder. He appreciated Herron, "a man of fine spirit, a worker for righteousness, [although], like Wilson, he broke down when [the new world order] proved a delusion."[57] His wife, of Swiss origin,[58] was a very cultured woman, who gave the villa a charming atmosphere and gave loving attention to her two sons. Everyone in the family spoke English, French, German, and Italian. One son was a musician and Herron's wife liked to sing. The Herrons often invited European dignitaries and professors to dinner, and Golder recalled the stimulating conversations which lasted late into the night. Golder, who never had a family, perhaps vicariously experienced one in this setting.

After Golder's stay with the Herrons, he then traveled to London,[59] Coblenz, and Berlin.[60] He arrived at Riga on 13 November; Cyril Quinn, assistant director of the ARA Russian unit, joined him there, and two days later they boarded the train for Moscow. They had a coupé to themselves, and at the Russian frontier customs officers came in. After casting a hurried glance at Golder's and Quinn's baggage, the customs officers began to tap on the walls. Golder observed one officer then climb on a bed and examine a ledge on which he found a broken screw. This small item aroused his suspicions, and he began to take off panels everywhere in sight. But before long, he grew tired, ready to leave. His partner, though, urged him to continue as Golder looked on in amusement. After a while, the officer discovered quite a treasure of contraband which had been tucked away behind other panels. This development led the officer to unscrew panels in several compartments. They hauled out so much loot that Golder estimated its worth at 300,000,000,000 rubles. Golder wrote Lutz, "Figure out the value in dollars if you like, I am too tired. The crowd of customs officials danced a regular war dance, for they will get a good share of the stuff." [61]

Golder returned to Moscow on 15 November. On 22 November, he had a meeting with Radek, who seemed "pleased to see me and urged me to stay and talk with him." [62] He said to Golder that the Soviet government had tired of discussions with other governments, such as at the Genoa and the Hague Conferences that summer, because they led nowhere. (These conferences, with the goal of solving the problem of European post–war reconstruction, had failed to establish mechanisms for loans and credits to Soviet Russia because of French and British hostility toward the Soviets over war debts. The United States had refused to officially attend the economic conferences.) Radek stated, according to Golder, "the Soviet is interested in deeds and not words and is ready to talk business with whomever comes along, . . . and looks with favor on foreign capital and will drive a bargain with it." [63]

Golder sent a letter of this conversation to Herter, while noting, "I wish to goodness I knew a little more the mind of Washington . . . ." [64] Then, in early December, Golder had another meeting with Radek, who informed him that Goodrich had sent an inquiry to the Soviet government: if the Soviets allowed a United States commission to travel to Russia, a Soviet commission would be permitted in the United States at a later date. Radek revealed to Golder that the Soviet government had agreed to this proposal. Golder wrote Herter, "[I find this proposal] very interesting and I am all ears and eyes." [65]

Golder waited for further information from Washington but none came. On 21 December, he wrote Herter, "You have lots of information but we never get any here. I have to go to Radek and the other communists to find out what is going on. It is not fair." [66] Five days later, Golder again complained, "The fact that I am kept in the dark as to what is going on at your end of the line makes my work stupid. I do not even know whether my letters reach destination."[67]

While experiencing frustration with Washington over insufficient information, Golder faced a new controversy. In July 1922, Hoover had decided to reduce the ARA's role in Soviet Russia because of a projected plentiful harvest in the Volga region. As the ARA scaled down its operations, the Soviet government embarked on a campaign to discredit the ARA, steering the "hearts and minds" of Russians away from American influence. This Soviet campaign was not a question of ingratitude but one of political expediency. The Soviets were not naive about Hoover's motives behind the ARA's economic intervention in Soviet Russia. The controversy, beginning tentatively in October 1922 (the reason for Golder's recent trips to London), became intense by January 1923.[68] Golder wrote Adams, on 4 January, "[The Soviets] want to get control of our supplies, direct our employees, and do everything in its name and for its glory."[69]

Golder believed that this discord between the Soviet government and the ARA would have a detrimental effect on how Western nations viewed the Bolsheviks. Soviet disrespect for the Riga Agreement would illustrate to United States policy–makers that the Soviets could not be trusted to carry out negotiated agreements. He wrote Adams:

> I have an idea of some of the schemes that are being talked about in Washington and the violation of the Riga Agreement will cause everything to fall through. But the [Soviets] do not see it or care.[70]

Golder was perhaps being too harsh. The Soviets were particularly sensitive to the dilemma of trying to encourage the Harding administration to reverse its non–recognition policy, while competing with the ARA. The Soviets, although disrupting ARA autonomy, did not bring forth a clearcut, open breach with the ARA. Instead, they conducted an erratic, uneven campaign. All the same, Golder angrily wrote to friends in Seattle, "The red gods are a disappointment and do not come up to the estimate that I had made of their ability."[71]

Golder then had another meeting with Radek on 1 February. Since their previous meeting in November, Radek had been in Western Europe for two months and out of touch with United States–Soviet relations. Golder inquired about Goodrich's cable regarding an American commission, which seemed to have come to nothing. Radek said that he did not have the latest information, but did say that a reciprocal Soviet commission had not been a condition. Golder wrote Herter that he "ventured to suggest to [Radek] that if relations between our two countries were not progressing, it might be due in part to the bad impression of the recent Russian dealings with the [ARA]."[72] Radek offered to inform Kamenev of Golder's observation. Even if Radek was cooperative, his information had not been insightful. Golder, far from Washington and an outsider in Moscow, felt lost on this stage of loose ends and false expectations.

As matters turned out, an official United States commission never did go to Soviet Russia. (Apparently, Goodrich had acted independently of the administration in proposing a new variation in exchanging commissions.) But sending unofficial commissions to the USSR[73] soon gained popularity among American and Soviet businessmen and government officials alike who wanted direct information. Golder's reports to Herter reflected the Soviet inclination to welcome unofficial United States commissions. For example, in a letter to Herter, dated 20 September 1922, Golder wrote that, "If no [official] commission can be allowed to go to America, [Krassin] would suggest that an unofficial commission of purely American businessmen should come to Russia to talk business."[74]

During the non–recognition period, from 1922 to 1933, congressmen, businessmen, and editors traveled to Russia. After they returned to the United States, a number of them embarrassed the State Department by advocating trade and even, on occasion, recognition, although the majority of businessmen did not advocate recognition. Moreover, as Hoover's Commerce Department eased restrictions against trade with the Soviets in the mid–20s, engineering companies, heavy machinery industries, and companies dealing with cotton, flour, automobiles, iron, and steel traded with Russia. Golder's observations to Goodrich in 1922 proved insightful:

> The only way [the Soviets] can save [Russia] is by calling in foreign capital and on the terms of the capitalists. The [party] will yield pretty much everything along economic lines. . . . I imagine foreign capitalists will have no quarrel with them on that score.[75]

When Golder returned to the Soviet Union in 1925, he observed the positive effect of the United States economic contact with Russia; he wrote Hoover, "I think it may be said with safety that the population as a whole is as well off today as it ever was in its history."[76] Finally, in 1933, Franklin D. Roosevelt circumvented public opinion, business opinion, and the State Department and granted recognition to the USSR as a countermove to Japanese imperialism in the Far East. While recognition had become official, the State Department still continued its ideological opposition against the Soviets.[77]

With United States–Soviet relations at a stalemate in January

1923, Golder accepted a new ARA assignment. That month, the chairman of the Dagestan Republic had come personally to the ARA office in Moscow, requesting help for the Dagestanian people. The ARA had asked Golder to go there and conduct a special investigation, since the ARA had established successful feeding operations in the most critical famine areas of Soviet Russia. Soviet authorities approved Golder's trip to Dagestan, a part of the USSR, without any complications. Little did Golder know that he would find himself challenged by the isolated, rugged, and mountainous Dagestan region, of which he had no knowledge of either its land or its people.[78]

Golder departed Moscow on 12 February, arriving in Petrovsk, the capital of Dagestan, four days later. Golder stayed at the Chairman's house for the next two days trying to ascertain the extent of Dagestan's famine in the mountains. This task proved difficult to accomplish, because the city had limited telegraphic communications and inadequate mail deliveries from tribesmen who seldom came down to Petrovsk. Golder therefore prepared to ascend the mountains of Dagestan, visiting the scattered towns and villages. He also knew that this investigation would involve forming personal impressions, since the tribesmen, for the most part illiterate, had no conception of modern statistics and had no records.[79]

At Petrovsk, Dagestan authorities gathered together several Dagestanians to accompany Golder—Abdulah, who acted as the liaison officer, Abdulrachman, a Dagestanian representative of the Commissariate of Education, Haji, a bodyguard, and two professional guides. Golder noted that each of them had a rifle, revolver, and *Kinzhal* (native dagger). This party was also accompanied by four mounted, malevolent–looking armed soldiers. The display of military hardware impressed Golder, but he thought this protection unnecessary. He wrote:

> When I got deeper into the mountains and heard stories of holdups and had the honor of looking in the face and shaking hands with some bandits, I came to the conclusion that the precautions were not altogether wasted.[80]

With this party, Golder traveled to Temir–Khan–Shura in the lowlands. He then began his ascent of the most rugged mountain ranges. He and his party traveled toward Levashi, and progressed slowly as the horses climbed up the steep terrain. Riding in carts and on horses, modes of travel as old as the dawn of civilization, the party traveled all day long. When they neared Levashi, a guard startled Golder by suddenly spurring his horse and galloping off at a reckless speed. Golder had no idea that the guard had abruptly departed to alert the inhabitants of Levashi of his arrival. Shortly afterwards, Golder rode through the streets, which he surprisingly found lined with curious spectators whose eyes followed this rare sight, an American of great prestige visiting their town.[81]

That evening local guides showed Golder the town's home for children and its hospital. After entering the children's home, he groped his way through the eerie darkness, since this sanctuary for orphaned children had neither candles nor lamps. He struck a match to find his direction. Proceeding slowly, he heard sounds. He then stepped into a room, from which the sounds had emanated, and discovered it crammed with children, dirty and half–clad, sitting on the floor "trying to eat their watery cornmeal soup." Golder inquired why the children had not been taken better care of. He learned that the home's former Russian personnel had disappeared, looking for employment in less desperate circumstances. Before leaving, they had selected native communist personnel, who had performed their duties apathetically, since they had little education and received paltry or no pay at all from the Dagestan Republic's famine relief committee. They would stay a few days, maybe a few weeks, "handing [their] duties to the cook or watchman."[82] Golder noted the consequence of the lack of caring supervision in his report: "[The children] run around the streets like little pigs looking for food. If the death rate among them has not been very high it is due largely to the pure air and excellent water."[83]

After Golder and his guides left the children's home, they moved on to the nearby hospital. Like the children's home, the building had neither lamps nor candles, again forcing Golder to use lighted matches for illuminating his pathway. In the troublesome process of burning match after match, he inspected different hospital rooms and found, with considerable astonishment, that this hospital seemed to have neither beds nor patients. He climbed the stairs to another floor. When he walked into a lighted room he startled four of the hospital's personnel who stood huddled around a fire. Golder asked to see the hospital's doctor, and they informed him of the doctor's frequent absence. Because of insufficient pay, the doctor had taken several other jobs in order to survive. Golder wrote that in the meantime,

> [The four medical personnel had been] eating up the supplies and refusing admission to sick people who did not bring with them their own provisions. There was but one patient in the building, and he had brought his own food and his wife to prepare it for him and probably take care of him.[84]

The following day, Golder arose at dawn, and he left his room to stroll around Levashi, a very picturesque community. As he returned toward his residence, a young woman stopped him. She said that she belonged to the Communist party and that the Tartar Republic had sent her to this town in order to indoctrinate its women. The Communist party had given her a large quantity of biaz, a cheap coarse, cotton sheeting, which was a very precious material in Dagestan. Golder wrote, "Salaries of officials are paid in biaz, food is purchased with biaz; and even wives are bought with biaz."[85] During local indoctrination meetings, the young communist had distributed biaz and had experienced tremendous success converting the women. She said, however, that the party had suddenly stopped sending her the highly valued cloth. As a result, her converts had relapsed to their former heretical convictions. She asked Golder, whom she thought was a fellow Communist, if he would replenish her supply of biaz. Golder, of course, could not fill her order, noting the contradiction between the "new gospel" and reality.

Late that morning, on 21 February, Golder departed Levashi with his party. As he traveled, Golder scanned the hilly, rocky, and sandy countryside. The land, he noted, had the disadvantage of being without valleys, having "only ravines and gorges that are as dry in February as our own Southwest in July."[86] He further noted a number of Dagestanians, to grow a few crops, had searched the mountainsides thoroughly for arable land and had cultivated a few strips of terrain, which they had enriched by transplanting fertile soil there from different part of the region. Here and there, Golder spotted patches of fruit trees and small hills of corn. Even during the pre-war days, the Dagestanians grew only a third or a fourth of their food; what they lacked, they had obtained by exchanging fruit, crafts from home industries, and work in neighboring parts of Russia for food. But the civil war had thoroughly disorganized this economic and social system. The carnage at Dagestan, or as Golder called it, the carnival of hate and blood, had been particularly sanguinary there because of the religious element—Bolshevik atheism vs. Moslem fervency.[87] He wrote:

> As a result of this carnage, the young and vigorous male population has greatly decreased and the number of widows and orphans greatly increased, the amount of livestock had been reduced by half and seeded area by two-thirds.[88]

Life in Dagestan had become more primitive than before World War I. Golder wrote, "In some villages, I have seen fire produced with steel and flint, houses lighted with pine knots, fields scratched over with wooden plows of the most primitive type, and tools of the stone age.[89] The Dagestanians, although not starving to death, suffered enormously from the years of war, and Golder admired their stoicism in facing a harsh world.

Golder reached Gunib on 21 February, a town high in the steep mountains—8,000 feet.[90] He tarried there for two days, resting the horses and visiting some of the surrounding villages. On the 23rd, he and four others rode horses to Chokh, twelve miles away, which was noted for its culture and local industry. After Golder and his party arrived at Chokh, he stayed with a relative of Abdulah, the liaison officer, whom Golder particularly liked because of his intelligence, discreetness, and charm. Once inside the relative's home, Golder literally found himself in a museum, "a fine, old building, with good rugs, a valuable collection of Dagestan weapons and many other interesting objects."[91] Here he experienced the joy of Dagestanian hospitality.

Golder became an honored *kunck*, a sacred institution, handed down from father to son, from generation to generation, which existed in every village for protecting visitors, strangers, and even enemies after they handed over their weapons. Golder wrote:

> I was told of a man who had killed another of a very powerful *tukhum* (clan) and, knowing that the clansman would soon be on his trail, fled to the home of the slain, where he gave his bloody *kinzhal* to the widow and demanded her protection. She held the avengers back until the Tsar's police came and led him out. After that she tried to stab him.[92]

Although an unusual case, Golder discovered that the host provided the *kunck* not only with protection but also with entertainment and comfort. Soon after his arrival, the host and the other male family members dusted his clothes, took off his shoes, poured water over his hands, showed him a comfortable guest room, and offered him delicious foods.

Less than an hour after Golder's arrival, a group of noted Chokhians came to visit the mysterious stranger. Then, a band of musicians slipped quietly into the house. As soon as they settled down, lavishly attired women sneaked in and moved to a corner, where they squatted. And then other Dagestanians streamed into the house. Golder, a bit confused, observed this slowly increasing population. Suddenly, the musicians began playing their native instruments, and some of the women moved onto the floor's center, where they danced to the music. Golder wrote, "[This was] the joy–giver of Dagestan which overcomes hunger and weariness."[93]

Golder, too, joined the festivities. The Dagestanians danced the

Lezginka, a popular native dance, with a number of variations. One particular variation held Golder's attention especially. He saw a man jump into the ring and dance with swift, controlled movements and rapid gesticulations, while holding a whip. After a while, Golder saw him toss the whip into a woman's lap. Golder wrote, "[She is] obligated to step out and dance or be whipped."[94] He noted that the woman who stepped into the ring turned swiftly as she held the whip and, being bound by convention, did not look up and kept an expressionless face. The man and woman danced together, until the woman released the man by tossing the whip to another man. The process continued successively as a number of dancers interchanged with each other. At one point, a young, demure, female dancer unexpectedly threw the whip at Golder, an act which brought a chorus of deafening cheers. He dared not dampen this spontaneous enthusiasm, and obligingly entered the ring, trying to dance, or, rather, to endure his awkwardness, shyness, and embarrassment. As soon as possible, he tossed the whip in front of the nearest woman. She got up, dancing along with Golder, who expected her to toss the whip, soon releasing him. He wrote, "She either enjoyed my company, or my misery, for she kept me hopping for what seemed to me a long time before she got me a [replacement]."[95] Finally, the woman tossed away the whip, and Golder returned to his seat with a mixture of glee and relief.

After the night of libation, music, and dancing, Golder sat down to breakfast the following morning. During the outdoor meal, he noticed the public crier, who stood conspicuously on a hill's slope, blowing a trumpet, whose sound reverberated in the mountains. Golder found out that the trumpet blasts alerted the local Dagestanians of a forthcoming meeting. Soon, dozens of people from the surrounding area filed into Chokh. Golder had not expected to attend this meeting, but Chokhian emissaries extended him and his party an invitation. He then discovered that this meeting had been especially convoked for him. When Golder went to the meeting, he turned his attention to this aul's (village's) spokesman, who, after describing gloomy economic scenes, asked Abdulah, as the Soviet government's representative, to tell the audience of the Soviet government's plans for economic assistance. "Abdulah," Golder wrote, "made them a long speech giving them more promises."[96] Unconvinced, the Dagestan spokesman exhorted Golder, whom he thought was a prominent communist, to spur the Soviet government into action. In trying to clarify matters, Golder disclaimed any membership with the Communist party and explained that he belonged to the American Relief Administration, an organization from the United States which had sent him there to determine the region's food requirements. None of

Women Dancing the Lezginka

the Dagestanians understood Golder, for, to them, the ARA was an incomprehensible abstraction. They imagined that Golder, with his security guards and official party, could only be an exalted communist. He knew how exasperating it would be to dispel the Dagestanians' misunderstanding, so he relented, playing the part of a Soviet official and promising to telegraph Moscow authorities about the plight in Dagestan.

On 24 February, Golder returned to Gunib from Chokh in the late afternoon, and discovered, to his amusement, "that the news of my night's [dancing] adventure had preceded me."[97] That evening, Golder enjoyed a pleasant time with Abdulah, who had been born in Gunib, and his mother, sister, and other family members. Just before Golder retired to his bed after the delightful evening, the household dog bayed at the moon and the superstitious Abdulah said, "I do not like it; it bodes no good."[98] Golder took note of this premonition, which soon dissolved as sleep overcame him.

The next day, Golder and his party, starting late, left Gunib and began a very difficult and steep climb. They reached the summit of the first ridge without any mishaps. Suddenly, Golder saw six, strapping women, each supporting two, thick sections of a log on their backs, crossing the pathway. The Dagestanians believed the passing women constituted an ill–omen. Thirty minutes later, the light, four wheel wagon in which Golder rode broke down. Repairs consumed more than an hour.

The party then continued on, and, for a moment, the country-side's scenery distracted Golder from thoughts of further misfortune; he saw the pastoral setting of an abandoned Russian fort and running beside it a swiftly flowing cool stream with many wild ducks. Then one of the wagon's horses became sick and had to be unhitched so that it could keep up with the party. The horse's condition, however, grew steadily worse and finally the animal fell. One of the Dagestanians claimed to be an expert regarding the care of horses. Golder watched as he pierced the horse's nostrils with an awl until they bled. The result, Golder noted, was worse than the cure; everybody had to pull and kick the stricken horse before it stood up again. At a native village, local doctors consulted each other on the horse's illness and determined that it suffered from constipation. Golder wrote, "One of the medicos, a big, strapping, savage–looking individual, pulled off his shuba, and twice in succession inserted his arm up to the elbow in the animal's vent."[99] This measure, too, was a miserable failure as the animal tottered. A group of Dagestanians tried to keep the animal on its feet, but it toppled over and had spasms, until someone mercifully slit the animal's throat. Golder wrote:

Five minute later, a dozen men were skinning it, and the women were preparing the pots for supper. Ali Khan (one of Golder's guides), who stood near me, and was quite broken up because of the loss of the horse, entrusted to him, said, "Watch the way the mouths of these wolves water." I was glad when we drove away from this bloody scene and from the company of these wild men.

These misfortunes spoiled what might otherwise have been a happy day. The sun was warm and agreeable, the mountains glorious and lofty, the air clear, the sky blue, and there was a wildness and primitiveness which was altogether inspiring.[100]

Golder finally rattled into Khunzakh late at night without his guards who had fled earlier because of the superstitious happenings, making the excuse that their horses had given out. In spite of the late hour, Golder, unafraid, woke up the head of the *Ispolkon* (local government), who took good care of him.

Before turning in that night, Golder decided to resolve a question that had been bothering him; he believed that the Dagestanians had a few odd notions about America and he wanted to know what they were. He asked if he might speak with the old, learned men of the community. The following morning, villagers brought to Golder an old man, who could barely walk, had poor eyesight, and was defective in hearing. The old man claimed to be one–hundred–and–twenty years old. Golder wrote, "Old people are not rare in Dagestan, and though feeble in body, they have minds as clear as those of their sons."[101]

Golder asked the old man, "Is America far from Dagestan?"

"So far," the old man answered, 'that no man can go there."

"But I am here," Golder said.

"Yes, I see. I suppose there must be a hole in the ground."[102]

Golder learned that America was the lower world, underneath Dagestan, and had no sunlight. Americans walked upside down, like flies, and worked hard, plowing their fields with oxen, guided by the light of lanterns hanging from their horns. America was a land of gold, silver, and precious stones, and Americans did good deeds and liked to help poor people everywhere. The "Tsar of Moscow" (Lenin) had a ladder so that one could climb down to America. Golder wrote:

When I learned [what] the Dagestanians thought of America, it became clear to me why I was an honored guest, and why I was almost as much of a curiosity to them as the first Europeans were to the Indians.[103]

Golder and his party next traveled toward Botlikh. On the 27th of February, they stayed at Tokh. About noon of the following day, they departed and just as his wagon ascended a steep ridge, Golder saw charging toward his party a troop of riders armed to the .teeth. He did not know what to expect: death, robbery, harassment, or protection. As Golder soon found out, these armed horsemen proved to be a greeting party from Botlikh, and Golder noted, "a little the worse for drink, to welcome the American from the lower world."[104] After exchanging salutations, the warriors lined up in front of Golder's party, acting as guards of honor, providing Golder with "the benefit of their music, fine riding, and choking dust."[105]

When this well–guarded ARA party arrived at Botlikh, Golder observed further evidence of his anticipated arrival. He noted that most of the town's citizens had come out to greet him. He saw veiled women atop roofs and men who lined the streets and bowed obsequiously. He wrote, "I doubted whether the freaks of [the circus of] Barnum and Bailey were eyed with more curiosity than the man from the land of gold, silver, and precious stones."[106]

During his stay at Botlikh, Golder considered this community the wildest of any he had passed through. Its members were happy-go–lucky and irresponsible, and excelled at fighting, drinking, and dancing. He especially thought the women were far less constrained by convention, unlike the women of Chokh. One night, Golder was invited to a wedding. He joined the Dagestanians at this ceremony as if he were a native and enthusiastically indulged in the conviviality, the delicious foods, and the abundant wine—a mere facade of plenty in this land of cruel poverty. In spite of reality, Golder toasted this joyous occasion several times, and noted how the women in dancing the *lezginka* "let [themselves] go, . . . [their] gestures, radiant faces and happy smiles, the movement of [their] bodies, expressed joyous emotion to such an extent that it becomes contagious."[107] During the dancing, Golder toasted one particular couple who had outshown, in his view, all the other ones. He wrote:

> When I sat down and the music started up again, the fair dancer, a beautiful and attractive woman, stepped up to the table and invited me to take a turn with her. I could not refuse that beaming, blushing face and tempting smile, and I stepped out.[108]

The audience became ecstatic over the professor's lack of shyness, his refusal to act like a stuffy official. After the dance when Golder returned to his seat, he heard a poet sing to the bride, "you are honored above all the other brides of Dagestan, for a stranger from the lower world danced at your wedding."[109]

Golder departed Botlikh soon after this festive night. He traveled to the valley of Temir–Khan–Shura, the city from which he had first climbed into the mountains of Dagestan. Golder wrote Colonel Haskell of this rigorous trip to Shura:

> Never before have I passed through such wild country, following such treacherous trails, climbed such steep mountains as on the two days of March 3rd and 4th, especially the 4th. When we finally jogged into Shura on the morning of the 5th, Abdulah had to go to bed, Abdulrachman was out of commission because of injuries received from falling off his horse and your humble servant, though suffering from a bad cold and feeling sore all over, was yet able to be about. The fact that I stood the trip so well raised my standing in the natives' eyes.[110]

The trip to Dagestan had offered Golder a physically challenging, interesting, and insightful experience. But emotionally, his thoughts clung tightly to the nearness of death surrounding the Dagestanians, especially the children. When he arrived at Petrovsk on 6 March, he learned, in response to a telegram he had sent to the ARA Moscow office ten days earlier regarding the Dagestanian famine, that a shipment of food, clothing, soap, and two train cars of medical and hospital supplies would arrive any day. After this shipment did arrive, Golder wrote:

> This promptness on our part was a bit too much for the Dagestanians, and they explained it, as they did our ability to walk on the ceiling, by saying that "the Americans are very clever and can do anything."[111]

Golder returned to Moscow on 13 March 1923. Two days later, he wrote Herter that he had had a fabulous experience with the Dagestanians. While proud of this experience, foreign affairs briefly concerned him again. For a month he had escaped the bewildering complexity of modern politics, living in a "primitive" world, perhaps a saner one in Golder's view. During Golder's absence from Moscow, the Harding administration had not retreated from its refusal to negotiate with the Soviets. In a letter to Golder, Goodrich described the "administration [as] drifting without wheel or compass"[112] in regards to Russia. Golder, on 15 March, wrote Herter of his own discouragement with the Harding administration's seeming paralysis regarding diplomatic and trade contact with the USSR. He wrote:

> The leading communists are most eager to come to an understanding with us, and they are ready to give their best

concessions and on the best terms, and reasonable capitalistic terms, but they cannot make general sweeping reforms
such as we demand. They are ready to give to each conces-
sioner individually what they cannot admit as a principle.
As one important communist told me, "We cannot go back
on ourselves and our theories to that extent; it would be
suicide for us as leaders and as a party." I think he stated
the case fairly.[113]

In January 1924, after Golder returned to the United States, and
gained a clearer perspective of United States opposition to recognition, he elaborated on the same theme in a letter to Herter:

> Why . . . do we not recognize Russia? Because the Bol-
> sheviks are unwilling to accept the conditions laid down by
> Secretary Hughes. He demands that before their sins can be
> forgiven they must repent, confess, and do penance. In other
> words, they must give up their legislation and in this way
> acknowledge before the whole world that they have done
> wrong. They can no more repudiate themselves than can
> other political leaders. To comply with Hughes' terms (as
> expressed in his 25 March 1921 Note), would mean not only
> political suicide [for the Bolsheviks] but in all likelihood as-
> sassination. But the Bolsheviks are ready to satisfy America
> in a practical way. They will not repeal their nationaliza-
> tion laws and recognize private ownership of real property
> but they will give a lease for 99 years or 999 years. They
> will not repeal certain laws which frighten the capitalist but
> they will make a special agreement with the investor which
> will fully protect him. They will not return to private own-
> ership concessions formerly held by Americans but they will
> compensate them in a way satisfactory to Americans. The
> Bolsheviks ask for a chance to save their face but Hughes
> holds them to his theology and hence the deadlock. It is
> rather a pity! No other people is so dear to the Russians
> as the American, for no other people has done so much for
> them during these hard years.[114]

After his trip to Dagestan, Golder learned that he would not be
in Soviet Russia much longer. Top ARA members, representing the
various famine districts, had submitted optimistic reports for a large
harvest of grain and vegetables in 1923. Most of the ARA personnel
would be leaving Russia in early spring and summer. Golder planned
to leave Russia in early May so that he could complete his itinerary
for the Hoover Collection in Europe. Adams, impatient with Golder's

long ARA and informant roles, had urged him to forego these assignments several times for over a year. But Golder's extra year in the USSR had been timely and productive for collecting documents there. During this year, he had collected many bundles of newspapers and periodicals, thousands of books, and scores of documents regarding Russian/Soviet history.[115]

That May, Golder departed Russia. He took the train to Odessa, where he boarded a U. S. destroyer in the Black Sea. As the destroyer drifted out to sea, Golder stood on the deck, watching the harbor, city, and countryside recede into obscurity. His departure, the memory of so many intense, bizarre, and human experiences, was extremely emotional. He wrote, "Tears almost came into my eyes at the thought of the misery and suffering endured by those big-hearted and fine people."[116]

The following day, Golder reached Constantinople and then he took passage aboard an Italian boat, sailing to Greece, where he had planned to pursue business related to the Hoover Collection. Golder traveled on to Athens by train, into this cradle of ancient culture, famous for the wisdom of its philosophers. But Golder, as he tackled his Hoover work, found little wisdom in contemporary Athens. The Greeks there seemed preoccupied with internal political struggles and national hatred of the Turks, Bulgarians, and Serbs. After speaking with heads of the Greek government, revolutionary leaders, commanders in the army, and party favorites, he wrote:

> It is about as easy to get my idea [of collecting documents] into their heads as the feeling of peace and good will towards their neighbors. They seem to be interested chiefly in war, in revolution, in profiteering, and such things.[117]

When Golder spoke with the Prime Minister, Dimitrios Counaris, the Prime Minister was so uninterested in discussing Greek documents that Golder steered the conversation to current events and asked him if there would be war between Greece and its adversaries? Golder wrote, "[The Prime Minister] gave a pious look and said, 'May God grant it.' "[118] Despite this discouragement, Golder relied on previous experience. Before leaving Athens, he entrusted his mission to a Madame Tsipouras, who had worked for Hoover at one time and who had connections with local government officials. Golder also asked the ARA staff in Athens to apply pressure on Greek authorities who controlled documentary sources. He wrote Adams, "By working together, we will get something done."[119]

From Athens, Golder traveled to Constantinople, Sofia,[120] Florence, and at the end of May, he arrived in London. While there, he wrote Lutz about an impoverished Russian countess whom he knew in the city. He related that in Russia she had come from a rich family, but that after the Bolshevik Revolution she had lost her wealth and lived a neurotic existence. He had found her in a Moscow hospital because of poor health and later in prison for protesting against a trial of clergymen.[121] Her sister in London had asked Golder to rescue the distressed Russian countess, and, with considerable difficulty, he had secured permission for her to leave Russia. Soon after Golder had reached London, he notified the Russian countess of his arrival. When she came to see him, he imagined that "she would jump on my neck and thank me for all I have done."[122] Instead, she jumped on Golder's back. He wrote, "[She] took me to task for bringing her out. 'Why did you not let me die in prison in Russia. It is a thousand times better than to hunt the streets of London for work.' "[123] She had had a falling out with the monarchist émigrés who might have helped her. Golder wrote, "She refuses to publish papers against the Bolos and therefore the monarchists, who have all the patronage and Russian jobs, have cut her cold."[124]

Golder, trying to be helpful, asked her to come to dinner with him. But she kept him waiting three quarters of an hour as she shed copious tears against her fate, and finally said, "I am going to take poison and die, that's what I will do."[125] Golder asked her to put off this extreme act and give him a chance to find her a job in America. She then calmed down somewhat. In disgust, Golder wrote Lutz, "Do you realize what a lot of crazy people these émigrés are? They are just morally sick and irresponsible."[126]

Following his trip to London, Golder sailed in cold and gloomy weather to Denmark. There he boarded a train for Berlin. When he arrived there, Golder suffered from a severe cold, owing to the unpleasant weather and crowded traveling conditions. He went to bed and, as he wrote, "doped myself with rum, quinine, and pills, and after passing a night of fever and fantastic dreams I was able to be up the next morning."[127] This solution allowed Golder to complete minimal business in Berlin, which consisted of supplementing his Russian periodical files, while he made personal observations of life in Berlin. He wrote,

> [For] the poor German who has neither dollars nor work life is difficult. I saw many of them standing in front of the meat shops and looking in. . . . In the train coming into Berlin there were posters showing the German [diplomats] with bleeding faces and under it, "notwithstanding all this, we do not bend."[128]

Poverty and resentment of the "peace" of Versailles among Germans made Golder wonder, as he had in 1920 during his trip to Berlin, what would happen to Germany.

From Berlin, Golder reached Copenhagen, Denmark on 5 June, and contacted Waldmar Westergaard, a professor at Pomona College and an expert on Scandinavian languages. Prior to his arrival, Golder had hired Westergaard to collect books and documents during his research trip to Scandinavia. After speaking with Westergaard, Golder discovered that he had bought a few books but had not collected any documents. Golder wrote, "I am deeply disappointed, for I had hoped that a good part of the work was done. We are to begin at the beginning."[129] Golder, relying on Westergaard's linguistic talents and contacts in Copenhagen, sought avenues leading to collecting success. They called on John D. Prince, a former professor of Slavic philology at Columbia University, who now headed the American Embassy at Copenhagen, and Golder asked Prince to write him a letter of introduction to the Danish foreign office. With this letter in hand, Golder and Westergaard went to the foreign office, where they used the letter to aid them in securing the office's war publications. This acquisition did not amount to a gold mine since Denmark had only peripheral involvement in the war. Still, every piece of information helped to complete a large, complex puzzle. Golder then had Prince write him another letter, introducing him this time to the Parliamentary Library. Prince did so, and shortly the two collectors were off in a rush to the Parliamentary Library. As previously, Westergaard handled any language barriers, but Prince's letter proved to be the dominating factor in the success of the negotiations. They left the building feeling certain that the Hoover would receive a set of parliamentary papers.

The following day, Golder visited Prince and expressed his appreciation and noticed that some of the foreign office's publications had already been delivered to the embassy. Subtly, Golder stated that Grew of the American Embassy at Berne had supervised the packing and shipment of Hoover materials. Prince caught the hint and offered to do likewise. His work done, Golder and Westergaard took advantage of a few hours of sunshine, walking along the waterfront and through the parks. Golder enjoyed the scenery, but wrote, "Westergaard is bubbling over with life and talks me off my feet, for I am not used to being much with people. When Prof. Hutchinson and I travel together we do not waste many words."[130]

Golder and Westergaard went on to collect documents in Norway and Sweden. In five days, they finished the whole Scandinavian assignment, and then Golder, wishing to reciprocate Westergaard for his able assistance, took him on a trip to meet scholars in Finland at Helsingfors, in Estonia at Reval, and in Latvia at Riga.[131] Following this excursion, Golder traveled alone to Berlin, where he joined Hutchinson. There Hutchinson asked Golder to accompany him to the Ruhr on a special mission for Hoover to investigate possible ARA food relief to the distressed Germans in this region.[132]

Golder decided to go, and for a week he visited such cities as Münster, Essen, Düsseldorf, and Dortmund as he investigated the Ruhr crisis. The German government had ordered the German mine workers of the Ruhr to strike, a so-called passive resistance to French control of the mines, a control which had occurred as a form of reparations following the war. In response, the French refused to permit train loads of food to be delivered to the German workers. At Essen, Golder wrote in his diary about an interview he had with German officials from the Health and Food Departments: "They emphasized the decline of health, due to under-nourishment, tuberculosis, and infant mortality being on the increase, especially since the French occupation."[133] In spite of the evidence of deprivation in the Ruhr region, Golder wrote Adams that, "should the ARA come into the Ruhr to help the suffering, it is bound to take sides with one or the other of the two parties. I, for one, do not recommend it."[134] In Germany, he saw ARA involvement as a huge political entanglement between the French, the Germans, the ARA, and, indirectly, the U. S. government, one in which the destitute might suffer greater calamities. (Hoover did not send the ARA to the Ruhr.)

After staying a week in Germany, Golder took a train to Florence, where he wished to expedite the completion of Herron's papers. Golder wrote Adams on 7 July, shortly after his arrival, "For the first time in three years I am really at rest and have a study and a bedroom. It is probably all the vacation I will get for some time."[135] But Golder found Herron in ill health, both physically and psychologically. Golder had written on an earlier visit,

> A number of people who have heard of Herron's plan to transfer his papers to us have given him a little worry by telling him it is not the right thing to do, it is not the safe thing to do, and other such unpleasant suggestions.[136]

Herron also suffered from neuralgia, a condition which affected his whole nervous system, causing him great pain and often requiring him to stay bed-ridden. Herron's illness and fears made him edgy. Golder wrote Adams, "We will have to be patient and gentle and in the end our patience will be rewarded."[137] Golder helped in organizing the materials, and often placated Herron with a kind, personal touch.

After staying at Herron's villa for three weeks, Golder departed with twelve big bundles of Herron's papers among his luggage.

With his bounty, Golder traveled to Rome. Fearing that Herron's papers might be confiscated at a border crossing, Golder took them to the American Embassy at Rome for their transfer to the United States through the diplomatic pouch.[138] A few days later, he ran into an ARA representative who had been in Athens and he said that the Greeks had offered a worthwhile Greek collection. Although lacking details of what had been collected, Golder was ecstatic. He wrote, "I am very happy, for the Greek collection completes our work in Europe. Every country with which I have had any dealings has come through."[139] In three years, Golder had collected millions of primary source documents, and his Russian/Soviet collection, as he had envisioned, represented the largest one outside Soviet Russia. Such a depository placed the Hoover War Collection on the archival map, elevated the prestige of Stanford University, and enhanced man's understanding of the past.[140]

Chapter VIII

The Unfulfilled Dream: The American–Russian Institute

Despite three years of living a dynamic existence, Golder did adjust quickly enough to quiet academic life at Stanford University. His life, although far less dramatic after his return, still had a harried tempo. Soon after Golder's arrival, he began preparing a new course on modern Russian history, including the March and November revolutions. He wanted students, who had so many misconceptions about modern Russia, to view Russian civilization as historical development rather than as historical aberration. For such a course, one of the few in the United States, he had extraordinary credentials—command of Russian, a Ph.D. in Russian history, publications in Russian diplomatic history, experience as a former "expert" on Russia for the Inquiry, and strong personal memories of Russia during the crucial historical periods of 1914, 1917, and 1921 to 1923. A student, Russell Buchanan, who became a distinguished history professor himself, wrote of Golder the teacher:

> My strongest reaction to him came from a course which he gave on the Russian Revolution. Both the course and the individual lectures were carefully organized, and most important to me, delivered with an objectivity seldom found in connection with this subject.[1]

Another student, Elsie Daly, wrote:

> [When] I arrived at Stanford . . . one of the first things my future husband told me was that I must sign up for Golder's . . . course on Russian history. My family was shocked, "What possible gain can there be in learning about Russia?" But I followed Jack's advice. There was a great deal of reading starting with [Sir Donald Mackenzie] Wallace's *Russian History.* I allotted an hour to each fifty pages, hit the course for a straight C, sat back and enjoyed Golder's beautifully organized lectures, interlaced with humor, and his splendid delivery, as I met Cossacks and Czars.[2]

Above all, Golder enjoyed his role as curator of the Hoover Library's Russian section; to this section, he eagerly gave his time, energy, and talent. As one might expect, the Russian collection brought him immense satisfaction since it represented the largest Russian/Soviet archival center outside of the USSR. Golder was the first historian in the world to open up archives for the study of the late Tsarist, Provisional Government, and Soviet periods. Without these records, our view of Russian/Soviet history would be far less comprehensive. During Golder's lifetime, many students and scholars from around the world, such as Bernard Pares, a British expert on Russia, came to Stanford and gleaned through Russian documents in the Hoover's small study room in the the main library.[3]

Due to Golder's success with collecting documents in the Soviet Union, not to mention Europe in general, Adams appointed Golder as the third member of the Hoover's directorate, which included Adams and Lutz. In this directorial role, Golder did not hesitate to suggest new ideas for implementation. One of his most innovative ideas involved establishing a network of permanent area curators in large European cities. Golder, supported by Lutz, persuaded Adams, who initially opposed the idea, to accept it. This decision proved to be very successful. The area curators, linguistically appropriate, aware of local archives, and interested in historical preservation, collected thousands of documents, and they did so without asking for any financial reward. Adams feared that they would do so. The prestige, rather than money, involved in belonging to the Hoover Library had a greater appeal to them.[4]

But Golder's foremost contribution to the Hoover Library concerned his sensitivity for continuous acquisitions of documentary materials in Europe, especially the USSR. Mabel Junkert, one of the Hoover's first secretaries, recalled that Golder, after his morning history class, came to her office and dictated letters to numerous European archival centers requesting documents. This frequent ordering resulted in bundles of government documents, newspapers, periodicals, pamphlets, memoirs, letters, diaries, books, and personal collections arriving at Palo Alto's train depot, all of which increased the Hoover Library's reputation for efficiency, depth, and perceptiveness in document collection.[5]

During Golder's first year after his return to Stanford, he also thought of establishing a Russian Institute at Stanford for the study of the Russian Revolution. He viewed the Russian Revolution of November 1917 as pivotal an event in history as the French Revolution, as a thorough political, economic, and social transformation of a civilization's traditions, the first attempt to create a socialist state in history, whose appeal spread far beyond its borders. He thought the information regarding the Soviet Union which trickled out of that country so full of distortions that outside observers in the United States and Europe could not form reliable judgments. To Golder, such judgments seemed extremely biased, either in support of or in opposition to the USSR because of the violent emotions following the old regime's fall. Golder hoped to promote through a Russian Institute non–emotional, non–political studies of Soviet policies since 1917. He wished to describe what the Soviet leaders wanted to achieve, how they faced problems, what sort of difficulties they encountered, and the causes of success. As Golder wrote:

> Some of us who were in Russia at the time of the famine and had an opportunity to observe conditions returned to America convinced that Bolshevism had a contribution to make to civilization and that it should be investigated openmindedly.[6]

Regarding a Russian Institute, Golder approached Stanford University's President, Ray Wilbur, stating that neither in the United States nor Europe did there exist an institute for studying the Russian Revolution. Golder wanted to seize the opportunity before Harvard University did so, and take advantage of the Hoover Library's unique Russian collection. He submitted to Wilbur the suggestion for establishing a Russian Institute at Stanford, and Wilbur, although Golder did not fully specify its scope, purpose, and objectives, agreed to support the idea. Then, in March 1925, Golder wrote to the Laura Spelman Rockefeller Memorial in an attempt to solicit funds for supporting a Russian Institute.[7]

In his letter to the Rockefeller Memorial, Golder amplified his plans for a Russian Institute. In the first place, he wanted American and Russian scholars to collaborate on topics concerning Soviet historical development. Secondly, he wished to restrict the studies to economic and social topics, at least initially, because of the Soviet government's sensitivity regarding political, religious, and educational subjects. Social and economic topics involved Soviet Russia's regeneration after the maelstrom of a world war, two revolutions, civil war, and famine. Soviet authorities might be prone to accept topics that discussed this extraordinary, if only partially successful, recovery. Third, Golder wanted to take advantage of the fact that many of the main actors who had participated in the Russian Revolution were still alive and had indispensable personal information. To make a Russian Institute operational, Golder stated that his institute required research assistants, secretaries, the purchase of books and documents, and asked the Rockefeller Memorial for $15,000 per annum.[8]

As Golder indicated in his letter, there existed the problem of

Soviet sensitivity for certain topics. His awareness of this problem stemmed from his days as an ARA representative when he had experienced Soviet repression, censorship, and interference. And yet, the Soviets had let the ARA conduct its work in the USSR without any formal rupture of relations, and at times the ARA and the Soviets had worked efficiently together. He therefore thought that a Russian Institute, a cultural enterprise, had an opportunity for success. Current Soviet society seemed to confirm this sentiment.[9]

After the repressive period of War Communism against the bourgeoisie during the Soviet Civil War, a period of restraint had taken place. Lenin had established his NEP policy as a retreat from imposing a communist society on Russia following the civil war. He did this for economic reasons; but he also calculated that NEP would have a cultural impact. He believed that a perpetuation of members of the bourgeois intelligentsia would aid Russia in raising its cultural standards in a society whose educational system and literacy had severely eroded during six years of war. Even after Lenin's death in 1924, NEP persisted in the USSR. However, the Workers' Opposition in the 1920s had many reservations regarding NEP; they were against the NEP bourgeoisie and the bureaucracy, which seemed to resemble a hierarchy of authority and status; the Opposition wished to end the social privileges and inequality of NEP and emphasized the grievances of working class youth as well as contempt for bourgeois literature and bourgeois schools, calling for communist vigilance and class war; they wanted to usher in the dream of socialism, while Lenin envisioned a gradual transformation. But, in 1925, the year Golder contacted the Rockefeller Memorial, Lenin's policy of treating the bourgeois intelligentsia in a conciliatory manner, at least certain "safe" members, against the new communist opposition, continued to prevail. Moscow in 1925, lively, energetic, and semi–prosperous, imposed little censorship on scholars.[10]

Nevertheless, Golder wanted to make sure that his organization remained free of censorship. But he did not wish to alarm the Rockefeller Memorial with such a question. Nor did he mention the fact that establishing a Russian Institute at Stanford, with the purpose of bringing Soviet scholars there, might antagonize the State Department. Even though Harding had died in August 1923, just before Golder returned to the United States, Hughes remained as Secretary of State under the Calvin Coolidge administration and maintained his ideological opposition to the Soviets. In 1925, the year after Coolidge won election to the Presidency, Frank D. Kellogg replaced Hughes; but the institutionalized policy of non–recognition of the USSR did not undergo any revision from Kellogg, who was as anti–Bolshevik as

Hughes.[11]

The impasse in United States–Soviet relations, however, underscored one of Golder's motives for establishing a Russian Institute. Golder wrote, "[One] of the main objectives we had . . . [was] to have at Stanford a center of information and channel of communication with Russia so as to be of help to our country when the time comes."[12] In other words, Golder thought the State Department's Russian Division had incomplete, distorted, and biased information for negotiating with the Soviets.

Neither the consideration of censorship nor the history of the State Department's ideological opposition to the Soviet regime discouraged the Rockefeller Memorial from supporting Golder's plan for a Russian Institute. In May 1925, its Board of Trustees granted him $12,000 to divide between a two year period for the scholarly investigation of the Russian Revolution, without any restrictions imposed by the Rockefeller Memorial and with the possibility of subsequent yearly funding. Besides this allocation, Golder also acquired six thousand dollars from Stanford University to divide between a two year period. Such cooperation from Stanford and the Rockefeller Memorial showed the growing American institutional interest in cultural relations with the USSR. The Rockefeller Memorial in the 1920s, for example, awarded fellowships to Soviet scientists so that they could study in the United States, Western Europe, or the USSR and also gave medical aid, laboratory equipment, and medical publications to Soviet scientific and medical institutions.[13]

After Golder secured the financial requirements for a Russian Institute, he scheduled a document collecting trip to Europe and the Soviet Union for August 1925. During this trip, he not only planned to collect documents but also to speak with Soviet government officials and Russian scholars regarding the establishment of a Russian Institute. Golder's travel plans became even more auspicious when the Russian Academy of Sciences invited him and Goodrich to attend its two hundredth anniversary. Golder later wrote about what this occasion meant to the Soviets:

> For the first time since 1914 the country had neither war nor famine and could satisfy its strong feelings of hospitality and welcome the stranger as a guest and not as an interventionist, child–feeder, or concession–hunter. For the first time since the formation of the revolutionary government the highest institutions of learning in the world recognized [the Academy] by assembling in [Russia's] capital and under the flag. For the first time in more than a decade Russian scholars had the possibility of meeting their colleagues from

abroad. . . . All elements of the population welcomed
the event and few begrudged the cost in time, labor, and
money.[14]

Golder accepted this invitation that would permit him to mingle with
Soviet scholars in Moscow during the celebration, presenting him with
a perfect opportunity to discuss the Russian Institute.

Golder left Stanford in August 1925 for the USSR. He took the
train to New York City, where he met Goodrich, and they boarded a
steamer, which transported them in comfortable, leisurely, and hos-
pitable fashion across the Atlantic to the European continent and
through the Baltic Sea. After his seaport docking, Golder took the
train to the Soviet–Finnish frontier, and from the outset of his contact
with the USSR he received preferential treatment. At the frontier, Soviet security officers waved aside any customs regulations for Golder,
and he received special low rates on the transportation lines. When
he arrived at Leningrad, a large committee welcomed him. He had
lodgings in a luxurious hotel, a guide to advise and help him, the
privilege of transmitting his messages at the post office and telegraph
office without charge; lastly, the police, as Golder wrote, "let [him]
break ordinances without arrest." He considered the special privileges thoughtful, an expression of good will, as well as the reflection
of a city's rejuvenation from the eerie silence of destruction, fear, and
despair which had pervaded the city during the Soviet Civil War and
famine. Indeed, Leningrad had a burgeoning hum of activity in 1925.
Golder wrote:

> I was struck first of all by the outward material prosperity.
> Streets are being repaired and cleaned, houses are painted
> and constructed, stores are opened and filled with goods.
> There is hustle and bustle in the streets, not unlike the years
> 1914–1917.[15]

The celebration of the Russian Academy's anniversary began on
5 September with a reception at the Academy of Sciences, a parade
on the Nevsky, and a concert of Beethoven's Ninth Symphony—all
joyous events to Golder. And that evening constituted the beginning
of a number of banquets. The first banquet was held at the Russian
Museum. After entering the building, he came across in one hallway
tables overflowing with delicacies and spirits: selections of caviar,
smoked ham, cured meats, domestic and imported cheese, pickled
vegetables and fruit, hot and cold dishes, cognac, vodka, and liquors.
Unable to resist the temptation of sampling this cornucopia, he whet-
ted his appetite and then walked into the main banquet room. He
found this room lavishly decorated with paintings and objects of art,

and sat down before what appeared to be a sea of the most delicious foods. The room was filled with sound—enchanting music, joyful laughter, and mirthful conversation. Everyone seemed to be effusive and convivial.[16]

Throughout the night toastmasters stood and lifted champagne glasses in celebration, indulging in propagandistic speeches, which, Golder wrote, "could not drown the music of the clinking glasses nor stop the outgushing of long pent up expressions of friendship."[17] Most of the participants turned a deaf ear to the speakers and paid attention to each other; Golder offered toast after toast to his table companions and engrossed himself in conversation. He wrote:

> Toward midnight I went, champagne bottle in hand, in search of . . . numerous friends to drain a glass of kindness. . . . We fell on each others' necks and with lips still moist with bonnie liquid we kissed and consecrated ourselves to science.[18]

Such endearment Golder valued above any other aspect of life. Finally, at dawn's early hour, he and Goodrich, as indulgent as his friend that night, headed in a staggering gait in the direction of their hotel. With harmonious gleefulness, they sang "For he is a jolly good fellow," and other frivolous songs. Golder wrote, "Governor Goodrich says that it was late when we went home, that he had to hold onto me. . . . Being an absent–minded professor I can hardly be expected to remember such details."[19]

From Leningrad, the Academy's celebrating party moved on to Moscow, where Golder experienced a lively sequence of excursions, parties, concerts, banquets, and speeches. He also mixed pleasure with business in Moscow, approaching Soviet scholars and political leaders regarding the establishment of a Russian Institute at Stanford. In this endeavor, he gained favorable impressions. After departing the Soviet Union in late September to collect documents in Europe, he remained optimistic that the Soviet government would approve a joint venture in scholarship through a Russian Institute. His presentiment proved to be correct. In November, while in Paris, the Soviet Embassy telephoned and informed him that the Soviet government had accepted his proposal for a Russian Institute.[20]

Two days after receiving this message, Golder wrote Wilbur at Stanford of the Soviet government's response and asked him to appoint Professor L. N. Litoshenko, a Russian agricultural economist, as an instructor for one year at Stanford University. While teaching there, Litoshenko would be collaborating with Lincoln Hutchinson, Golder's ARA compatriot and an economic expert, on a history of

Soviet land policy. Golder, thinking that this topic, which reflected Soviet Russia's triumph against the devastation of famine and the wastage of war, would elicit Soviet enthusiasm, had no way of knowing that Soviet agricultural policy would shortly become involved in a bitter political controversy in the Soviet Union.[21]

Wilbur complied with Golder's request and appointed Litoshenko as a history instructor at Stanford. On top of this development, Golder received a note in Paris on 12 December from Madame Olga D. Kameneva, President of the USSR Society for Cultural Relations with Foreign Countries. She inquired about negotiating an agreement involving her organization with the Russian Institute, formalizing the previous oral agreement from the Soviet Embassy. Golder favored this approach because such an organization attached to the Russian Institute would augment the cultural links between the United States and Soviet Russia that already involved, by 1925, sporadic contacts among actors, artists, scientists, and musicians.[22]

In his return letter, Golder wrote that he accepted Kameneva's proposal. He then mentioned that Stanford University and the Rockefeller Memorial would provide the Russian Institute with supporting funds. He also informed her that Litoshenko had been appointed a lecturer at Stanford, where he would work on an agricultural study, and that Stanford University Press would publish the manuscript under the auspicies of the Russian Institute. He further stated that Stanford University would not publish any forthcoming study until the Society had read over the manuscript. But Golder, who feared that ideological misunderstandings might jeopardize the success of a Stanford University–Soviet cultural relationship, stated that the jointly authored studies should not become instruments for propagandizing institutional viewpoints. He wanted American and Russian scholars to be free of the imposition of capitalist and communist ideology. To prevent such an occurrence, he asked Madame Kameneva to sign a formal agreement between Stanford University and the Society which permitted individual authors to work with autonomy within the organizational structure, reaching their own conclusions.[23]

For the next several months, Golder collected documents in Europe and then returned to the Stanford campus in April 1926. The time needed for organizing new archives, administrative duties, and soliciting documents for the Hoover Library, as well as teaching obligations, kept him tied to the university for a year. He planned, though, to embark on another trip to the USSR in 1927 to negotiate an agreement with the Society for Cultural Relations. In the meantime, Golder sent Litoshenko $700 to help defray traveling expenses during his trip to the United States. In May 1926, Litoshenko and his wife departed Moscow, and sixty days later they arrived at Stanford, no doubt a welcomed relief from such a long trip. Litoshenko's new environment did not disappoint him, with its rustic surroundings, resplendent Spanish architecture, and inquisitive faculty and student body. In collaboration with Hutchinson, the Soviet scholar labored over writing and careful research at the Hoover Library; he also lectured, held meetings with students and faculty, and took trips to the nearby pleasant coastal towns. Indirectly and directly, Golder always encouraged the policy of visiting scholars at Stanford, considering this university a stimulating environment for scholars of merit.[24]

After a year at Stanford, Litoshenko departed the campus in order to continue research on the agricultural manuscript in the Soviet Union. Golder now worked toward sealing an agreement with the Society for Cultural Relations, wishing the publication of the Litoshenko–Hutchinson manuscript to occur without any unnecessary complications. In early August, Golder submitted to Wilbur a working agreement that he would use for negotiations with the Society. Wilbur approved this agreement, although he suggested to Golder that he ought to send a copy to the State Department for its evaluation in light of the controversial nature of trying to establish cultural ties with a country suffering the opprobrium of United States nonrecognition. Golder mailed the document in abridged form to the State Department, and on 19 August he received a telegram from the Secretary of State, Frank Kellogg: "Cannot express approval of project described in your letter of August twelfth."[25] Golder wrote in dejection the following day to Goodrich, "I am very sorry. I do not see on what grounds it meets with the disapproval of the Department of State."[26] For Golder, cultural ties seemed quite innocuous. Suddenly, he faced a potential quagmire even before he had begun his trip.

Golder decided to try to resolve this objection by personally conferring with the State Department. In the summer of 1927, he and Hutchinson departed Stanford for the USSR and conveniently made a stopover at Washington. They arrived there in late August, and Golder spoke with William Castle, Chief of the Division of Western European Affairs in the State Department, regarding Kellogg's disapproval of negotiating a cultural agreement with the USSR. Castle relieved Golder of any fears surrounding Kellogg's opposition when he suggested to the historian that the State Department had no objection as long as an agency of the Soviet government, such as the Society for Cultural Relations, signed the agreement, rather than an official diplomatic representative. While the State Department certainly did not promote cultural contact with the USSR at an official level, it was permitting contact behind the veneer of opposition; increasingly, American students, professors, unofficial delegations, business, technical, and labor leaders, and the curious tourist were traveling to the USSR.[27]

After Golder and Hutchinson reached Moscow on 27 September, they tried to contact Madame Kameneva, but learned that she had departed Russia temporarily on a special assignment. Golder wrote, "She apparently attached enough importance to our coming to leave word to be kept informed by telegraph of all our plans and moves."[28] In her absence, Golder explained the purpose of his visit and gave a copy of the proposed agreement to the acting President of the Society for Cultural Relations. Golder, though, did not just merely wait for Madame Kameneva's return. He made inquiries elsewhere regarding the nature of the Society for Cultural Relations. He wrote after his investigations, "The Society for Cultural Relations is not a simple and as innocent an organization as might appear. Madame Kameneva is largely a figurehead,"[29] even though married to Lev Kamenev, the high-ranking Soviet political leader, as well as being Leon Trotsky's sister. As Golder discovered, the Society formed part of an intricate network of diplomatic and political organizations: Intourist, the Foreign Office, the Comintern (an international revolutionary bureau), the Central Statistical Board, the secret police, and military intelligence. The inter-relationships of the Soviet government, like any civilization, challenged Golder.

Golder's investigative trail led him to V. Ossinsky, the former Commissar of Agriculture, who presently headed the USSR Central Statistical Board. Since Ossinsky had considerable decision-making power in regards to the Society, Golder submitted a copy of the proposed agreement as well as the study by Litoshenko and Hutchinson to him for suggestions and criticism. After Ossinsky read the manuscript, Golder wrote:

> Ossinsky found much fault with the study. Some of his objections were on matters of fact but most of them were on matters of opinion. He was under the impression that our economists were more bent on uncovering Soviet shortcomings than on discovering the truth.[30]

Golder, quite naturally, defended the manuscript, since he feared the imposition of censorship. Ossinsky then communicated his views to other Soviets connected with Golder's negotiations. After Golder met with a number of Soviet negotiators, he believed that the question of objectionable manuscripts would be a touchy one, since they had insisted on having control of Litoshenko's manuscripts before publication. It was at this conference that Golder, too, became aware of the influence of Soviet politics on Russia's cultural life after 1925.[31]

Indeed, political reality in Moscow had become stormy over an economic crisis. After 1925, a series of bad harvests and lack of foreign credits had brought a decline in the USSR's economy, deepening the so–called scissors crisis, in spite of increased trade between the United States and the USSR. Industrial production, just beginning to stir in 1925, could not as yet meet the growing need of farmers' requirements for equipment and material goods. What equipment that did exist cost an exorbitant rate. Industrial problems threatened to break the link between town and country, with the peasant refusing to sell food and industry falling into stagnation. In September 1927, the Soviets intensely sought a solution to this crisis. Joseph Stalin, a Politburo member, advocated further concessions to capitalism under NEP, while Leon Trotsky, also a Politburo member, viewed the continuation of small trade and the growth of the kulaks, capitalistic farmers, as they gained control over labor and rural Soviets, a political and economic threat; he favored the advancement of socialism through state controlled industrialization and collectivization of farmland. As the struggle between the two factions increased, a Communist party member like Ossinsky feared the political consequences of being associated with approving a controversial book such as the agricultural study. It could be called into question by either the supporters of NEP or the supporters of the socialist dream. One might find his whole political career in jeopardy.[32] In this ambiguous and uncertain world, the Soviet negotiations therefore needed guarantees of control over manuscripts in order to give themselves a measure of security.

When Golder participated in further negotiations, he often came across the Soviet fear of the political consequences of uncontrolled publications. At the same time, the Soviets generally indicated that they wished contact with such an organization as the Russian Institute. Despite official hostility toward the USSR from the State Department, the Soviets favorably noticed that Hoover's Commerce Department under the Coolidge administration had expanded trade with the USSR in 1925. The Soviet government, desirous of broader trade relations to pump desperately needed capital into industrial and agricultural development, continued to endorse contact with the United States. Cultural contact with the United States therefore appealed to Soviet negotiators. In his case, Golder wondered which force, reconciliation or fear, NEP or class war, would win out.[33]

Then, in the middle of October, Golder and Hutchinson conferred with the acting President of the Society for Cultural Relations, who assured them that an agreement satisfactory to Golder would be concluded as soon as Madame Kameneva returned to Moscow on 25 October. This meeting encouraged Golder to be hopeful of such an outcome. While negotiations were at a standstill, Hutchinson had to leave Moscow because of commitments he had to fulfill in western Europe. Golder would have to face the Soviet negotiators alone. He accompanied Hutchinson as far as Finland, and, on his way back to Moscow, Golder stopped at Leningrad for a few days to complete matters involving the Hoover Library. When he arrived at Moscow on 25 October, Madame Kameneva had not yet returned to the city. Three days later, she arrived and on 29 October, Golder met with her. He wrote, "I quickly discovered that during the fortnight that had passed fear had [gotten] the upperhand. Madame Kameneva gave little hope that an agreement such as we desired could be made." [34]

Considering his previous negotiations with the Soviets, Golder decided to draw up a new document, one which embodied his main point of no censorship and which removed all Soviet responsibility for published statements. But perhaps all this was wishful thinking on Golder's part. He then met with F. Rothstein, a Foreign Office official; without at first being aware of the new document, he, too, complained about the problem of responsibility and repeated Soviet eagerness for contact with the United States. At this point, Golder read the new document and Rothstein said, "Fine, such an understanding Madame Kameneva will accept." [35] Golder wrote:

> I was quite pleased with myself. I seemed to have gained everything and lost nothing. For us the quest of an organization was merely a means to an end and if we could gain the end without a cumbersome organization so much the better. [36]

As Golder found out, he rejoiced too soon. He presented the new document to Madame Kameneva on 2 November, and she asked for a day to have the document translated and to prepare a reply. When Golder met with her the following day, Madame Kameneva proved to be in an ugly mood. Instead of giving Golder a definite reply, she scolded him: what right had he to ask guarantees for the Russian professors? "Are they not dearer to me than to you? Haven't I always protected them? This is not famine time when Americans could dictate terms to us." [37] She raved for a while longer and then, as Golder noted, she helplessly concluded that she would sign any document that her superiors asked her to sign.

Madame Kameneva had clearly made it a point to defend Soviet cultural policy–making against what she considered American cultural intervention. But Golder had no intention of trying to impose a capitalist ideological bias on the Russian Institute's historians. Golder then explored possible motives behind Kameneva's obstinacy and evasiveness. He wrote:

> At this time Madame Kameneva was in deep trouble. Her husband (Kamenev) and brother (Trotsky), leader of the opposition, were under fire and she herself under a cloud. Our affair worried her. If she broke with us, she would be severely blamed. If she gave in and something unfavorable to the Soviets were published, she would be held responsible.[38]

After his meeting with Madame Kameneva, Golder came to the realization that his negotiations edged closer to failure. And yet, he still thought he might be able to provoke the Soviets into signing an agreement. On 3 November, he advertised that he planned to depart the USSR on 7 November, the anniversary of the Bolshevik Revolution. He based his hoped-for Soviet volte-face on the assumption that the news of his near departure, signaling the end of negotiations, might bring forth enough pressure on Soviet negotiators to sign an agreement. Golder wrote:

> By this time [my] negotiations had aroused considerable interest. The Moscow papers had made the most of it, had painted in flowing colors the possibility of . . . a Russo–American organization. From different parts of the Empire came offers of service and collections. The one international act that Russians of all classes desire is a re-establishment of friendly relations with America. The work of the ARA, our prosperity, our efficiency, our part in world affairs have impressed themselves on the minds of the Russians. To be the friend of America, to be like an American is an ideal of most Russians, even Communists. The news that a Russo–American Institute was about to be formed filled them with joy and the rumor that negotiations had failed cast them into gloom. Such important Communists as Sokolnikov and Nevski, who saw eye to eye with me, pleaded with those in authority to yield, but to no avail.[39]

On the afternoon of 4 November, a non-communist professor, who had been one of Lenin's boyhood friends, visited Golder. The professor said that he had recently stressed to Georgi Chicherin, the Commissar of Foreign Affairs, that letting such a rare opportunity of establishing cultural ties with Stanford University pass by appeared to him as a great loss. An hour after this Russian's departure, Golder received a phone call from the Foreign Office to meet with Chicherin at five o'clock that day.

At five, Golder visited the astute diplomat noted for being above Communisty party intrigue. Chicherin, smitten by Russia's diplomatic isolation after France and Great Britain had severed diplomatic relations with the USSR in 1927 as a result of an International Red Scare, let Golder know that he thought highly of establishing a joint organization. Even though Chicherin seemed excited by the idea, Golder said that he had heard such enthusiasm previously but that nothing had happened to formalize an agreement. He said, "I am tired of hanging around and am going home." Chicherin responded, "Remain a few days longer and we will get the matter straightened out." Golder balked at this plea, convinced that Soviet hesitation seemed inalterable. Chicherin reacted with desperation, "But this is important, and I am deeply interested." Golder said impertinehtly, "I wish your associates would see it in that light." Chicherin said, "They do see it, but they are afraid of your university publications,"[40] and politely asked Golder to bear with the annoying negotiating process a few days longer than his scheduled departure on 7 November.

The following day, Rothstein informed Golder through a messenger that he should not lose patience and be assured that an agreement would be worked out. Golder thought Chicherin had acted on his behalf, and the news brought him cheer. But that evening, Golder ran into Maxim Litvinov at an opera, and Litvinov, in conflict with Chicherin as one of Stalin's allies and destined to replace Chicherin in 1930 as Commissar of Foreign Affairs, informed Golder that he viewed the negotiation's outcome with pessimism. The rapidly changing viewpoints made Golder dizzy.[41]

The next day, a phone call from the Foreign Office roused Golder from his sleep at three in the morning. Chicherin, an unconventional diplomat, had the habit of conducting foreign office business throughout the night rather than during normal working hours. His secretary instructed Golder to be at the Foreign Office at two o'clock that afternoon. Golder hoped that at long last an agreement could be worked out, although, in reality, he had little to be optimistic about considering the confusing political atmosphere in Moscow.[42]

At two o'clock, Golder met with Rothstein and Ossinsky at the Foreign Office. Golder used his original agreement (without the responsibility clause) as the basis for negotiations, since Chicherin seemed so determined to have a joint organization. During the negotiations, Golder relinquished the minor points in order to fight for the major ones, especially the question of censorship, while trying to be as respectful as possible. He wrote:

I tried in every way to bring about an agreement of good

will, realizing that it was worth more in the long run than fine words. Without good will an agreement with the Soviets is no better than a scrap of paper.[43]

After three hours of a give–and–take session with the Soviets, Golder thought he had made progress as he professed friendship on the one hand and sternness on the other. The negotiators, though, did not settle on a definite agreement and set a date for another meeting.

When this first meeting broke up, Golder returned to his hotel room. There he developed his strategy for the upcoming meeting. He took the original agreement and rewrote paragraph five regarding the question of censorship so that this question would be open to suggestions. He also wrote down a list of suggestions which had come under consideration at the previous meeting for discussion during the next meeting. Golder purposely left the censorship question open in the original agreement because he wished to incorporate paragraph seven of the meeting's suggestions into the original agreement. The Soviets, too, could offer a countersolution or leave the question unsettled, but Golder was counting on his solution prevailing. Paragraph seven read:

> [Golder] suggested that each manuscript prepared in America should be sent to Russia for corrections and suggestions. These corrections and suggestions would reduce to a minimum the points of difference. If after that there should still remain differences in point of view then the Russians should write out their differences in the form of a review not to exceed in length one tenth of the manuscript and that this review should be published with the manuscript.[44]

With this suggestion firmly in Golder's mind, he met with Rothstein on 9 November.

Rothstein accepted the agreement with the open–ended paragraph regarding censorship, while offering no solution to clarify the ambiguity. When Golder offered his suggestion to be used to solve the censorship question, Rothstein said that he accepted the proposal in theory, but he preferred to leave the censorship question unsettled on the assumption that the publication of manuscripts would occur without disagreements. Golder wrote, "This view I could not accept, for I was certain that there would be disagreements and unless a method of dealing with them were provided beforehand, there would be endless disputes and hard feelings with each manuscript."[45] After Golder let this view be known, Rothstein asked for time to consider the matter with Ossinsky. Golder, however, had made up his mind to leave Moscow that evening, and Rothstein, fearful of a complete break of the negotiating process, stated that he would notify Golder in Leningrad of what decision the Soviets had come to.

When Golder returned to his hotel, he received a message from Madame Kameneva which requested that he see her. When he did so, she apologized for the delay involving the negotiations, complaining that he drove a hard bargain; she pledged her support and again promised to sign whatever document her superiors asked her to sign. This repetitious performance did not impress Golder, and he made no effort to be conciliatory.

That night, Golder took the train to Leningrad. After arriving there, he planned to stay three days to find out if by a miraculous chance the Soviet negotiators would come around to his point of view. Late on the afternoon of the second day, 11 November, a Mr. Salzkind, Commissar of the Leningrad Branch of the Foreign Office, summoned Golder. Salzkind read a telegram, written by Madame Kamenva and sent by Rothstein, which declined Golder's method for handling controversies and proposed leaving the censorship question open. Predictably, Golder found the officer unacceptable, and Salzkind telephoned Golder's response to Moscow authorities.[46]

The Soviet rejection of Golder's conception of a Russian Institute, of course, disappointed him. At the same time, he thought that extraordinary forces had plagued his negotiating experience in the Soviet Union. In November 1927, Stalin actively pursued the policy of bringing charges against the Workers' Opposition, which led to expulsions from the party, and to the arrest, internment, and exile of Opposition members. Trotsky, Kamenev, and Zinoviev, leaders of the Workers' Opposition in 1927, were all discredited by Stalin's campaign. The War Scare of 1927, which involved Soviet fears of foreign intervention, the controversy over Stalin's advocacy of Soviet self–sufficiency in a hostile world, which the Opposition rejected as incompatible with world revolution, and Trotsky's futile attempt to being about an insurrection against the party's right wing, enabled Stalin's faction to render the Opposition leaders powerless. As Stalin's faction spread fears over party loyalty and beliefs, Golder noted the resulting confusion and insecurity among the party's rank–and–file, a confusion which had contributed to so much hestitation by the Soviet negotiators. He wrote:

> It was . . . interesting to note how responsibility was passed from one person to another and in the end no one would assume it. The internal fight in the Party has reached the stage where its members are not quite certain where they stand and what to do. What is good Communist theory today may be unpardonable heresy tomorrow.[47]

After Golder returned to Stanford University in early December 1927, he felt compelled by the USSR's political climate to reappraise his views on manuscript policy. Hutchinson, on the other hand, had a different view. Golder wrote: "Professor Hutchinson is of the opinion that there is little use of trying to have anything to do with the Bolsheviks and that so far as he is concerned he is through with them."[48] Hutchinson resigned from further relationship with the Russian Institute. But Golder would not let go; he had an obsession with scholarship and communication between the Soviet Union and the United States, and wanted to expedite his plan in some form. He therefore decided to relinquish his fight for rules governing manuscript censorship, and on 5 January he cabled the Society for Cultural Relations that he accepted Rothstein's version of leaving manuscript policy an open question, as embodied in Golder's revised agreement of 9 November, which Rothstein had agreed would be acceptable.

Four days later, Golder mailed the agreement to be signed by Madame Kameneva and informed her of certain requests. In the first place, he urged the completion of Litoshenko's manuscript in accordance with Ossinsky's objections and proposed that Litoshenko prepare at Stanford University a study of Soviet commerce from 1917 to 1927. Golder further suggested the undertaking of projects in fields of Soviet economic experimentation: public finance, currency policy, control of foreign and domestic trade, and industrial policy. In this direction, he requested that G. Sokolníkov, the former Commissar of Finance, be asked to compete a study of Soviet public finance. Golder also wished to set in motion a series of studies regarding Soviet society, and requested that Professor S. A. Zilov be asked to complete a study about the status of women and children in Soviet Russia and that Zilov be given permission to begin this study at Stanford University. Golder tried to be positive in his outlook concerning the successful completion of these studies, but he believed that his success depended on at least tenuous Soviet cooperation.[49]

In early 1928, Wilbur again supported Litoshenko's nomination as a lecturer for Stanford's history department during 1928–29. Then in late January, Golder received a cable from Madame Kameneva which stated that the Society for Cultural Relations accepted the binding agreement he had referred to in his cable. After finally accomplishing a formalization of cultural relations, Golder placed considerable value on Litoshenko's trip to the United States, since this trip would indicate to a certain extent Soviet cooperation; the agreement, soon to be signed by Stanford University and the Society, had a clause providing for unrestricted travel. In a letter dated 27 January, Golder informed Litoshenko that, instead of coming to Stanford in the fall as originally planned, he should begin work there late that summer.[50]

While involved with numerous activities, Golder, during February, waited for a letter from Litoshenko indicating when he would be departing the Soviet Union. In the meantime, he received a formal letter from Madame Kameneva which stressed the Society's full cooperation. She further stated that Ossinsky, along with Litoshenko, would revise the agricultural manuscript before Litoshenko departed for the United States. About the same time, in April, he received a note from Sokolnikov which stated that he would complete a public finance study.[51] Zilov, in a letter, committed himself, too. Finally, in late April, Golder learned that Litoshenko had been given permission to travel abroad. All this news excited Golder.

Then, in May, Golder received a telegram mentioning that Zilov might not be able to leave the USSR for a research trip to Stanford. A formal letter followed the telegram:

> On the question of the position of women and children in the Soviet Union there arose doubts as to the competence of Professor Zilov to give an all–sided picture of this important question. . . . Therefore, we thought that . . . it would be far more practical and profitable to select, for this mission, a scientist, who, of course, can be found here, and can present this question in its final and most complete light.[52]

Of course, Golder viewed Zilov's disqualification as a threat to the Russian Institute rather than as a preferable change.

Golder's assessment had important implications not only in regards to the Russian Institute but also for the Soviet Union. Zilov had fallen into a storm of wide–ranging changes in the USSR. Stalin, having defeated the Opposition, did not wish to share power with the party's right wing in the Politburo. Perhaps in reaction to the War Scare and the worsening economic crisis, and, to separate himself from the right wing as a leader in his own right, Stalin repudiated NEP and proposed the First Five–Year Plan that encompassed rapid industrialization and collectivization. The signals for this transformation of the USSR also ignited a cultural revolution, beginning in 1928, which encouraged proletarian hegemony in culture, education, and the managerial–professional strata, opening up unparalleled opportunities for hundreds of thousands of workers and communists of working–class origin.[53] Stalin associated himself with this cultural revolution, since it served the Soviet regime's requirements for extensive education, especially in technical skills, in order to bring coherence to economic reconstruction. This cultural revolution, which demanded ideological purity, posed a direct confrontation to Golder's collaborative view of a Russian Institute, a view which evoked the NEP world of the old intelligentsia.[54]

Golder, aware of the undercurrent of class war in the USSR, did not at this time take any action regarding Zilov's disqualification with Soviet authorities. For the next six weeks, he busied himself in researching and writing a scholarly paper, which he would deliver in Hawaii as part of a commemoration for the 150th anniversary of Captain Cook's discovery of Hawaii. In early August, Golder sailed to Hawaii in anticipation of an exciting vacation. After arriving there, he thoroughly enjoyed this adventure as he traveled to the different islands, ate exotic foods, met old and new friends, and indulged in lively conversation. On 17 August, he delivered his paper, entitled, "Proposals for Russian Occupation of the Hawaiian Islands," a nineteenth century topic which was well received with applause.[55]

When the commemoration came to an end, Golder decided to extend his stay in Hawaii. He accepted a wedding invitation from Dr. Thomas Bailey, who, as a student at Stanford University, had been a reader for Golder's Russian history course and had assisted him with editing a book concerning the Mormons;[56] in 1928, Bailey taught American history at the University of Hawaii. On 28 August, Golder attended Bailey's wedding. After the ceremony, Golder mirthfully said to Bailey in the wedding line, "We brought you along this far; now we leave you to the machinations of your wife."[57]

Golder returned to Stanford in early September, wondering if Litoshenko would be there. But the Russian had not arrived. In response, Golder now acted on Zilov's disqualification and Litoshenko's failure to arrive, mailing an urgent letter to Boris Skvirsky, who was a Soviet diplomatic agent in Washington, D. C., although non-accredited by the State Department. Golder asked him to wire Rothstein, explaining the detrimental effect refusing Litoshenko travel permission would have on the Russian Institute. Golder also stated to Skvirsky that he planned a trip to the USSR in the spring of 1929 so that he could speak with Madame Kameneva regarding the lack of cooperation. In the meantime, Golder depended on his intermediary, Skvirsky, to elicit a change of policy from the Society for Cultural Relations.[58]

While Golder waited for developments, he prepared a course on eastern Europe. Typically, he put a high premium on staying busy. And yet, on this occasion, he slowed down somewhat, since a severe cold, which he thought he had caught during his return voyage from Hawaii, harassed him. For over a year, Golder had been concerned about his health, thinking that, at the age of 51, he had the superb

Frank Golder with Friends at Stanford University, 1928

advantage of experience, knowledge, and documents to write several compelling books on Russian/Soviet history. Golder's cold, intensified instead of subsiding as the days passed by, causing him to worry. One day, as he was walking down a hallway, Golder spotted a student of his, Edward White; Golder walked over to him and said, "Mr. White, I think you are working too hard. Take care of your health,"[59] a pronouncement which thoroughly puzzled White.

Soon, Golder's cold sapped his strength so much that he decided on 18 September to remain in bed at his campus apartment until he felt well enough for resuming work. But Golder's cold failed to abate. Finally, he was examined by a doctor at a hospital at Palo Alto, who discovered that Golder had lung cancer. After this diagnosis, doctors placed him in the hospital for observation and concealed from him the seriousness of his condition.[60]

Golder's pain from his illness intensified during October after his hospitalization. But, in spite of pain, isolation, and apprehension, Golder tried to proceed with the Russian Institute. Skvirsky had acted on Golder's request to prod Rothstein concerning Litoshenko's trip, but to no avail. Golder learned through Skvirsky that Soviet officials had explained the delay of Litoshenko's trip because Ossinsky had not been available to participate in correcting Litoshenko's manuscript. From his sickbed, Golder continued to correspond with Skvirsky as he clung to the belief, however elusive, that perhaps the unofficial Soviet representative could somehow smooth out the controversy. This controversy remained unsettled in Golder's mind until 15 November when he found out that Soviet officials had actually denied Litoshenko travel status. Litoshenko's forthcoming contact with Western influence could not go unnoticed in the increasingly popular public campaign against non–Marxist historians and non–Marxist historiography, and as Marxist scholars stressed the theme of class conflict and class war during the cultural revolution.[61]

A few days after receiving the disappointing news regarding Litoshenko's trip, Golder dictated a letter for Madame Kameneva on 22 November:

> This decision [to prevent Litoshenko's trip] is contrary to earlier assurances and inconsistent with the policy of cooperation which had been assured. It indicates on the part of the Russian authorities a lack of interest in or even hostility to the project of the Russian–American Institute; and that this attitude if maintained will make it impossible ro retain the support of the institutions on which the whole project depends. If we cannot invite a Russian scholar to this country of whom we have confidence and who could cooperate

with us, then there is no use whatever to form an institute.[62]

Following this letter, Golder dictated a brief note on 28 November for Litoshenko: "I am heartbroken over the fact that you have not been granted permission to leave the country." Golder added, "I am very sorry to tell you that I have been quite ill ever since the first of September and I have been in bed most of the time. That explains the lack of vigor in pushing the matter."[63] This letter was one of the last Golder would compose.

In a few days, Golder's pain had become so intense that doctors drugged him with opiates, and they predicted that he would succumb to his illness in a few weeks. When Golder could speak coherently, many friends visited him for brief periods. Lutz, his closest friend, cut short a collecting trip in Europe to be with him. Golder's brother, Congressman Benjamin Golder of Philadelphia, and his sister, Sara, from New York, stayed near him. Herbert Hoover, the President-elect, stopped in Palo Alto before beginning his good-will tour of Latin America and visited the stricken historian. Such kind visits encouraged Golder to struggle bravely against his illness that had come without explanation or comprehension.[64] At the beginning of January 1929, Golder's condition became critical and he died Monday morning on 7 January.

When Golder died, the Hoover lost not only a major scholar in the field of Russian history, but also a warm, considerate, and unassuming man. His colleagues had respected him for his compassion, trust, and keen intellect. He was not an authoritarian personality, but, if the occasion demanded him to be so, he could be outspoken. His modesty had evolved from his experience in Alaska; the hardships he had endured had been humbling; he had developed respect for nature and an appreciation for the sanctity of human values and cultures; this appreciation had sparked his interest in history. Alaska had also influenced him to be adventuresome; he had an insatiable appetite for adventure, for discovery of the unknown and for accepting challenges. It was his gusto for life, people, and history which had brought him into contact with one of the major events of the twentieth century: the Russian Revolution. He had been a man of the world, not a brilliant academician; he had not bedazzled his audience with oratory nor had he created new ideas, but he did create historical archives which would touch the lives of many.

After Golder's death, someone had to fill his place at the Hoover War Library. Harold Fisher, Golder's associate in the ARA and history colleague at Stanford, took over the Hoover's Russian section and the Russian Institute. In January, Fisher set to work trying to accomplish Golder's goals for the Russian Institute. He wrote

Madame Kameneva expressing Golder's discouragement over the Institute's future. Fisher, prior to this letter, had learned that Ossinsky had submitted his criticisms regarding the agricultural manuscript to Litoshenko, and now he asked that Litoshenko be granted a passport. Fisher also stressed the importance of a consultation between Litoshenko and Hutchinson to put the final touches on the text before publication, warning her that the Rockefeller Memorial might cease supporting the Russian Institute if no progress could be shown for the previous year. Fisher further tried to goad Chicherin into action with a letter dated 4 February 1929.

Fisher failed to receive any response from either Madame Kameneva or Chicherin; Chicherin was in ill health and being eclipsed by Litvinov in the Foreign Office. And in 1929, the cultural revolution had brought about a thorough Marxist hegemony in scholarship. As a result of the silence, Fisher traveled to the Soviet Union in the summer of 1929. Although he tried to persuade members of the Society for Cultural Relations on the necessity of cooperation, his trip proved to be a failure. Then, in December 1929, Fisher learned that the Soviets had terminated the agreement with Stanford University concerning the Russian Institute. After this severance, Fisher sought out different ways of using the Rockefeller funds, buying books, documents, memoirs, personal collections, periodicals, newspapers, and other source materials in Europe and the USSR which dealt with Soviet history. The Russian Institute also translated a number of works from Russian into English regarding Russian/Soviet history. Fisher was able to continue the Russian Institute's work until 1940, when the Rockefeller Memorial ceased supporting the Institute.[65]

While Fisher had been moderately successful in maintaining the Russian Institute, Golder had provided the groundwork for the attempt to broaden awareness of Soviet Russia. Golder's experience in Russia in 1914 and 1917 had made him aware of the world in transition. 1914 was a turning point in history. He had observed Russia in peace, war, and revolution: a world of tradition in 1914, a world undermining those traditions to win an all–consuming war, and a world responding to the European chaos through revolution, which had led to the first socialist state in Western Europe. His experience with the Inquiry had also deepened his interest in the wider world and his understanding of the lack of intellectual, educational, and archival resources in the United States for scholars, diplomats, and politicians to deal with the complexities of the post–war world. It was Hoover, through his money, prestige, and power—via Adams— who had opened new doors for Golder. By way of his connection with them, he had become a collector of documents, a member of the ARA, and a participant in Soviet–American relations, which had enabled him to play a part in history as participant and bibliophile. He had collected millions of documents which contributed to a comprehensive view of late Tsarist Russia, western, central and eastern Europe in World War I, the Provisional Government in Russia, the Bolshevik Revolution, the Soviet Civil War, the Soviet famine, and the reconstruction of Soviet society. He had helped Archibald Cary Coolidge to achieve his goal of spreading education and knowledge beyond the dominion of Harvard University, in this case, all the way to the west coast, where Golder had taught classes on Russian history, developed fabulous archives on eastern Europe, and established the first institute for studying Soviet Russia in the United States. Golder had also wished that there would be diplomatic, economic, and cultural harmony between the United States and Soviet Russia instead of prevailing hostilities perpetuated through the traditional policies of propaganda, warfare, and economic boycotts. Living in a world of radical change, intense emotions, and pervasive ignorance, Golder had sought to bring forth understanding, even if, at times, he had been overwhelmed by inexplicable forces and events himself.

Notes to Chapter I

1 Harold H. Fisher, "Frank A. Golder, 1877–1929," *The Journal of Modern History* 14 (June 1929): 243. Cited hereafter as Fisher, "Golder." Edward Channing to Harold H. Fisher, 8 May 1929, p. 1, personal files of A. G. Wachhold, Santa Barbara, California. Mrs. Samuel Golder to A. G. Wachhold, n.d., p. 1, *Ibid.* Mrs. Charles Solomon to A. G. Wachhold, 20 July 1976, p. 1, *Ibid.* Richard Minch to Stanford University, 12 February 1929, p. 1, Golder Correspondence, Internal Records, Box 94, Hoover Institution, Stanford, California. Cited hereafter as HIR.

2 Richard Minch to Stanford University, 12 February 1929, p. 1, Golder Correspondence, HIR. Mrs. Charles Solomon to A. G. Wachhold, 20 July 1976, p. 1. Joseph Brandes, *Immigrants to Freedom: Jewish Communities in Rural New Jersey Since 1882* (Philadelphia: The Jewish Publication Society of America, 1971), p. 274. Cited hereafter as Brandes, *Immigrants.*

3 Harold Fisher, rough draft of biographical sketch of Golder, p. 2, Personal Files of A. G. Wachhold. Harold Fisher to Benjamin Golder, 24 February 1930, p. 1, Golder Correspondence, HIR, Box 94. *Georgetown College Catalogue, 1895–1896*, p. 6, Georgetown College Library, Georgetown, Kentucky. Brandes, *Immigrants*, p. 274.

4 R. G. Rudenburg to Harold Fisher, 21 October 1930, p. 1, Golder Correspondence, HIR, Box 94. Golder, Reminiscence on Alaska, p. 1, Golder Papers, Box 19, Hoover Institution, Stanford, California. Cited hereafter as GP.

5 Golder, Reminiscence on Alaska, p. 1, GP, Box 19. Golder, Reminiscence on Pete Nelson, p. 1, Golder Correspondence, HIR, Box 94.

6 Ted Hinckley, *The Americanization of Alaska, 1867–1897* (Palo Alto: Pacific Books, 1972), pp. 96–97, 99, 121, 157, 159, 198–199. Charles P. Poole, "Two Centuries of Education in Alaska," (Ph. D. dissertation, University of Washington, 1947), p. 29. Robert Laird Stewart, *Sheldon Jackson: Pathfinder and Prospector of the Missionary Vanguard on the Rocky Mountains and Alaska* (New York: Fleming H. Revell, 1908). Ted Hinckley, "The Alaska

Labors of Sheldon Jackson, 1877–1890," (Ph. D. dissertation, University of Indiana, 1961), pp. 114–115.

[7] Hamilton to Golder, 1 August 1899, p. 1, National Archives, Washington, D.C., Record Group 75. Cited hereafter as RG 75.

[8] Glen Smith, "Education for the Natives of Alaska: The Work of the United States Bureau of Education, 1884–1931," *Journal of the West* 6 (July 1967): 443.

[9] Golder, Reminiscence on Pete Nelson, pp. 2–3, Golder Correspondence, HIR, Box 94. Golder later developed an appreciation for Nelson after the two men became friends. Golder wrote, "Pete was the only other person at [Unga Village] with an interest in cultural matters. He seemed to know Shakespeare from cover to cover, for he was always illustrating the points in his discussion by quotations from this author. Pete took a kindly interest in me partly because my naivety amused him, partly because I reminded him of his own youth, and partly because he realized that I needed him. I realized [after I left Alaska], more than I did then, how much he did for me. He was lonely and came to see me often. He talked most interestingly and I learned a great deal of life from him." See, *Ibid.*, p. 6.

[10] *Ibid.*, p. 4.

[11] *Ibid.*, p. 5.

[12] *Ibid.*

[13] U. S. Office of Education, *Report of the Commissioner of Education, the Year 1900–1901* (Washington, D.C.: Government Printing Office, 1902), p. 1465. *Ibid., 1899–1900*, p. 1741.

[14] Charles Huse, Golder's friend at Harvard University when they were students together, wrote, "Golder . . . was called upon to help the natives in all sorts of problems. For example, when they fell sick, they would send for him to prescribe for them. He ascribed his success as a doctor to the fact that their trouble arose from over–eating in most cases and could be relieved by the simple remedies he knew. His success in curing the daughter of a chief brought him no little renown." See, Huse to Harold Fisher, 3 August 1929, p. 1, Golder Correspondence, HIR, Box 94.

[15] Golder, Reminiscence on Alaska, p. 2, GP, Box 19.

[16] *Ibid.*

[17] Golder, Reminiscence on Pete Nelson, p. 6, Golder Correspondence, HIR, Box 94. Golder, Alaska Diary, 14, 24 November 1899, GP, Box 19.

[18] After one dinner with friends, Golder wrote in his diary, "Took with Sinnott dinner with Judge Isham. Had year old beef steak.

Smelled very strong, but said I enjoyed it." See, Golder, Alaska Diary, 27 December 1899, GP, Box 19.

[19] Golder, Alaska Diary, 1 January 1900, *ibid.* Golder became so depressed and resigned to his fate that he recorded in his diary, "Lonely in soul. No one that knows my feeling. I wonder if it wouldn't be best after all to spend the remainder of my life here."

[20] Golder, Alaska Diary, 29 April 1900, *ibid.*

[21] Golder, Alaska Diary, 2 September 1900, *ibid.*

[22] Golder, Alaska Diary, 22 September 1900, *ibid.*

[23] Golder, Alaska Diary, 1 October 1900, *ibid.*

[24] Golder, Reminiscence on Alaska, p. 4, GP, Box 19. Golder to Hamilton, 15 June 1901, p. 1, RG 75.

[25] Golder, Reminiscence on Alaska, p. 4, GP, Box 19.

[26] Golder, "Tom Williams: Fortune Hunter," *Boston University Beacon*, n.d., p. 14, Golder Correspondence, HIR, Box 94. Robert Louis Stevenson, *The Merry Men and Other Tales and Fables* (London: Chatto, 1877), pp. 2–29.

[27] Golder, Reminiscence on Alaska, p. 6, GP, Box 19.

[28] *Ibid.*

[29] *Ibid.*

[30] *Ibid.*, p. 7.

[31] Golder to Hamilton, 15 June 1901, pp. 1–2, RG 75. Hamilton to Golder, 13 July 1901, p. 1, RG 75.

[32] Golder to John Brady, 18 October 1901, Frame 862, Roll 9, *Alaska Territorial Papers* (Washington, D.C.: National Archives Microfilm Publications, 1963). Cited hereafter as ATP.

[33] M. C. Brown to John Brady, 25 November 1901, *ibid.* Golder, Reminiscence on Alaska, p. 10, GP, Box 19.

[34] Golder, Reminiscence on Alaska, p. 13, GP, Box 19.

[35] *Ibid,* p. 14.

[36] *Ibid.*, p. 8.

[37] *Ibid.*

[38] Marie Jenson to Golder, 1902, p. 1, Golder Correspondence, HIR, Box 94.

[39] Golder, Reminiscence on Alaska, p. 9, GP, Box 19.

[40] *Ibid.*, p. 10.

[41] *Ibid.*

[42] *Ibid.*, p. 11.

[43] *Ibid.*, p. 12.

[44] *Ibid.*, p. 13.

[45] *Ibid.*

[46] *Ibid.*, p. 14.

[47] *Ibid.*, p. 15. After Golder returned to the United States, he wrote to President Theodore Roosevelt about the crude American interference with native Alaskans: "If they are not to be permitted to live in peace, they ought at least be allowed to die in peace." See, Golder to Roosevelt, 29 March 1903, Frame 734, Roll 7, ATP. Golder to Secretary of Interior, 25 March 1903, Frame 734, *ibid.* Golder, "A Plea for the Indians of Alaska," in *Red Man and Helper*, cc. 1903, Scrapbook, Sheldon Jackson Collection, Vol. 32, p.82, Presbyterian Historical Society, Princeton Theological Seminary, Princeton, New Jersey.

Notes to Chapter II

[1] Charles Huse to Harold Fisher, 3 August 1929, p. 2, GP, Box 19. Lincoln Hutchinson, "Frank A. Golder," *ARA Association Review* 4 (February 1929): 42.

[2] Charles Huse to Harold Fisher, 3 August 1929, p. 1, GP, Box 19. Edward Channing to Harold Fisher, 8 May 1929, p. 1, *ibid.* Later in life, Golder wrote several articles regarding Alaska and was considered a leading historian of Alaska. See, Golder, "A Survey of Alaska, 1743–1799," *Washington Historical Quarterly* 4 (April 1913): 83–93. "Mining in Alaska before 1867," *Washington Historical Review* 7 (July 1916): 233–238. His most influential article on Alaska is, "The Purchase of Alaska," *American Historical Review* 25 (April 1920): 411–425.

[3] Jackson to Golder, 25 February 1903, p. 1, RG 75.

[4] Fisher, "Frank Golder," p. 254. Robert F. Byrnes, *Awakening American Education to the World: The Role of Archibald Cary Coolidge, 1866–1928* (Notre Dame: University of Notre Dame Press, 1982), pp. 49, 68. Cited hereafter as Byrnes, *Coolidge.* Byrnes writes, "[Coolidge] trained able men who succeeded him at Harvard and many who introduced the study of Russia . . . into colleges and universities throughout the United States. The standards he set helped give Russian studies a stamp of quality and distinction at their formative stage." See, *ibid.*, p. 49.

[5] Golder, Résumé, Washington State University Archives, Pullman, Washington. Cited hereafter as WSUA.

[6] Golder, *Paris*, n.d., Scrapbook, Golder Correspondence, HIR, Box 94. Golder, *Russian Expansion on the Pacific, 1641–1850*, (Cleveland: Arthur Clark, 1914), p. 337.

[7] Golder, *Paris*, n.d., Scrapbook, Golder Correspondence, HIR, Box 94.

[8] *Ibid.*

[9] *Ibid.*

10 Golder, Notebook, GP, Box 10. Edward Channing to Harold Fisher, 8 May 1929, p. 1, GP, Box 19.

11 "Mr. Golder's Resignation," *Tempe Normal Student,* 18 October 1907, Vol. III, p. 1. Minutes, Board of Education, Tempe Normal School of Arizona, Arizona State University Archives, Tempe, Arizona. Cites hereafter as ASUA.

12 For Golder's Alaskan folklore tales see, Golder, "A Kodiak Island Story: The White–Faced Bear," *Journal of American Folklore* 20 (October–December 1907): 336–339. "Aleutian Stories," *Journal of American Folklore,* 20 (July–September 1905): 215–222. "Eskimo and Aleut Stories from Alaska," *Journal of American Folklore* 22 (January–March 1909): 10–24. "Primitive Warfare Among the Natives of Western Alaska," *Journal of American Folklore* 22 (July–September 1909): 336–339. "Tales from Kodiak Island I," *Journal of American Folklore* 16 (April–June 1903): 16–31. "Tales from Kodiak Island II," *Journal of American Folklore* 16 (April–June 1903): 81–103. "The Songs and Stories of the Aleuts, with Translations from Veniaminov," *Journal of American Folklore* 20 (April–June 1907): 132–142. "Tlingit Myths," *Journal of American Folklore* 20 (October–December 1907): 290–295.

13 Students to the Board of Trustees, 31 January 1907, pp. 1–2, ASUA.

14 "Mr. Golder's Resignation," *Tempe Normal Student,* 18 October 1907, Vol. III, p. 1.

15 Edward Channing to Harold Fisher, 8 May 1929, p. 1, GP, Box 10. Fisher, "Frank Golder," p. 254. Golder, Russian Voyages in the North Pacific Ocean to Determine the Relation between Asia and America, (Ph. D. dissertation, Harvard University, 1909), p. 3, University Archives, Harvard University.

16 Golder, Résumé, WSUA. Golder, Notebook, GP, Box 10. Edward Channing to Harold Fisher, 8 May 1929, p. 1, GP, Box 19. Golder, Across Arizona's Desert on Horseback, GP, Box 19. Interview with Dr. Thomas Barclay, Emeritus Professor of Political Science at Stanford University, Palo Alto, California, 10 September 1977.

17 Hart to Harold Fisher, 29 April 1929, p. 2, Golder Correspondence, HIR, Box 94. Golder remained a bachelor throughout his life, although a lady's man. He could not be considered handsome, but women were attracted to his wide traveling experiences and cosmopolitan personality. Golder had a philosophy about marriage, "Either you devote all your life to one woman, or to history." See, Interview with Charles B. Burdick, His-

tory Professor at San Jose State University, San Jose, California, 24 August 1976, and Interview with Dr. Carl Brand, Emeritus Professor of History at Stanford University, Stanford, California, 28 March 1976. Ivy Lewellan, Remarkable Men Who Served the State College in Doctor Holland's Early Regime, Holland Papers, WSUA. Cited hereafter as HP.

A former student of Golder's at Washington State wrote, "A memory of Golder's sense of humor was of meeting him some years after my graduation at a little gathering of alumni and friends. The conversation included reminiscences of college events and personalities. I told of an eight o'clock class taught by a former . . . professor now pretty much dead wood who always gave the same lectures, from course to course, in a deadly monotone, through which most members of the class slept. I was not being inspired and found myself in the state of mind in which my only remaining interest seemed simply to get a grade. But I did read the accompanying text each preceding evening. As a sort of experiment, I figured out a few questions on the subject—I hoped—and as the class slept I asked the questions. Apparently the old professor was so astonished that anyone in that class could ask an *intelligent* question, he concluded I was a good student, excused me from the final examination, and gave me an A. After our group laughed, Dr. Golder burst my bubble by inquiring, "How do you know your questions were intelligent?" See, L. B. Vincent to Wachhold, 9 May 1976, Personal Files of A. G. Wachhold, Santa Barbara, California.

18 *Yearbook, 12, 1913, Report of the Department of Historical Research, Plans for 1914*, p. 161, Carnegie Institution of Washington, D.C., 1914, Carnegie Institution Archives, Washington, D. C., Golder, ed., *Guide to Materials for American History in Russian Archives*, Vol. 1, with an introduction by John F. Jameson (Washington, D.C.: Carnegie Institution, 1917), pp. iii–iv.

19 Tsuyoshi Hasegawa, *The February Revolution: Petrograd 1917* (Seattle: University of Washington Press, 1981), pp. 6–7. Cited hereafter as Hasegawa, *The February Revolution.* R. R. Palmer and Joel Colton, *A History of the Modern World* (New York: Alfred A. Knopf, 1978), pp. 700–702, 704. Cited hereafter as Palmer, *Modern World.*

20 Golder, Russian Diary, May 1914, GP, Box 19. Golder to E. A. Bryan, 9 March 1914, pp. 3–4, Bryan Papers, WSUA. Cited hereafter as BP. Stephen F. Cohen, *Bukharin and the Bolshevik Revolution: A Political Bibliography, 1888–1939* (New York: Alfred A. Knopf, 1973), p. 7.

[21] Golder, Russian Diary, May 1914, GP, Box 19.

[22] *Ibid.*

[23] *Ibid.*

[24] *Ibid.*

[25] *Ibid.*

[26] *Ibid.* George Vernadsky, Reminiscences of F. A. Golder, p. 2., Golder Correspondence, HIR, Box 94.

[27] Golder to E. A. Bryan, 9 March 1914, pp. 1–2, BP, WSUA.

[28] Golder, Russian Diary, May 1914, GP, Box 19.

[29] *Ibid.*

[30] Golder's association with Vernadsky also provided the American historian with an opportunity to illustrate his pugilistic skills. Vernadsky wrote, "I remember our strolling one night at the Nicholas Quai on Basil Island. Our party consisted of four persons. Golder was walking with a young Russian lady. A drunken hooligan passing by said something rough. Golder immediately got him and did not return to his companion before having stroked him in the nape of the neck. All passed with lightning speed and nobody else had time to interfere. I remember that everybody was pleased by such quick action." See, Vernadsky, Reminiscences of F. A. Golder, p. 3, Golder Correspondence, HIR, Box 94.

[31] Golder to E. A. Bryan, 9 March 1914, pp. 4–5, BP, WSUA.

[32] *Ibid.*

[33] *Ibid.* Hasegawa, *The February Revolution*, pp. 9–10, 106–107.

[34] Hasegawa, *The February Revolution*, p. 10.

[35] Golder, Russian Diary, 11 July 1914, GP, Box 19.

[36] Golder wrote of this experience, "The fact that I came to look into the history of these missionaries aroused the interest of the Valaam monks. They placed all their papers before me, the same papers which were used years ago by one of their number in writing the saintly story of the missionaries. In this account many documents were given in the original but the writer forgot to mention that he edited certain portions of them and left out others. It is of such material and by such writers that lives of saints are written. One can trace the growth of this particular legend from one document to another." See, Golder, Russian Diary, July 1914, GP, Box 19.

Golder wrote a short history of the missionaries, led by a Father Herman. About his version, Golder wrote, "This is not a critical study of the life of Father Herman but the monastery version. In this respect it does not differ from the lives of other saints. Golder had the charming story privately printed as a pamphlet and sent copies of it to friends as a Christmas card. It was Golder's habit to write an enchanting episode of his or someone else's life in celebration of the Christmas season. See, Golder, *Father Herman: Alaska's Saint*, pp. 1–20, WSUA.

37 Golder, Russian Diary, July 1914, GP, Box 19.

38 Nicholas V. Riasanovsky, *A History of Russia* (London: Oxford University Press, 1969), pp. 461–464. Palmer, *Modern World*, pp. 654–665. Golder, Russian Diary, 30–31, 1914, GP, Box 19.

39 Golder, Russian Diary, 1 August 1914, GP, Box 19.

40 Golder, Russian Diary, 31 July 1914, *ibid.*

41 Golder, Russian Diary, 2 August 1914, *ibid.* Robert K. Massie, *Nicholas and Alexandra* (New York: Dell Co., 1967: A Dell Book, 1969), pp. 77–78. Cited hereafter as Massie, *Nicholas and Alexandra.* Hasegawa, *The February Revolution*, p. 4.

42 Golder, Russian Diary, 15 November 1914, GP, Box 19.

43 Golder, Russian Diary, 16 November 1914, *ibid.*

44 Golder, Russian Diary, 20 November 1914, *ibid.*

45 *Ibid.*

46 Golder, Russian Diary, 22 November 1914, *ibid.*

47 Robert Warth, *The Allies and the Russian Revolution: From the Fall of the Monarchy to the Peace of Brest–Litovsk* (New York: Russell & Russell, 1973), p. 5. Michael T. Florinsky, *Russia: A Short History* (London: Macmillan, 1969), p. 393. Palmer, *Modern World*, p. 705.

48 Golder, Russian Diary, 23 November 1914, GP, Box 19.

49 Golder, Russian Diary, 27 November 1914, *ibid.*

50 Golder, Russian Diary, 2 December 1914, *ibid.*

51 *Ibid.*

52 Golder, Russian Diary, 5 December 1914, *ibid.*

53 Golder, Russian Diary, 7 December 1914, *ibid.*

54 Golder, Russian Diary, 9 December 1914, *ibid.* Newspaper Clipping, "Liberal Christianity and Types of Character," *China Press* (Shanghai), 15 December 1914, GP, Box 9. Newspaper Clipping, "Continuous Stream of Troops in 16 Day Passage on Trans-Siberian: Rich Historical Discoveries," *China Press* (Shanghai), 19 December 1914, GP, Box 9.

Notes to Chapter III

1 John F. Jameson to Hugh Gibson, 8 October 1917, U. S. Department of State, Records of the American Commission to Negotiate the Peace, Record Group 256, National Archives, Washington, D.C., Golder, Russian Diary, 22 February 1917, GP, Box 33.

[2] These publications are, Golder, "The Russian Fleet and the Civil War," *American Historical Review* 20 (July 1915): 801–802. "Catherine II and the American Revolution," *American Historical Review* 21 (October 1915): 92–96. "The Russian Offer of Mediation in the War of 1912," *Political Science Quarterly* 31 (September 1916): 380–391. *The Attitude of the Russian Government toward Alaska*, in *The Pacific Ocean History*, H. Morse Stephens and Herbert E. Bolton, eds., (New York: Macmillan, 1917), pp. 269–275. The American historian, Thomas Bailey, a history professor at Stanford University, vigorously defended Golder's article on the Russian fleet, an article which created quite a splash in its day, because years after its publication popular fancy persisted in believing that the Russian fleet had come to the United States in 1863 to aid the Union. Golder contended that the fleet had sought neutral ports in case of war with Britain and France over a crisis involving Poland. From U. S. ports, the fleet could have ravaged its adversaries with the advantage of clear water. See, Thomas Bailey, "The Russian Fleet Myth Reexamined," *Mississippi Valley Historical Reveiw* 38 (June 1957): 81–90. Interview with Thomas Bailey, Emeritus Professor of History at Stanford University, Stanford, California, 11 April 1976.

[3] This book was published in 1914 (the first monograph by an American on Russia). Golder was the first non–Russian scholar after Hubert Howe Bancroft to interest himself in Russian eastward expansion. Golder accepted the traditional European view that Vitus Bering's two voyages were of a geographical nature, establishing beyond a doubt the separation of the continents of Asia and America. For years, Golder was the authority cited by non–Russian authors who wrote accounts of Bering's voyages. In the 1950s, Raymond H. Fisher began to challenge the traditional view, and in 1977, he published an excellent study on Bering's voyages. Fisher asserted that the geographical question was not the primary reason for the voyages; Peter the Great commissioned Bering to gather information in order to "establish Russian sovereignty in northwest America to the end of exploiting its fur and mineral resources." See, Raymond H. Fisher, *Bering's Voyages: Whither and Why* (Seattle: University of Washington Press, 1977), pp. 152, 18–19, 114–115. Fisher, "Semen Dezhnev and Professor Golder," *Pacific Historical Review* 25 (August 1956): 281–292. Fisher, *The Voyage of Semen Dezhnev in 1648: Bering's Precursor* (London: The Hakluyt Society, 1981), pp. 277–289.

[4] Vernadsky wrote such books as *Ancient Russia, Kievan Rus-*

sia, The Mongols and Russia, and *History of Russia.* Philip E. Mosely, *The Growth of Russian Studies,* in *American Research on Russia,* Harold H. Fisher, ed., (Bloomington: Indiana University Press, 1959), pp. 1–2. John S. Curtis, *History, ibid.,* pp. 23–24.

5   John F. Jameson to Hugh Gibson, 8 October 1917, RG 256. Golder, *Bering's Voyages* Vol. II: *Steller's Journal of the Sea Voyages from Kamchatka to America and Return on the Second Expedition, 1741–1742* (New York: American Geographical Society, 1925), pp. vii–x, 1–7.

6   Golder, Russian Diary, 4 March 1917, GP, Box 19. Golder to H. Eliot, 18 March 1917, GP, Box 12. When Golder discovered there was also a widespread food shortage in Petrograd, he wrote, "Embarrassing to go for dinner; one is afraid he eats too much." See, Golder, Russian Diary, 6 March 1917, GP. Box 19.

7   Frank Golder, Samuel Harper, and Alexander Petrunkevich, *The Russian Revolution* (Cambridge: Harvard University Press, 1918), p. 56. Cited hereafter as Golder, *Russian Revolution.*

8   Hasegawa, *The February Revolution,* p. 201. Palmer, *Modern History,* pp. 704–706. Golder, *Russian Revolution,* pp. 47–59. Golder, Russian Diary, 8–9 March 1917, GP, Box 19.

9   Golder, *Russian Revolution,* p. 58.

10   *Ibid.,* pp. 58–59.

11   The March Russian Revolution is also known as the February Revolution, since according to the Julian calendar, used in Russia until 1918, this revolution occurred in February. Dates used in this account are according to the Gregorian calendar (new style), thirteen days behind the Julian calendar (old style) in the twentieth century.

12   Golder, *Russian Revolution,* p. 60.

13   *Ibid.,* p. 63. Golder to H. Eliot, 18 March 1917, p. 1, GP, Box 12. Hasegawa, *The February Revolution,* pp. 215, 217, 222–223, 230–231. William H. Chamberlain, *The Russian Revolution,* Vol. I: *1917–1918, From the Overthrow of the Czar to the Assumption of Power by the Bolsheviks* (New York: Universal Library, 1965), p. 65. Cited hereafter as Chamberlin, *Russian Revolution,* Vol. 1. Leon Trotsky, *The Russian Revolution,* Trans. Max Eastman (New York: Doubleday, 1932; Anchor Books, 1959), pp. 97–98.

14   Golder, *Russian Revolution,* p. 64.

15   *Ibid.,* p. 65. Golder to H. Eliot, 18 March 1917, GP, Box 12.

16   Golder, *Russian Revolution,* pp. 64–65. Golder to H. Eliot, 18 March 1917, pp. 1–2, GP, Box 12.

17   Golder, *Russian Revolution,* p. 65.

[18] Hasegawa, *The February Revolution*, pp. 107, 247–248. Chamberlin, *Russian Revolution*, Vol. 1, pp. 76, 131. Golder, *Russian Revolution*, p. 66. Louis Fischer, *The Life of Lenin* (New York: Harper & Row, 1964), p. 94. Cited hereafter as Fischer, *Lenin.*

[19] Golder, *Russian Revolution*, p. 67. Hasegawa, *The February Revolution*, p. 263. Massie, *Nicholas and Alexandra*, p. 400.

[20] Golder, *Russian Revolution*, p. 66. Hasegawa, *The February Revolution*, p. 263. Golder, Russian Diary, 11 March 1917, GP, Box 19.

[21] Golder, *Russian Revolution*, p. 67. Golder, Russian Diary, 11 March 1917, GP, Box 19.

[22] Golder, *Russian Revolution*, p. 68. Golder, Russian Diary, 11 March 1917, GP, Box 19. Hasegawa, *The February Revolution*, pp. 268–269.

[23] Golder, *Russian Revolution*, p. 69.

[24] Hasegawa, *The February Revolution*, pp. 278–281. Chamberlin, *Russian Revolution*, Vol. 1, pp. 78–79. Trotsky, *Russian Revolution*, pp. 119–120.

[25] Golder, *Russian Revolution*, p. 69. Golder to H. Eliot, 18, March 1917, p. 2, GP, Box 12.

[26] Golder, *Russian Revolution*, p. 69.

[27] *Ibid.*

[28] Golder to H. Eliot, 18 March 1917, p. 4, GP, Box 12.

[29] Golder, *Russian Revolution*, p. 70.

[30] Palmer, *Modern World*, p. 706. Hasegawa, *The February Revolution*, p. 507.

[31] Golder to Friends, 20 March 1917, p. 1, GP, Box 33.

[32] Golder, *Russian Revolution*, pp. 71, 73.

[33] Golder to H. Eliot, 18 March 1917, p. 4, GP, Box 12. Golder, Russian Diary, 13, 14, 16 March 1917, GP, Box 19.

[34] Golder, *Russian Revolution*, p. 78. Rex Wade, *The Russian Search for Peace, February–October 1917* (Stanford: Stanford University Press, 1969), pp. 51–74. Cited hereafter as Wade, *Russian Search for Peace.*

[35] Golder to Friends, 20 March 1917, p. 1, GP, Box 33. Chamberlin, *Russian Revolution*, Vol 1, p. 100. Wade, *Russian Search for Peace*, p. 143. Adam B. Ulam, *A History of Soviet Russia* (New York: Praeger, 1976), p. 2.

[36] Golder to K., 8 June 1917, p. 4, GP, Box 12.

[37] Golder to H. Eliot, 18 March 1917, p. 4, GP, Box 12.

[38] John F. Jameson to James Shotwell, 8 October 1917, p. 3, RG, 256.

39 Golder, Russian Diary, 12 April 1917, GP, Box 19. Of the Russian army Golder wrote, "The officer who is here (at the apartment where Golder was staying) thinks that the officers and soldiers are worn out, that their nerves are on edge and that they cannot hold out for more than six months. If peace does not come soon, they will lay down their arms." See, Golder, Russian Diary, 5 April 1917, *ibid.* Chamberlin, *Russian Revolution*, Vol. 1, pp. 103–105. Palmer, *Modern World*, pp. 706–707.

40 Chamberlin, *Russian Revolution*, Vol. 1, pp. 116, 118, 137. Edmond Wilson, *To the Finland Station* (New York: Frarrar, Straus & Giroux, 1968), pp. 541, 547–550. Fisher, *Lenin*, pp. 127–128.

41 Golder, Russian Diary, 3 May 1917, GP, Box 19.

42 Golder, Russian Diary, 18 April 1917, *ibid.* Christopher Lasch, *The American Liberals and the Russian Revolution* (New York: Columbia University Press, 1962), p. 45. Cited hereafter as Lasch, *Liberals*.

43 Golder, Russian Diary, 14 May 1917, GP, Box 19. Lincoln Steffens, *Autobiography of Lincoln Steffens* (New York: Harcourt, Brace & World, 1931), pp. 764–765. U. S. Department of State, *Foreign Relations of the United States: Russia, 1918*, Vol III (Washington, D. C.: Government Printing Office, 1932), David Francis to Robert Lansing, 6 April 1917, pp. 2–3. Cited hereafter as *FRUS*. Robert Lansing to David Francis, 17 May 1917, *ibid.*, pp. 9–10. Wade, *Russian Search for Peace*, p. 74. Betty Miller Unterberger, *America's Siberian Expedition, 1918–1920: A Study in National Policy* (New York: Greenwood Press, 1969), pp. 9–10. Otis L Graham, Jr., *The Great Campaigns: Reform and War in America, 1900–1928* (Englewood Cliffs, New Jersey: Prentice–Hall, 1971), p. 57. By October 1917, on the eve of the Bolshevik Revlution, the commitment of American financial support to the Provisional Government reached $325 million in credit. The Provisional Government spent over $187 million of this credit. See, James K. Libbey, *Alexander Gumberg and Soviet-American Relations, 1917–1933* (Lexington: University Press of Kentucky, 1977), p. 3. Cited hereafter as Libbey, *Gumberg*.

44 Golder, Russian Diary, 31 May 1917, GP, Box 19. Jacqueline St. John, "John F. Stevens: American Assistance to Russian and Siberian Railroads, 1917–1922," (Ph. D. dissertation, University of Oklahoma, 1969), pp. 113–116.

45 John F. Stevens, Report on the Stevens Mission, n.d., pp. 1–2, John F. Stevens Papers, Box 1, Hoover Institution, Stanford,

California. Cited hereafter as SP. Robert Lansing to Francis, 16 April 1917, *FRUS, 1918, Russia,* Vol. 111, p. 185. Russian Embassy to State, 21 April 1917, *ibid.,* p. 187. Francis to Robert Lansing, 15 May 1917, *ibid.,* pp. 189–190. William Appleman Williams, *American–Russian Relations, 1781–1947* (New York: Rinehart, 1952), p. 92. Massie, *Nicholas and Alexandra,* p. 398. Golder, Russian Diary, 31 May 1917, GP, Box 19.

[46] George Vernadsky, Reminiscences of F. A. Golder, p. 5, Golder Correspondence, HIR, Box 94. Golder to H. Eliot, 31 May 1917, p. 1, GP, Box 12. Golder to E. D. Holland, 17 May 1917, p. 1, HP.

[47] Golder to E. D. Holland, 17 May 1917, p. 1, HP.

[48] George Vernadsky, Reminiscences of F. A. Golder, p. 5, Golder Correspondence, HIR, Box 94.

[49] Golder, Russian Diary, 26, 28 to 31 May 1917, GP, Box 19.

[50] Golder to K., 8 June 1917, p. 1, GP, Box 33, Golder, Russian Diary, 26 May 1917, GP, Box 19.

[51] Golder, Russian Diary, 2 to 12 June 1917, *ibid.* John F. Stevens, Report on the Stevens Mission, pp. 5–7, SP. George Kennan, *Soviet–American Relations, 1917–1920,* Vol. I: *Russia Leaves the War* (Princeton University Press, 1956), pp. 284–285.

[52] Golder to H. Eliot, 25 June 1917, p. 1, GP, Box 33.

[53] *Ibid.*

[54] *Ibid.*

[55] Chamberlin, *Russian Revolution,* Vol. I, pp. 152–153, 162–163. Golder, Russian Diary, 1 to 4 July, GP, Box 19.

[56] Golder, Russian Diary, 5, 12 July 1917, GP, Box 19. William Darling, Diary, 11 July 1917, Hoover Institution, Stanford, California. Cited hereafter as Darling, Diary. Chamberlin, *Russian Revolution,* Vol. I, pp. 163–164.

[57] Rex Wade writes, "[Miliukov] held that since inept prosecution of the war had caused the fall of the old regime, the primary task of the new government should be the vigorous and efficient conduct of the war to a final and decisive victory. He was confident that this goal could be achieved; not only would the new govenment be more competent than the old, it would generate popular enthusiasm and the will to win the war." See, Wade *Russian Search for Peace,* pp. 10–11.

[58] Golder, Russian Diary, 5, 12 July 1917, GP, Box 19. Darling,Diary, 13 July 1917.

[59] Golder, Russian Diary, 16 July 1917, GP, Box 19. Chamberlin, *Russian Revolution,* Vol. I, pp. 159, 163–164, 167.

[60] Golder to H. Eliot, 25 June 1917, p. 1, GP, Box 12. Golder, Russian Diary, 16 July 1917, GP, Box 19.

[61] Golder, Russian Diary, 28 July 1917, 31 July to 5 August 1917, GP, Box 19. Chamberlin, *Russian Revolution*, Vol. I, pp. 181–185. Rex Wade writes, "Many contemporary observers testify to (Miliukov's) self–confidence and assertiveness. This never left him, even in defeat. In 1925 he was asked by the American historian Frank A. Golder if he thought anybody could have saved the situation in the summer of 1917 (at which time he was no longer in the government). [Golder wrote], 'He hesitated a bit and finally said that he could have.' When I pushed him a little, he did not make it clear to me how." See footnote in Wade, *Russian Search for Peace,* p. 10.

[62] Palmer, *Modern History,* p. 708. Alexander Kerensky, *The Catastrophe: Kerensky's Own Story of the Russian Revolution* (New York: D. Appleton, 1927), pp. 336–337. Cited hereafter as Kerensky, *Catastrophe.* In 1925, Golder spoke with Kerensky in Paris regarding his role in the Provisional Government. Golder wrote in his diary, "Had Kerensky for luncheon. He said that in 1917 he and his friends had two choices—one was to make peace and save themselves and Russia. The other was to go on and help save the allies. Even with all that has happened . . . [Kerensky thought that] the future will show that he was right in [taking] the road he did." See Golder, Diary, 26 May 1925, GP, Box 19.

[63] George Vernadsky, Reminiscences of F. A. Golder, pp. 5–6. Golder Correspondence, HIR, Box 94. Palmer, *Modern History,* p. 708. Golder, Russian Diary, 14 August 1917, GP, Box 19. Golder, "The Tragic Failure of Soviet Policies," *Current History* 14 (February 1924): 776. Cited hereafter as Golder, "Tragic Failure of Soviet Policies." The editor of this journal changed Golder's original title to the one above, making the article appear to be anti–Soviet. He also included photographs with anti–Soviet captions. When the article was published and Golder saw the changes, he strongly objected to what the editor had done, since Golder was trying to gain support for Soviet studies.

[64] Golder, Russian Diary, 15, 16 August 1917, GP, Box 19.

[65] *Ibid.* Francis to Robert Lansing, Note from Stevens to Willard, 25 June 1917, *FRUS, 1918, Russia,* Vol. III, p. 192. Francis to Robert Lansing, Note from Stevens to Willard, 30 July 1917, *ibid.,* pp. 194–195. Robert Lansing to Francis, 5 October 1917, *ibid.,* p. 201.

[66] William Chamberlin, *The Russian Revolution,* Vol. II: *1918–1921, From the Civil War to the Consolidation of Power* (New

York: Universal Library, 1965), p. 85. Massie, *Nicholas and Alexandra*, pp. 467–471. Kerensky, *Catastrophe*, pp. 258–278.

[67] Golder, Russia Diary, 15, 17 August 1917, GP, Box 19.

[68] Golder, Russian Diary, 15, 20 August 1917, *ibid.* Chamberlin, *Russian Revolution*, Vol. I, p. 278.

[69] Golder, Russian Diary, 20 August 1917, GP, Box 19. While in Krasnoyarsk, Golder spoke with an ordinary soldier. He wrote that the soldier said, "Kerensky had no right to send the Emperor away without consulting the people." Golder commented, "Kerenski is not the idol of the Krasnoiarskers. Everyone is tired of the war, tired of the soldiers, tired of living." See, *ibid.* Dimitri von Mohrenschildt, "The Early American Observers of the Russian Revolution, 1917–1921," *Russian Review* 3 (1943): 64–67.

[70] Golder, Russian Diary, 21 to 30 August 1917, GP, Box 19.

Notes to Chapter IV

[1] John F. Jameson to Hugh Gibson, 8 October 1917, pp. 3–4. U. S. Department of State, Records of the American Commission to Negotiate the Peace, National Archives, Washington, D. C., Record Group 256. Cited hereafter as Record Group 256. Peter G. Filene, *Americans and the Soviet Experiment, 1917–1933* (Cambridge: Harvard University Press, 1967), pp. 13–14. Cited hereafter as Filene, *Soviet Experiment.* Lasch, *Liberals*, p. 57.

[2] Golder's research in Russian in 1917 had not been futile regarding his assignment for the American Geographical Society. During the summer of 1917, he located a copy of Georg Steller's journal in the archives of the Russian Academy of Sciences at Petrograd. Golder wrote, "Steller's acount of his experiences with Bering during his second voyage is the most interesting of all the papers that have come down to us. The Naval officers' log books contain the dry facts of the voyage, but Steller's journal gives the spirit · of it, the *inside* story . . ." Golder compiled and helped translate his collected materials on Bering's voyages for two unique volumes. See, Golder, *Bering's Voyages*, Vol. I: *The Log Books and Official Reports of the First and Second Expedition, 1725–1730 and 1733–1742* (New York: American Geographical Society, 1922) and *Bering's Voyages*, Vol. II: *Steller's Journal of the Sea Voyage from Kamchatka to America and Return on the Second Expedition, 1741–1742* (New York: American Geographical Society, 1925). Charles V. Piper to Golder, 5 January 1917, pp. 1–2, Charles V. Piper Papers, WSUA. Fisher, *Bering's Voyages*, p. 128.

3   John F. Jameson to Hugh Gibson, 8 October 1917, p. 3, RG 256.
    Golder, "Failure of Soviet Policy," p. 3. Mohrenschildt, "Early
    American Observers of the Russian Revolution," pp. 64–74.

4   Lawrence E. Gelfand, *The Inquiry: American Preparation for
    Peace, 1917–1919* (New Haven: Yale University Press, 1963),
    pp. 181, 313–314. Cited hereafter as Gelfand, *Inquiry*.

5   Jameson to James T. Shotwell, 8 October 1917, p. 3, RG 256.
    White to Golder, 4 February 1905, pp. 1–2, GP, Box 13. Gelfand,
    Inquiry, pp. 39–42.

6   James to Shotwell, 8 October 1917, pp. 3–4, RG 256. Gelfand,
    Inquiry, pp. 44–45.

7   Shotwell to Golder, 15, 17 November 1917, telegrams, RG 256.

8   Robert Byrnes writes, "The division included ten men who had
    obtained their Ph.D.'s with [Coolidge]: Andrews, Blakeslee, 'Fay,
    Golder, Kerner, Lord, Lybyer, Shipman, Steefel, and Tyler. In
    fact, all those in The Inquiry who wrote reports on Russia had
    studied with him." See, Byrnes, *Coolidge*, p. 166. Golder to E.
    Holland, 23 November 1917, p. 1, RG 256. Shotwell to Golder,
    3 Decemer 1917, p. 1, *ibid.*

9   Quotes in Gelfand, *Inquiry*, pp., 56, 35, 48, 89. Robert Byrnes
    writes, "The work of The Inquiry demonstrates how little infor-
    mation was readily available and how few specialists the United
    States possessed on Central and Eastern Europe. In 1920, only
    eighteen American historians had received Ph.D.'s for theses on
    Russia and Central and Eastern Europe." See, Byrnes, *Coolidge*,
    p. 167. Coolidge, *Archibald Cary Coolidge*, pp. 158, 172–174,
    193–199.

10 Shotwell to Golder, 3 January 1918, p. 1, RG 256. Golder to
    Shotwell, 17 December 1917, p. 1, *ibid.* Shotwell to Golder, 20
    December 1917, p. 1, *ibid.* Mezes to Holland, 15 January 1918,
    p. 1, *ibid.* Holland to Mezes, 1 February 1918, p. 1, *ibid.*

11 Gelfand, *Inquiry*, pp. 49–52, 55, 92. Robert Lansing, the Sec-
    retary of State, set the tone for U. S. ideological opposition to
    the new Soviet regime, an opposition which became an institu-
    tionalized policy in the State Department under his, Bainbridge
    Colby's, and Charles Evans Hughes' direction. Lansing wrote,
    "Bolshevism is the most hideous and monstrous thing that the
    human mind has ever conceived. It appeals to the basest pas-
    sions and finds its adherents among the criminal, the depraved,
    and mentally unfit. It is opposed to nationality and represents
    a great international movement of ignorant masses to overthrow
    government everywhere and destroy the present social order. Ac-
    cording to this doctrine [of Bolshevism], life, property, family

ties, personal conduct, all the sacred rights are subject to the ar-
bitrary will of the proletariat." Quoted in Gelfand, *Inquiry*, pp.
212–213. For an excellent discussion of the clash between Wilso-
nianism and Leninism in the twentieth century, see, Charles B.
Burdick, *Aesop, Wilson, and Lenin: The End of the World*, Second Annual President's Scholar's Address, 23 April 1975, San
Jose State University, pp. 3–15. Cited hereafter as Burdick,
Wilson and Lenin.

12 Golder's reports for the Inquiry are located in Box 12 of his
papers at the Hoover Institution, Stanford, California. They
are: The Ukrainians, 1 February 1918, 13 pp. Don Province, 8
April 1918, 30 pp., Appendix to the Don Province, 11 April 1918,
30 pp. Report of Siberia, 25 May 1918, 150 pp. This report is
not located at the Hoover Institution but is among the Inquiry
papers at Yale University Archives. Lithuania, 20 August 1918,
98 pp., with appendix, 58 pp. Lithuanian Parties in America,
12 April 1918, 7 pp. Ukraine, 1 November 1918, 121 pp., with
appendix, 65 pp. Lithuania: The Question of Independence, 11
November 1918, 11 pp. Western Russia and Poland, n.d., 10 pp.
A Survey of the Ukrainian Situation, n.d., 16 pp. Special Report
on Russia, n.d., 4 pp.

13 In 1919, Golder wrote, "The poor peasants are not interested either in cultural development or in national independence; many
of them do not even understand the meaning of these words.
What they want is steady work, good wages, and plenty to eat.
They hate landlords of all nationalities, and they have no reason to think that a bishop of their own people would treat them
with more consideration than one of another people. Ninety percent of every nationality in Europe is more interested in social
than national problems in the question of food and wages than
in culture and independence. This explains the success of Bolshevism with its appeal to throw over the clergy and the bourgeoisie because they are the landholders, the privileged classes,
the capitalists, the reputed oppressors of the working people."
See, Golder, "Will the Unrestricted Self–Determination of All
National Groups Bring World Peace and Order," *Journal of International Relations* 10 (January 1920): 284. Golder, Western
Russia and Poland, n.d., GP, Box 12., offers recommendations
for the territorial and political settlement of Poland, Finland,
Estonia, Livonia, and Lithuania. Golder, Ukraine, 1 November
1918, p. 15, *ibid*. Gelfand, *Inquiry*, pp. 213–214.

14 Golder to Lippmann, 25 May 1918, p. 1, RG 256. Lippman to
Golder, 17 May 1918, p. 1, *ibid*. Jzlupa to Golder, n.d., p. 1, GP,

Box 2. Golder did write to the former Russian Provisional Government's Embassy in Washington, D.C. (the U. S. government supplied the embassy with funds after the Bolshevik Revolution to keep it operational for political purposes, as an anti–Bolshevik propaganda center), but received only evasive responses.

[15] Golder to Lippmann, 11 April 1918, p. 1, RG 256. William Bentinck–Smith, *Building a Great Library: The Coolidge Years at Harvard* (Cambridge: Harvard University Press, 1976), pp. 126–128.

[16] Lippmann to Golder, 4 April 1918, p. 1, RG 256. Golder to Lippmann, 1 April 1918, p. 1, *ibid.*

[17] Golder to E. Holland, 16 July 1917, p. 1, HP.

[18] Golder to Bowman, 24 November 1918, p. 1, RG 256. Gelfand, *Inquiry*, pp. 162–163.

[19] Golder to Bowman, 24 November 1918, p. 1, RG 256. Gelfand, *Inquiry*, p. 58. Isaiah Bowman, as director of the American Geographical Society, for which Golder was preparing a study on Vitus Bering, reacted sympathetically toward Golder's letter of protest, and also wanted to know how much progress he had made with the Bering project. From time to time, Golder worked on the project while involved with the Inquiry. See, Bowman to Golder, 17 November 1919, p. 1, RG 256.

[20] Gelfand, *Inquiry*, p. 162.

[21] John M. Thompson records that Wilson in 1919 received a memorandum on the Russian situation from Robert Lord, his technical advisor on Russia at the Paris Peace Conference, dated 16 January. Thompson states that "Lord's report, while full of accurate data, tended to stress Soviet weakness in its interpretations." In fact, at the time of the Soviet Civil War, the Bolsheviks were eager to be conciliatory to the Allies and make peace, although gaining victories in the war and gaining growing support for the Soviet regime from those disillusioned with White Russian policies or repelled by foreign intervention. See, John M. Thompson, *Russia, Bolshevism, and the Versailles Peace* (Princeton: Princeton University Press, 1966), p. 100, footnote #62. Lord, in *Some Problems of the Peace Conference* (Cambridge: Harvard University Press, 1922), p. 171, did mention the problem of disposing of Russian territory without Soviet Russia's consent, but fell on the excuse that "there was no recognized Russian government with which a voluntary settlement could be negotiated." Gelfand, *Inquiry*, pp. 55, 92, 162. Thompson writes that Wilson followed his own dictates regarding Russia: "There is no evidence that Wilson paid any attention to the suggestions of either his experts

or his admirals." See, Thompson, *Bolshevism and the Versailles Peace*, p. 48, footnote #35.

22 Ulam, *Soviet History*, p. 34. Williams, *American–Russian Relations*, pp. 102–129, 163–175. William Appleman Williams, *American Invervention: Strictly Anti–Bolshevik*, in Betty M. Unterberger, ed., *American Intervention in the Russian Civil War* (Lexington, Mass.: Heath, 1969), pp. 83–97. William S. Graves, *America's Siberian Adventure, 1918–1920* (New York: Jonathan Cape and Harrison Smith, 1931), pp. 191–195. Thompson, *Bolshevism and the Versailles Peace*, pp. 207–251.

23 Golder, Biographical Sketch, p. 2, HUA. In 1919, Golder wrote Lansing, asking for permission to publish Inquiry reports of his on Lithuania and on the Ukraine. Lansing, for reasons of secrecy, did not give Golder the requested permission. See, Lansing to Golder, 18 August 1919, p. 1, GP, Box 19. Golder to E. E. Bernays, n.d., GP, Box 2.

Golder published four articles between 1919 and 1921. They are: "The Russian Revolution," *University Magazine*, Washington State University 13 (April 1919): 56–70. "Will the Unrestricted Self–Determination of all National Groups Bring Peace and Order?" *Journal of International Relations* 10 (January 1920):278–288. "The Purchase of Alaska," *American Historical Review* 25 (April 1920): 411–425, an excellent article, which is still useful for an introduction to the topic, although the author describes the purchase from a political rather than an economic perspective. "The American Civil War through the Eyes of a Russian Diplomat," *American Historical Review* 26 (April 1921): 454–463.

24 Since 1919, the Hoover Institution has undergone several name changes. In the first few years, the library was known as the Hoover War Collection. From 1921 through the academic year 1936–37, it was called the Hoover War Library; through 1941–42, it was called the Hoover Library on War, Revolution, and Peace; through 1946, the Hoover Library on War, Revolution, and Peace and the Hoover Research Institute; through 1955-56, the Hoover Institute and Library on War, Revolution, and Peace; and since 1956–57 it has been formally named the Hoover Institution on War, Revolution, and Peace. Such name changes reflect the Hoover Institution's changing and expanding collections.

25 Adams to Ralph Lutz, 17 January 1920, p. 1, Administrative Subject File, HIR, Box 156. Adams to Edgar Robinson, 1920, p. 1, Edgar Robinson Collection, Box 59, Stanford University Archives, Stanford, California. Cited hereafter as SUA. Ray Ly-

man Wilbur to Golder, 28 Febuary 1920, Wilbur Papers, SUA, Box 37. Charles B. Burdick, *Ralph H. Lutz and the Hoover Institution* (Stanford: Hoover Institution Press, 1974), pp. 8–9, 35–39. Cited hereafter as Burdick, *Lutz.* Benjamin Weissman, *Herbert Hoover and Famine Relief to Soviet Russia* (Stanford: Hoover Institution Press, 1974), pp. 19–20. Cited hereafter as Weissman, *Hoover and the Soviet Famine.* Ephraim D. Adams, *The Hoover War Collection: A Report and Analysis* (Stanford: Stanford University Press, 1921), p. 72. Cited hereafter as Adams, *Report.* Nina Almond and H. H. Fisher, *Special Collections in the Hoover Library on War, Revolution, and Peace* (Stanford: Stanford University Press, 1940), pp. 16–17. Cited hereafter as Almond, *Hoover Library.*

[26] Burdick, *Lutz,* pp. 10–39.

[27] Golder to Adams, 19 August 1920, p. 1, GP, Box 32. Adams to Golder, 17 August 1920, p. 1, GP, Box 19. Adams to Golder, 12 November 1920, p. 2, GP, Box 32. Burdick, *Lutz,* pp. 30–40. Interview with Charles B. Burdick, Professor of History at San Jose State Univesity, 24 August 1976, San Jose, California.

[28] Ephraim D. Adams, Digest of the Work of F. A. Golder in Connection with the American Relief Administration and Hoover War Collection, quotes a number of Golder's letters, p. 1; a copy of this digest is in the personal files of the author. At the project's outset, Professor Charles Burdick of San Jose State University gave the author a small Golder archive. Cited hereafter as Adams, Digest. Filene, *Soviet Experiment,* p. 62. Robert K. Murray, *Red Scare: A Study in National Hysteria, 1919–1920* (Minneapolis: University of Minnesota Press, 1955). Guy Alchon, lecture on the 1920s in the U. S., 2 April 1982, University of California, Santa Barbara. Martens to Secretary of State, 32 March 1920, *FRUS, 1920,* Vol. III, pp. 455–457. Memorandum by Mr. Basil Miles, in charge of Russian Affairs, Division of Near Eastern Affairs, Department of State, 24 June 1919, *ibid.,* pp. 146–147. Acting Secretary of State to the Ambassador of Great Britain, 16 December 1920, *ibid.* p. 480. Martens' real purpose in the United States had nothing to do with establishing a propaganda bureau or bureaus advocating the overthrow of the United States. His mission involved negotiating (and he did so) trade connections between American businessmen and Soviet Russia, since his country had suffered major economic destruction during World War I and the Soviet Civil War. In January 1921, U. S. agents deported Martens. See, Martens to Acting Secretary of State, Memorandum, 18 March 1919, *ibid.,* pp. 134–141. Act-

ing Secretary of State to Commission to Negotiate the Peace, 5 June 1919, *ibid.*, pp. 144–145. Frederick Lewis Schuman, *American Policy Toward Russia Since 1917: A Study of Diplomatic History, International Law, and Public Opinion* (New York: International Publishers, 1928), pp. 185–195, presents a justifiably favorable account of Martens. Cited hereafter as Schuman, *American Policy Toward Russia.*

29 For example, Golovin told Golder during a conversation in Paris on 29 September 1920 that both the Reds and the Whites appealed to the lowest passions to win the Soviet Civil War. Thus, Golder had a chance to view the civil war with a certain objectivity from an eye–witness. See, Golder, Diary, 29 September 1920, GP, Box 19. In a letter to Adams, Golder wrote, "The Soviet Civil War has come to the point where brutality is matched against brutality. It is a savage drama that is being played." See, Golder to Adams, 6 October 1920, p. 1, GP, Box 32.

30 Thus began Golovin's long association with the Hoover Library, whose repositories he enriched with documentary treasures on Tsarist policy, Russian military activities, and Russian diplomatic developments. See, Burdick, *Lutz*, p. 90. Golder to H. Eliot, September 1920, pp. 1–2, GP, Box 12. Golder to Adams, 16 September 1920, pp. 1–2, GP, Box 32. Adams to Wilbur, 13 September 1926, p. 3, Wilbur Papers, SUA, Box 65. Lutz to Wilbur, 16 December 1926, p. 1, *ibid.*

31 Golder to Adams, 21 September 1920, p. 1, GP, Box 32. Golder to Lutz, 23 September 1920, p. 2, Personal Files of A. G. Wachhold. Arthur P. Mendel, ed., *Political Memoirs, 1905–1917, by Paul Miliukov* (Ann Arbor: University of Michigan Press, 1967), pp. xiv, p. 198. Cited hereafter as Mendel, *Miliukov's Memoirs.*

32 Golder, Diary, 24 September 1920, GP. Box 19. Thompson, *Russia and the Versailles Peace*, pp. 362–363, 370. These negotiations eventually led to the Anglo–Soviet trade agreements of 1921.

33 Adams, Digest, p. 2. During the summer of 1920, Hoover tried to negotiate with Soviet authorities about feeding children in territory controlled by the Bolsheviks after the outbreak of the Polish–Soviet War in April 1920. The ARA had been feeding thousands of children in territory occupied by the Polish army in Soviet Russia and in Poland itself. In July, the tide of battle turned against the Poles, and the Bolshevik army overran the ARA relief station. Hoover wanted the ARA to continue operations in Soviet Russia, but needed an agreement to do so. The Soviet government, in September, responded favorably to per-

mitting the ARA to stay in Soviet Russia, although not trusting
Hoover, whose ARA had supplied food, gasoline, and clothing
to the advancing White armies in northern Europe during the
Soviet Civil War and to Poland during its war with Soviet Russia. However, by September, the Polish army struck back at
the Bolshevik army of occupation, driving the Bolsheviks from
Poland and thereby removing the threat to the ARA stations.
Hoover, only concerned about children in Poland and Polish oc-
cupied Soviet territory, would cut off negotiations with the Soviets shortly after Golder's visit with Krassin. While in London,
Golder had no knowledge that Hoover would leave him in a negotiating void. See, Weissman, *Hoover and the Soviet Famine*, pp.
37–39. Golder, Diary, 24 September 1920, GP, Box 19. Walter
Brown to Russian Trade Delegation, letter of introduction, 23
September 1920, pp. 1–2, BAEF Papers, Correspondence Series,
Hoover Presidential Library, West Branch, Iowa. Cited hereafter
as HPL. Herbert Hoover, *The Memoirs of Herbert Hoover* Vol.
I: *Years of Adventure, 1874–1920* (New York: Macmillan, 1951):
pp. 411–420. Cited hereafter as Hoover, *Years of Adventure.*

[34] Golder, Diary, 24 September 1920, GP, Box 19. Golder to Adams,
25 September 1920, p. 1, GP, Box 32. Adams, Digest, p. 2.

[35] Golder wrote, "Paris looks the same, but it does not feel the
same—the old gaiety is gone with the students. The Latin Quarter where I had lived and to which I have returned is full of people
but not students. Happily, I found my old friend the artist and
his housekeeper and I feel quite happy with them." See, Golder
to H. Eliot, 1 October 1920, p. 1, GP, Box 12. Golder to Adams,
25 September 1920, p. 1, GP, Box 32.

[36] Golder to Adams, 28 September 1920, p. 1, GP, Box 32.

[37] Adams, *Report*, pp. 10–15. Golder to Adams, 28 September
1920, p. 1, GP, Box 32. Adams, Digest, p. 2. Lutz to Wilbur,
16 December 1926, p. 1, Wilbur Papers, SUA, Box 65.

[38] Golder to Adams, 4 October 1920, p. 1, GP, Box 32. Alexander
DeConde, *A History of American Foreign Policy* Vol. II: *Global
Power, 1900 to the Present* (New York: Charles Scribner's Sons,
1978), pp. 67–68.

[39] Golder, Diary, 3 October 1920, GP, Box 19. Golder to Adams,
4 October 1920, p. 1, GP, Box 32. Palmer, *World History*, pp.
682–283. Henry T. Allen, *My Rhineland Journal* (New York:
Houghton Mifflin Co., 1923), pp. 115–116. Keith Nelson, *Victors Divided: America and the Allies in Germany, 1918–1923*
(Berkeley: University of California Press, 1975), pp. 254–261.

[40] Golder to Adams, 6 October 1920, p. 1, GP, Box 32. Golder,

Diary, 5 October 1920, GP, Box 19.
41 Golder to Adams, 6 October 1920, p. 1, GP, Box 32. Palmer, *World History*, pp. 743–744.
42 Golder to Adams, 19 October 1920, p. 14, GP, Box 33. Golder to Adams, 6 October 1920, p. 1, GP, Box 32. Golder, Diary, 6 October 1920, GP, Box 19. Donald W. Treadgold, *Twentieth Century Russia* (Chicago: Rand McNally & Co., 1972), pp. 196–197. Adams, *Report*, p. 54. Adams, Digest, p. 4.
43 Golder to Adams, 12 October 1920, p. 6, GP, Box 33. Golder to Adams, 8 October 1920, p. 8, *ibid.*
44 Golder to Adams, 10 October 1920, p. 6, *ibid.*
45 Golder, Diary, 9, 10 October 1920, GP, Box 19. Adams, Digest, p. 5. Joseph D. Dwyer, *Russia, The Soviet Union, and Eastern Europe: A Survey of Holdings at the Hoover Institution on War, Revolution, and Peace* (Stanford: Hoover Institution Press, 1980), pp. 9–13. Cited hereafter as Dwyer, *Russia, Soviet Union, and Eastern European Collections at the Hoover Institution.*
46 Golder to Adams, 12 October 1920, p. 9, GP, Box 33.
47 Golder, Diary, 12 October 1920, GP, Box 19. Albert Tarulis, *American–Baltic Relations, 1918–1922: The Struggle over Recognition* (Washington, D.C.: The Catholic University Press, 1965), p. 207.
48 Golder, Diary, 12 October 1920, GP, Box 19. Murray A. Rothbard, *Hoover's 1919 Food Diplomacy in Retrospect*, in Lawrence E. Gelfand, ed., *Herbert Hoover: The Great War and Its Aftermath* (Iowa City: University of Iowa Press, 1979), pp. 101–102. Cited hereafter as Gelfand, *Hoover and the Great War.* Herbert Hoover, *The Ordeal of Woodrow Wilson* (New York: McGraw–Hill, 1958), pp. 126–134. Cited hereafter as Hoover, *Wilson.* Herbert Hoover, *An American Epic*, Vol. III: *The Battle on the Front Line and Famine in Forty–Nine Nations, 1914–1923* (Chicago: Henry Regnery, 1961), pp. 301–309. Cited hereafter as Hoover, *An American Epic.* In the 1930s, Ulmanis set up a Fascist state in Latvia, and during World War II the Soviets captured and executed him.
49 Golder to Adams, 12 October 1920, p. 9, GP, Box 33. Golder, Diary, 12 October 1920, GP, Box 19.
50 Golder, Diary, 12 October 1920, GP, Box 19. Golder to Adams, 12 October 1920, pp. 9–10, Box 33.
51 Golder, Diary, 12 October 1920, GP, Box 19.
52 Golder to Adams, 12 October 1920, p. 10, GP, Box 33. Poland gained White Russia, north of the Ukraine, part of the Ukraine, and a broad area, including Vilna, all the way to the

Latvian border.

53 Walter Brown to Golder, 11 October 1920, telegram, BAEF Papers, Correspondence Series, HPL. Golder, Diary, 13 October 1920, GP, Box 19.

54 While the Soviets did arrest a few Americans, the U. S. government during the Red Scare arrested and deported hundreds of suspected Reds. Golder to H. Eliot, 17 October 1920, p. 1, GP, Box 12. Golder to Walter Brown, 31 December 1920, p. 1, BAEF Papers, Correspondence Series, HPL. Golder to Walter Brown, 18 August 1920, p. 1, *ibid.* Golder thought that the State Department had a hand in objecting to him entering Soviet Russia. In August 1920, Bainbridge Colby, the Secretary of State who replaced Lansing in the Wilson administration, wrote his famous "Colby Note," stating officially the United States' policy of non-recognition. In part, the Note stated that "the existing regime in Russia is based upon the negation of every principle of honor and good faith . . . whose conceptions of international relations are so alien to the United States own, so utterly repugnant to the United States moral sense." See, Colby to Avenzzana, 10 August 1920, *FRUS, 1920,* Vol. III, pp. 463–468.

55 Golder to Adams, 17 October 1920, p. 11, GP, Box 33, Golder to Adams, 19 October 1920, p. 14, *ibid.* Adams, *Report,* p. 73. Adams, Digest, p. 7.

56 Golder to Adams, 22 October 1920, p. 1, GP, Box 32.

57 Golder to Adams, 19 October 1920, p. 14, GP, Box 33.

58 Golder to Adams, 19 October 1920, p. 14, GP, Box 33. Wojciech Zalewski writes, "In [Golder's] mind, there was a very thin line between the collecting scope of the Hoover and that of the University Library. 'We agreed,' he wrote [Adams], 'that some material in Russian history must be bought.' The Russian Revolution, he argued, had to be understood in light of preceding Russian history." See, Wojciech Zalewski, unpublished monograph on Slavic collecting at Stanford libraries and the Hoover Institution, p. 71. This monograph contains only a small portion of Golder's gargantuan collecting efforts. Adams, Digest, p. 6. Adams to Golder, 4 December 1920, p. 2, *ibid.* Golder to Adams, 21 December 1920, p. 1, General Correspondence, HIR, Box 8. Golder to Lutz, 10 December 1920, p. 1, *ibid.* Lutz to Adams, 20 July 1922, p. 1, Administrative Subject File, HIR, Box 156. Golder also received $5,000 from the Library of Congress to buy books, a sum which he spent to enrich this library. See, Adams, Digest, p. 8. Regarding books, Golder wrote, "The State Library at Riga has an unusual collection of books. When the Bolsheviks

came here a little over two years ago, they went through every house and took . . . books for the purpose of making one national public library. They never carried out the scheme and as a result the new state has come into the possession of these books, some very valuable, most of them old." See, Adams, *Digest*, p. 8.

59 Golder, Diary, October 1920, GP, Box 19.

60 Golder wrote in his diary, "Hoover has a regard for Holsti for he gave me a personal letter to Holsti and to no other European. Holsti has an interesting Hoover story. He said that during the Peace Conference he came to see Hoover to ask him for food for Finland, which was then (1919) in great want. After listening to him, Hoover touched a button and one of his officials appeared: "Where is ship so and so, giving the name of the vessel. The official retired and returned in a moment to report the latitude and longitude of said ship. 'Order the captain to change course and go to Helsingfors and unload the cargo,' said Hoover." See, Golder, Diary, 1 November 1920, GP, Box 19. Hoover, *Wilson*, pp. 123–126. Hoover, *An American Epic*, pp. 27–36.

61 Golder, Miliukov Collection, 6 November 1920, pp. 1–2, GP, Box 32.

62 After Golder had taken the time and effort to recover Miliukov's collection, Miliukov later demanded several thousand dollars for the collection from the Hoover. Golder haggled with Miliukov, but to no avail. According to Wojciech Zalewski, "Golder [by 1928] gave up altogether his hopes that the Miliukov Collection would remain at Stanford. He prepared a list of its contents, to facilitate its sale to another library. When the list was ready in July 1928, he wrote to Miliukov: 'I am impressed with the value of it, but I am sorry to say that we at Stanford have no money to purchase it. Much as we regret it, we will have to let it go.' Soon after, Miliukov did sell his collection, to the Library of the University of California, Berkeley, where it remains today." See, Wojciech Zalewski, unpublished monograph on Slavic collecting at Stanford libraries and the Hoover Institution, p. 74 Paul Gary, "The Development of the Hoove Institution on War, Revolution, and Peace Library, 1919–1944," (Ph.D. dissertation, University of California, Berkeley, 1974), pp. 158–159. Mendel, *Miliukov's Memoirs*, p. 198. Audrey Philips, *Guide to Special Collections: University of California, Berkeley, Library* (Metuchen, N.J.: Scarecrow Press, 1973), p. 33.

63 Adams, *Digest*, p. 9.

Notes to Chapter V

[1] Golder to Adams, 19 November 1920, p. 1, GP, Box 32. Despite his enjoyable social life, Golder did lament the lack of female companionship. He wrote to Henrietta Eliot, a friend at Seattle, Washington, "I am just back from the opera where a Finnish opera based on an epic poem was given. It was good but, of course, I wished so much that you could have been with me. Indeed there is hardly any day when I do not wish it. This roving life has an interesting side, but it would be very much more interesting if two people could see it together." See, Golder to H. Eliot, 9 November 1920, p. 1, GP, Box 12.

[2] Golder to Adams, 19 November 1920, pp. 1–3, GP, Box 32. Golder to Lutz, 10 December 1920, p. 2. General Correspondence, HIR, Box 8.

[3] Golder had a useful conception regarding duplicates, a conception which became standard Hoover policy. He wrote Adams, "We are going to have duplicates; in some cases I get duplicates purposely so that we may have them in order to exchange with the Library of Congress and other libraries. Some of the things we need are not to be bought and can only be had by exchange and we must have equally valuable material to exchange with. If we do not exchange it, we can easily dispose of any material we do not want. In some cases, duplication is unavoidable. In order to get the material we need I have to order it in two or three places to make sure of getting any at all." See, Golder to Adams, 7 November 1920, p. 3, GP, Box 32.

[4] Golder wrote, "These new small Baltic States are worth studying. I am learning much of value and may one day have the time to write it up." Golder never found the time to do so. See, Golder to H. Eliot, 9 November 1920, p. 1, GP, Box 12. Dwyer, *Russian, Soviet Union, and Eastern European Collections at the Hoover Institution*, pp. 1–13.

[5] Wilson abandoned his previous policy of self–determination in the Baltic States for a variety of reasons. Secretary Bainbridge Colby, in his Colby Note of 10 August 1920, announced that the Wilson administration would not allow the territorial dismemberment of Russia, which the Allied governments wished to do during the Soviet Civil War; Colby's Note was designed to prevent the Bolshevik regime from strengthening itself through an appeal to nationalism; to uphold territorial inviolability which would encourage the Russian people to revolt against commu-

nist tyranny, (and also to keep the Japanese out of Siberia); to gain the gratitude of the Russian people for this preservation of Russian territories; and to bring Russia intact into the fold of democracy and capitalism. See, Joan Hoff–Wilson, *Ideology and Economics: U. S. Relations with the Soviet Union, 1918– 1933* (Columbia: University of Missouri Press, 1974), pp. 14–17. Cited hereafter as Hoff–Wilson, *Ideology.* Schuman, *American Policy Toward Russia,* pp. 182, 207–208, 216. Golder to Adams, 3 December 1920, p. 16, GP, Box 33. Golder to H. Eliot, 9 November 1920, p. 1, GP, Box 12.

6 Golder to Adams, 3 December 1920, p. 16, GP, Box 33.

7 Golder to Adams, 9 December 1920, p. 17, GP, Box 33. Golder also vented his irritation toward certain book dealers. He wrote, "I get quite tired at times, especially when I have to buy books. These Jew dealers with whom one has business dealings, they assume that I am a millionaire and keep repeating 'what is a dollar to you.' " See, Golder to Lutz, 10 December 1920, p. 3, GP, Box 32.

8 Golder to Adams, 9 December 1920, p. 17, GP, Box 33.

9 *Ibid.* Burdick, *Wilson and Lenin,* pp. 3–4.

10 Golder to Adams, 17 December 1920, p. 1, GP, Box 32. Golder to Lutz, 20 December 1920, p. 1, *ibid.* Golder to Lutz, 6 January 1921, p. 18, GP, Box 33.

11 Golder to H. Eliot, 6 January 1921, p. 1, GP, Box 12. Golder to Lutz, 20 December 1920, p. 1, GP, Box 32.

12 Golder to Adams, 22 December 1920, pp. 1–2, GP, Box 32. Adams to Golder, 16 December 1920, pp. 1, 5, GP, Box 32. Golder to Adams, 17 December 1920, p. 1, *ibid.* Lutz to Golder, 20 December 1920, p. 1, *ibid.*

13 Golder to Adams, 21 December 1920, pp. 1–2, *ibid.* Golder to Adams, 22 December 1920, p. 1, *ibid.*

14 Golder to Bertling, 29 December 1920, p. 1, GP, Box 32. Golder to Lutz, 6 January 1921, p. 18, GP, Box 33. Golder to Lutz, 20 December 1920, p. 1, GP, Box 32. Golder to Lutz, 23 December 1920, p. 1, *ibid.* Golder to Lutz, 7 January 1921, p. 1, *ibid.*

15 Golder to Adams, 17 January 1921, p. 1, GP, Box 32. Golder to Adams, 6 January 1921, p. 18, Box 33. Golder did not like Allied treatment of the Turks, who had fought on the side of the Central Powers—Germany and Austria. Golder wrote, "The Allies with their soldiers are in possession and they treat the Turks as if they had no right to exist." See, Golder, Diary, 14 January 1921, GP, Box 19.

16 Firuz Kazemzadeh, *The Struggle for Transcaucasia, 1917–1921*

(New York: Philosophical Library, 1951), pp. 294–313. Richard
Pipes, *The Formation of the Soviet Union: Communism and
Nationalism, 1917–1923* (Cambridge: Harvard University Press,
1964), pp. 210–241. David Land, *A Modern History of Soviet
Georgia* (New York: Grove Press, 1962), pp. 230–234.

17 Golder to Adams, 30 January 1921, pp. 31, 32, GP, Box 33.
Golder, Diary, 22 January 1921, GP, Box 19.

18 Golder to Adams, 30 January 1921, p. 32, GP, Box 33.

19 *Ibid.*

20 Golder, Diary, 29 January 1921, GP, Box 19.

21 Golder to Adams, 30 January 1921, p. 33, GP, Box 33.

22 *Ibid.*, p. 34.

23 Golder to Adams, 20 February 1921, p. 1, GP, Box 33.

24 *Ibid.*

25 Golder to Adams, 20 February 1921, p. 1, GP, Box 32.

26 *Ibid.*

27 *Ibid.*, pp. 1–2.

28 *Ibid.*, p. 2.

29 Golder, Diary, 7 February 1921, GP, Box 19.

30 Regarding a Red army invasion of Georgia, Golder wrote, "Every
day or so a rumor starts that the Bolos are going to attack. I
think the Bolos just now have bigger game than the Georgians
and I doubt whether they will waste much energy on them. Later
on they can handle them. Just the same the Bolo situation is
not very encouraging." See, Golder to Adams, 30 January 1921,
p. 29, GP, Box 33.

31 Golder to Adams, 30 January 1921, p. 38, GP, Box 33.

32 Golder to campus newspaper, Washington State College, Pullman, 24 February 1921, p. 5, WSUA.

33 Golder to Adams, 20 February 1921, p. 2, GP, Box 32.

34 *Ibid.*

35 Golder to campus newspaper, Washington State College, Pullman, 24 February 1921, p. 1, WSUA.

36 *Ibid.*

37 *Ibid.*

38 *Ibid.* Golder did not condemn the Turks for Constantinople's
turmoil. He wrote, "From this description one need not jump
to the conclusion that the Turks are to blame for this state of
affairs. The fact that the city is in the control of the Allies has
not helped much; it has brought in hundreds of carpetbaggers. .
. . The Italians and Greeks, in their pretty uniforms, look as if
they had conquered the world." See, Golder to Adams, 6 March
1921, p. 1, GP, Box 32.

[39] Golder to Adams, 6 March 1921, p. 1, GP, Box 32.

[40] Golder to Adams, 11 March 1921, pp. 2–3, GP, Box 32.

[41] While in Constantinople, Golder wrote Adams concerning his policy of purchasing manuscripts. "In regards to manuscripts I have adopted [the policy of paying] nothing for them. . . . I am a bit suspicious of those who have manuscripts to sell; from my experience I find that those who really possess valuable papers have no objection to giving us a copy." See, Golder to Adams, 6 March 1921, p. 3, GP, Box 32.

[42] Golder to Adams, 6 March 1921, p. 1, GP, Box 32.

[43] Golder to Adams, 24 March 1921, p. 56, GP, Box 33.

[44] Golder to Adams, 6 March 1921, p. 1, GP, Box 32. Golder to Adams, 11 March 1921, p. 3, GP, Box 32.

[45] Golder to Adams, 6 March 1921, p. 1, GP, Box 32. Golder to Adams, 11 March 1921, p. 1, GP, Box 32.

[46] Golder to Adams, 26 April 1921, p. 1, GP, Box 32. Stephanov to Golder, 17 July 1921, p. 2, GP, Box 32.

[47] Golder to Adams, 16 March 1921, pp. 1–2, GP, Box 32.

[48] Golder to Adams, 18 March 1921, p. 47, GP, Box 33. Nissan Oren, *Revolution Administered: Agrarianism and Communism in Bulgaria* (Baltimore: John Hopkins University Press, 1973), pp. 5–12. Cited hereafter as Oren, *Bulgaria.*

[49] Golder to Adams, 18 March 1921, p. 47, GP, Box 33. From March to November 1919, Hoover had sent food relief to Bulgaria. See, Hoover, *An American Epic,* Vol. III, pp. 128–130.

[50] Golder, Diary, 17 March 1921, GP, Box 19. Golder to Adams, 18 March 1921, p. 50, GP, Box 33. Golder to Adams, 24 March 1921, p. 55, GP, Box 33.

[51] Golder, Diary, 18 March 1921, GP, Box 19. Oren, *Bulgaria,* p. 61.

[52] Golder, Diary, 18 March 1921, GP, Box 19. Golder to Adams, 18 March 1921, p. 52, GP, Box 33. Golder later invited King Boris to come to Stanford University as a guest speaker. Golder wrote Adams, "In regards to the visit of the King of Bulgaria to America, I may tell you what our charge d'affaires, Mr. Wilson, told me. He said the King was eager to go but did not wish to go in the company of the Prime Minister, Stamboulisky, for fear the latter would humiliate him. I can well believe it, judging from the way he ordered about his secretary and disregarded the wishes of His Majesty." Boris never did visit Stanford University. See, Golder to Adams, 24 March 1921, p. 55, GP, Box 33.

[53] Golder to Adams, 21 March 1921, p. 53, GP, Box 33. Golder to Brewster of Standard Oil, 19 March 1921, p. 1, GP, Box 32.

54 Golder, Diary, 23 March 1921, GP, Box 19.
55 Hoover, *An American Epic*, Vol. III, pp. 367, 364–365, 140.
Hoover abhorred any government that resembled the reactionary,
pre–Wilsonian political order. However, while the Romanian
army departed from Hungary, the Romanians handed the Hungarian government over to Admiral Nicholas Horthy, who imposed a White Terror on Hungary far more extensive than Bela
Kun's Red Terror. Hoover failed to mention this episode in his
memoirs. See, Rothbard, *Hoover's Food Diplomacy*, in Gelfand,
Hoover and the Great War, pp. 100–101.
56 Golder to Adams, 30 March 1921, pp. 58–59, GP, Box 33. Adams
to Golder, 12 November 1920, p. 1, GP, Box 32. Hoover, *An
American Epic*, Vol. III, pp. 373–374.
57 Golder to Adams, 30 March 1921, pp. 58–59, GP, Box 33.
58 *Ibid.* Nicolae Iorga, *My American Lectures* (Bucharest: State
Printing Office, 1932), pp. 5–9. Golder also received an assignment from Geneal Golovine that brought him a certain amount
of apprehension. He wrote, "When I came to Bucharest I was
commissioned by General Golovin to secure the archives of the
Russian army in Romania. This archive consisted of several hundred boxes. To tell you (Adams) the truth, I was afraid we would
have an elephant on our hands. (Railway and postal services in
eastern Europe had become so problematic that Golder had to
rely on the American legation at Bucharest to ship out his materials, but the legation could only handle a few of his packages each
week.) I secretly hoped it would be refused to me. The other day,
I called with my credentials on General Heroys, the custodian of
the archives, and explained my mission. He was very nice and
expressed his regret because last summer the whole [collection]
was sent to the Crimea, so sure was he that Wrangel would win.
That almost settled that, but not quite. He still has a number
of valuable papers which he is offering us and also a box of war
books. One of the papers, a report by the commander–in–chief of
the Russian army in Romania, is promised for shipment tomorrow and other are to follow." See, Golder to Adams, 30 March
1921, p. 60, GP, Box 33.
59 Golder to Adams, 5 April 1921, pp. 63, 64, GP, Box 33.
60 Adams to Golder, 12 November 1920, p. 1, GP, Box 32. R.
W. Seton–Watson, *A History of the Roumanians* (Cambridge:
Cambridge University Press, 1934), pp. 526–550.
61 Golder to Adams, 30 March 1921, pp. 58, 61, GP, Box 33.
Hoover to Adams, 3 January 1921, Telegram, BAEF Papers,
Correspondence Series, Golder, HPL.

62 Dwyer, *Russian, Soviet Union, and Eastern European Collections at the Hoover Institution*, p. 209. Frank B. Singleton and Muriel Heppel, *Yugoslavia* (New York: Praeger, 1961), pp. 150, 156, 159.

63 Golder to Adams, 5 April 1921, p. 64, GP, Box 33. Golder to Adams, 10 April 1921, p. 68, *ibid.*

64 Golder to Adams, 10 April 1921, p. 70, *ibid.*

65 Golder to Lutz, 10 April 1921, pp. 72, 73–74, 78, *ibid.* Golder also commented about Zagreb, "The women are good to look upon and be it said to their credit they do not try to look through you as the women of certain cities." See, *ibid.*, p. 72.

66 Golder to Lutz, 10 April 1921, p. 73, *ibid.*

67 Golder to Adams, 19 April 1921, pp. 85, 83, *ibid.* Golder to Adams, 15 April 1921, pp. 77–78. While at Zagreb, Golder wrote that he received an "invitation of some . . . artists, [and] I visited their studios this morning and was delighted with what I saw. I understand now as I never have before how these people felt towards the Habsburgs. Every picture, every poem is full of the spirit of nationalism and idealism." See, *ibid.*, p. 78. Golder, Diary, 19 April 1921, GP, Box 33.

68 Golder to Adams, 30 April 1921, p. 1, GP, Box 32. Golder to Walter Brown, 18 August 1921, p. 1, BAEF Papers, Correspondence Series, Golder, HPL. Logan to Walter Brown, 28 July 1921, Cablegram, *ibid.* Walter Brown to Edgar Rickard, 29 July 1921, *ibid.*

69 Golder to Adams, 10 July 1921, p. 3, Box 32. Because of Golder's rapid travels in Europe and the small Hoover staff, he often had to work as if blindfolded without a continuous flow of information from the Hoover regarding his acquisitions that had arrived there. He wrote Lutz on 15 May 1921, "What is the next job? How is the collection coming on and what do you expect of me? Are we rounding out the collection? Are there gaps to be filled? Any information of that kind would be highly appreciated. I am so close to the work that I do not always see as I wish I could. Do not be afraid to make criticisms and suggestions. I am afraid I have scared Adams off from making criticism for I have not had any for a long time." See, Golder to Lutz, 15 May 1921, p. 3, GP, Box 32.

70 Hoover wrote, "Secretary of State Charles Evans Hughes, my colleague, agreed with me that the only possible source of relief (the ARA) should respond to this call of human suffering, that there was a remote possibility that a generous action by a free people might have some moderating influence upon the bloody

regime in the Kremlin, with its daily conspiracies against the free world, and that we should distinguish between 140,000,000 terrorized Russian people and the one or two million Communists who oppressed them." See, Hoover, *An American Epic*, Vol. III, p. 427. James P. Goodrich, "The plight of Russia," *The Outlook* 130 (11 January 1922): 66–68. Weissman, *Hoover and the Soviet Famine*, pp. 46–73. Charles Milton Edmondson, "Soviet Famine Relief Measure, 1921–1923," Ph. D. Dissertation, Florida State University, August 1970, pp. 51–52. Leon Trotsky, *My Life: An Attempt at an Autobiography* (New York: Charles Scribner's Sons, 1930), pp. 395, 465.

71 Golder to Lutz, 13 August 1921, p. 2, GP, Box 32.

72 *Ibid.*

73 Golder to Lutz, 18 August 1921, p. 1, GP, Box 32.

74 *Ibid.*

75 Golder to Walter Brown, 18 August 1921, p. 2, BAEF Papers, Correspondence Series, Golder, HPL.

76 Golder wrote Lutz, "All come to tell me how deeply interested they are in Hoover's scheme (of establishing an archival center so that scholars could describe World War I in all its phases so that future wars would be avoided) and how ready they are to cooperate. After talking to them about [this] it became evident that each visitor has a scheme of his own with which to save the world for peace and democracy and they would appreciate it very much if Hoover or some other American would finance it and in this way there would come about true cooperation. I usually refer them to you or to Hoover when I cannot get rid of them any other way. You do not have to talk to them, I do. Some of these poor professors who call are rather pitiful, full heads and empty stomachs and it makes my heart ache to watch them. Many of them do not earn more than 8,000 kronon a month or the equivalent of eight dollars, and on such pay one can starve." See, Golder to Lutz, 20 August 1921, p. 2, GP, Box 32.

77 Golder to Lutz, 20 August 1921, p. 2, GP, Box 32.

78 Golder to Adams, 27 August 1921, p. 1, GP, Box 32. Walter Brown to Miller, 26 August 1921, Telegram, BAEF Papers, Correspondence Series, Golder, HPL.

Notes to Chapter VI

1 Jacqueline St John, "John F. Stevens: American Assistance to Russian and Siberian Railroads, 1917–1922," (Ph.D. dissertation, University of Oklahoma, 1969), pp. 1–273.

2 Weissman, *Hoover and the Soviet Famine*, p. 36. Hoover, *An American Epic*, Vol. III, pp. 166–171.

3 Frank Golder and Lincoln Hutchinson, *On the Trail of the Russian Famine* (Stanford: Stanford University Press, 1927), pp. 27–28. This is a diary account of Golder's experiences during the Soviet famine. Cited hereafter as Golder, *Famine*.

4 *Ibid.*, p. 28.

5 The Tartar Republic was, in name, an autonomous government that had risen out of the Bolshevik principle of self–determination, but in reality the Republic was very closely tied to Moscow, receiving funds from the Soviet government and dependent on the Red army for its military protection.

6 Golder, *Famine*, pp. 28–35. Bill Shafroth, Inspection Trip to Volga, ARA Russian Unit, pp. 1–9, Box 87, Hoover Institution, Stanford, California. Cited hereafter as ARA Russian Unit. Shafroth, Article II: Kazan and the Tartar Socialist Soviet Republic, pp. 1–5, ARA Russian Unit, Box 87.

7 On the famine around Kazan, Shafroth wrote in his report, "periodic shortages have occurred which the peasants have always been able to tide over by the reserve stocks or by help from the [Tsarist] government. But this year there were no reserves, drought surplus stocks have been requisitioned, and the terrible drought all along the Volga River had brought a crop failure unexampled in the modern history of Russia, with no reserve supplies to meet the situation." See, Shafroth, Kazan . . . , p. 5, ARA Russian Unit, Box 87.

8 Shafroth, Inspection Trip to the Volga, p. 8, ARA Russian Unit, Box 87.

9 Golder recorded in his diary what one of these peasants said, "We cheered, we clapped our hands [during the revolution], and here we are dying of hunger and going hundreds of verts for a sack of potatoes and carrying it on our backs. We drove off the [landlords], we plundered his house, putting his picture and mirrors into our cow barns, we divided his land; and what is the result? We are famishing, the land is untilled, and the country is becoming a graveyard. Fools, we Russians are; we are not fit for freedom. God has turned his face from us, and the civilized world regards us as unclean, as the children of the devil. It is a good thing we are dying. We get what we deserve." See, Golder, *Famine*, p. 43.

10 Golder, *Famine*, p. 42. The peasants also told Golder that "the hunger is so great in Simbirsk that some mothers have abandoned their children in the marketplace, while others have killed them

and then committed suicide." See, *ibid.*
11 *Ibid.*
12 Hoff–Wilson writes, "during [1917 and 1921] 90 percent of Russian industrial and agrarian production was disrupted or destroyed, but most contemporary observers did not realize that this economic disintegration was a product more of the war than of Bolshevik rule. Moreover, the significant, if erratic, industrialization of the Russian economy in the late nineteenth century had made substantial progress by the eve of World War I, and that progress ultimately gave the Bolsheviks a solid base upon which to build, once they brought the revolution, civil war, armed intervention, and famine under control. Any new government would have faced economic chaos for a few years; the Bolsheviks under Lenin provided no exception. See, Hoff–Wilson, *Ideology*, p. 4.
13 Golder, *Famine*, p. 103.
14 *Ibid.*, p. 43.
15 *Ibid.*, p. 47.
16 Weissman, *Hoover and the Soviet Famine*, p. 95.
17 Golder, *Famine*, p. 49.
18 *Ibid.*, p. 50.
19 *Ibid.*, pp. 55–57.
20 Golder to Holland, 26 October 1921, p. 1, HP, WSUA.
21 Shafroth, Article IV: Eight Months in the Russian Famine Area, pp. 4–6, ARA Russian Unit, Box 87. Golder, *Famine*, p. 69.
22 Peter G. Filene writes, "What [Hoover] said about the European Children's Relief in 1921 also held true for Russian relief: American charity 'had planted the American flag in the hearts of all those little ones' and it is a greater protection to the United States than battleships.' This preoccupation with identifying relief as American explains his demand that the ARA be independent of Soviet control and that all American relief groups be subordinate to the ARA. For Wilson, words served as the vanguard of democracy in Russia; for Hoover, food was the vanguard." See, Filene, *Soviet Experiment*, p. 78.
Weissman quotes Leon Trotsky as saying, "Of course, help to the starving is spontaneous philanthropy, but there are few real philantropists—even among American Quakers. (Hoover came from a Quaker background.) Philanthropy is tied to business, to enterprises, to interests—if not today, then tomorrow." Weissman adds, "Trotsky compared relief workers to the advance guard of missionaries that precedes soldiers and merchants; the goal of relief missionaries of 1921 was obviously to open the Russian market to the bourgeoisie and thus to relieve 'the great and un-

precedented trade–industrial crisis all over the world, especially in America and England.' " See, Weissman, *Hoover and the Soviet Famine.*, pp. 18–19.

23 Weissman, *Hoover and the Soviet Famine*, pp. 39–40.

24 Shafroth, Article V: Eight Months in the Russian Famine, pp. 2–6, ARA Russian Unit, Box 87.

25 *Ibid.* p. 2.

26 *Ibid.*, pp. 5–6. Golder, *Famine*, pp. 72–73.

27 Golder, *Famine*, p. 74.

28 Golder to H. Eliot, 3 October 1921, p. 4, GP, Box 12.

29 Golder to Adams, 3 October 1921, p. 1, GP, Box 32.

30 Golder to Adams, 3 October 1921, p. 111, GP, Box 33.

31 Golder to Lutz, 3 October 1921, p. 115, *ibid.*

32 Golder to H. Eliot, 8 October 1921, p. 3, GP, Box 12. James P. Goodrich, "Impressions of the Bolshevik Regime," *The Century* (May 1922): 64–65.

33 Hoover, *Memoirs*, Vol. 2, p. 23. From this trip, Goodrich would later recommend to Hoover that fifteen to twenty million adults and children in Russia would perish unless the ARA expanded its feeding operations.

34 Golder, *Famine*, p. 75.

35 *Ibid.*, p. 98.

36 *Ibid.*, p. 100.

37 *Ibid.*

38 *Ibid.*, p. 101.

39 Golder to Adams, 7 November 1921, GP, Box 33. A few days earlier, Golder wrote to the President of Washington State College, Holland, "I wish you could see the land of the famine region. It puts our Palouse soil to shame. . . . In some parts the black soil is four to five feet deep. Yet, notwithstanding all these blessings, thousands are dying of hunger. (Between one to two million Russians died during the famine.) There are many reasons for this, one of them being poor agricultural methods. There is more than enough rain for dry farming purposes but these people know nothing about it. They possess poor tools, some are still wooden and primitive, and with these the surface of the soil is scratched and the seed put in and when tender roots are formed the sun comes out and burns them. If some of our farmers were let loose here for a few years they would make enough to live in Pasadena the rest of their days." See, Golder to Holland, 26 October 1921, p. 2, HP, WSUA.

40 Golder to Adams, 16 November 1921, p. 1, BAEF Papers, Hoover Institution Collectors: Golder, HPL. Within the ARA

itself there was discord. Weissman writes, the ARA in Europe "had become accustomed to a loosely structured organization. Occasionally, the Chief (Hoover) would visit the scene of operations to check that his policies were being effectively carried out. This was not possible in Russia, and none of the ARA officials in Moscow had the stature that insured reflexive obedience. Hoover may have had this in mind when he chose to bypass the ARA staff in appointing a high–ranking regular army officer as head of the Russian mission." See, Weissman, *Hoover and the Soviet Famine*, p. 83. Golder wrote of Haskell's appointment, "It was a mistake to put Colonel Haskell and his military crowd in command here. The old ARA men chafe under it, and resent it, and as a result the morale is not what it should be." See, Golder to Adams, 3 October 1921, p. 111, Box 33.

41 Weissman, *Hoover and the Soviet Famine*, pp. 93–95.

42 Golder to Adams, 16 November 1921, p. 1, BAEF Papers, Hoover Institution Collectors: Golder, HPL.

43 Golder did object to the participants' carelessness at this party. He wrote, "The pitiful part of it all is that we are housed in a museum where there are many rare treasures and beautiful things, finest furniture, and the pigs are crawling all over it, throwing cigarettes around and more of the like." See, Golder to Lutz, 24 November 1921, p. 130, GP, Box 33.

44 Golder, Investigation in the Ukraine, 4 December 1921, p. 1, Box 264, ARA Russian Unit. Weissman, *Hoover and the Soviet Famine*, pp. 83–94.

45 Golder, *Famine*, p. 119, Golder, Record of Interviews in Kharkov, 4 December 1921, pp. 1–3, Box 264, ARA Russian Unit.

46 Quoted in, Harold Fisher, *The Famine in Soviet Russia, 1919–1923* (New York: Macmillan, 1927), p. 250. Cited hereafter as Fisher, *Famine in Soviet Russia*. Golder, Record of Interviews in Kharkov, 4 December 1921, pp. 1–3, ARA Russian Unit, Box 264. Golder and Lincoln Hutchinson, Ukraine Preliminary Report, 7 December 1921, pp. 1–5, *ibid.*, Box 85.

47 Golder, Record of Interviews in Kharkov, 4 December 1921, p. 3, Box 264, ARA Russian Unit.

48 Golder and Lincoln Hutchinson, Ukraine Preliminary Report, 7 December 1921, p. 4, ARA Russian Unit.

49 Fisher, *Famine in Soviet Russia*, pp. 252–253. Lincoln Hutchinson, Report on the Ukraine, 19 January 1922, pp. 1–5, Box 85, ARA Russian Unit. Weissman, *Hoover and the Soviet Famine*, pp. 94–95. On Ukrainian nationalism, Golder wrote, "The Ukrainian nationalist movement has little to recommend it. There

is less physical difference between the North and South Russians than between the North and South Germans, or Italians. For many years the movement was limited to a few parlor nationalists, socialists, and other disgruntled professors and students; but when the authorities tried to suppress it the number of the nationalists increased. At the time of the outbreak of the war probably ninety–nine percent of the inhabitants of Russian Ukraine were untouched by the nationalist movement. The Russian revolution with the propaganda of self–determination, also the establishment of a separate Ukrainian government by the Germans, and the creation of a Ukrainian state with definite boundaries, have all helped to spread the idea of nationalism among the lower classes. The local politicians and office seekers may be depended upon to spread the separatist idea and stand in the way of a strongly centralized Russia." See, Golder, *Famine*, p. 115.

50 Golder to Lutz, 6 October 1921, p. 116, GP, Box 33. Libbey, *Gumberg*, p. 127. Golder wrote Adams, "Stanford University must make a special effort to buy now, while buying is cheap and collections are thrown on the market. It is the opportunity of the century." See, Golder to Adams, 19 October 1921, p. 14, GP, Box 32.

51 Golder to Lutz, 6 October 1921, p. 116, GP, Box 33. Concerning book purchases, Golder also wrote Adams, "Let me add that I will probably use up all the balance of the [$2,000], and some more. I hold myself personally responsible for these purchases and pay for them with my own money. We have a very rare opportunity in Russia, and I am going to take advantage of it to the full, and some day the scholars everywhere will come to Stanford to study and thank us." See, Golder to Adams, 23 October 1921, p. 119, GP, Box 33.

52 Golder to Adams, 30 December 1921, p. 143, GP, Box 33.

53 Golder to Adams, 8 December 1921, p. 132, *ibid.*

54 Golder to Adams, 22 December 1921, p. 138, *ibid.*

55 *Ibid.*

56 *Ibid.* Golder had become discouraged with the Bolsheviks, whom he thought spent too much time on theoretical rather than practical matters. He wrote, "The country is in ruins, and I wish I could see sunshine ahead. So much suffering, so much talking, so much arresting, so much stealing, so much demoralizing one finds nowhere else, and while Rome burns the [Soviets] leaders fiddle." See, Golder to Lutz, 15 December 1921, p. 134, GP, Box 33. Golder also wrote, "Our men in the field report terrible conditions. Disease and death are spreading and whole villages

are becoming empty. Now is not the time to theorize but to work along old lines. Unless there is a change to practical ways of life there is no hope. I am not defending capitalism with all its evils but I insist in a time like this the old way is the good way." See, Golder to H. Eliot, 2 December 1921, p. 1, GP, Box 12.

[57] Golder, The Ivanov's: A Christmas Story, pp. 1–2, HP, WUSA. Golder to H. Eliot, 22 December 1921, p. 2, GP, Box 12.

[58] Weissman writes, "There was . . . . the strong possibility that a large congressional appropriation would have a beneficial effect on farm prices and ultimately on the [U. S.] economy as a whole. To Hoover, the effect of the appropriation on the national economy was not immaterial." In spite of the fact that the Red Scare still aroused intolerance, there was not overwhelming opposition to the bill. Hoover sent his agents and leaders of agricultural groups to lobby for the passage of the bill. See, Weissman, *Hoover and the Soviet Famine*, pp. 97–98.

[59] Golder to Lutz, 3 October 1921, p. 109, GP, Box 33.

[60] Weissman, *Hoover and the Soviet Famine*, pp. 110, 113.

[61] Golder to Adams, 30 December 1921, p. 145, GP, Box 33.

[62] While in Soviet Russia, Golder tried to keep in contact with collecting matters in other European countries. He wrote Adams, "Enclosed you will find a long list of materials which has been presented to us by the authorities at Vilna (Poland). Will you please acknowledge it. . . . Our friends in the ARA mission at Warsaw have written me to say that the material is being sent." Golder to Lutz, 22 December 1921, p. 136, GP, Box 33.

[63] Golder, *Famine*, p. 147. Golder to Lutz, 1 January 1922, p. 174, GP, Box 33.

[64] Golder, *Famine*, p. 148.

[65] Golder to Lutz, 1 January 1922, pp. 179–180, GP, Box 33. In his diary on 19 January 1922, Golder wrote less critically of the proletariat and culture. "It should be said to the credit of the Soviet that it has given the workman an idea of art that he did not have before. When the revolution broke out, the operas, ballets, and plays were thrown open to the proletariat, who greatly enjoyed them." See, Golder, *Famine*, p. 158.

[66] *Ibid.* The following day, Golder found a different audience at a ballet. He wrote, "On New Year's Eve . . . workingmen were allowed to come in free, but on New Year's night a high admission fee was charged and Ivan could not afford to attend. The many profiteers who were present were well dressed, some in evening clothes, and many of them wore diamonds and pearls of the old aristocracy and bourgeoisie. This new rich class is as

yet less cultured, less gentlemanly than the old, but it is more unscrupulous and more grasping." See, Golder, *Famine*, p. 150. Golder also could not tolerate bourgeois pretensions. He wrote, "While at the opera tonight (21 January 1922) I saw a classic example of parvenuism. In a prominent box sat a speculator with his richly dressed wife. They placed in front of them a box of delicious sweets, and in the presence of the [proletariat] onlookers peeled an orange (oranges are as rare in Petrograd as in the Arctic), put it on the sweets, and walked out." See, Golder, *Famine*, p. 159.

67 Golder, *Famine*, p. 147.
68 *Ibid.* Golder to Lutz, 1 January 1922, p. 174, GP, Box 33.
69 Golder to Adams, 30 January 1922, p. 212, GP, Box 33. Golder to Lutz, 4 January 1922, p. 183, GP, Box 33.
70 Golder to Lutz, 4 January 1922, p. 183, *ibid.*
71 Golder to Adams, 30 January 1922, p. 212, GP, Box 33. Golder wrote Adams, too, "I am telling you all this not to praise my work, for I have made many mistakes, but to explain what we have, for it will please you."
72 Golder to Adams, 11 January 1922, p. 196, GP, Box 33.
73 Golder to Adams, 30 January 1922, p. 210, *ibid.* Fisher, *Famine in Soviet Russia*, p. 281.
74 Golder to Lutz, 31 January 1922, p. 215, GP, Box 33.
75 Golder, *Famine*, p. 160. Golder to Lutz, 1 February 1922, p. 217, GP, Box 33.
76 Golder, *Famine*, p. 160. Golder to Lutz, 1 February 22, p. 218, GP, Box 33. Golder wrote that Colonel Haskell, "was mad and went to talk to the representative of the Soviet government and, though I did not hear his language, yet, from reports that have come to me, I dare say it was picturesque. . . ." See, *ibid.*
77 Golder, *Famine*, p. 161.
78 *Ibid.*
79 *Ibid.* Exhaustion always seemed to hang over Golder, and he often became cold. Illness might come at any time. He wrote, though, humorously about how he took care of himself: "I have had the same suit of clothes (two) on me ever since September, and the wind is beginning to find openings; my overcoat is a second hand chauffeur's coat that the Red Cross in Riga gave me, and my fur cap is the kind the Mushiks wear. It has advantages, for I look quite like a Bolo and the highwaymen of Petrograd let me pass." See, Golder to Adams, 30 January 1922, p. 213, GP, Box 33.
80 Golder, *Famine.*, p. 164.

[81] *Ibid.*, pp. 164–165.

[82] *Ibid.*, p. 165.

[83] *Ibid.*

[84] *Ibid.*

[85] *Ibid.*, p. 174.

[86] Quoted in Fisher, *Famine in Soviet Russia*, p. 282. Golder and Lincoln Hutchinson, "Investigation of Food Conditions in Transcausia," 13 March 1922, pp. 1–8, ARA Russian Unit, Box 85. Golder to H. Eliot, 13 March 1922, pp. 1–2, GP, Box 12. Golder, Diary, 18 February, GP, Box 15. Golder reported an example of class conflict regarding professors. "Lately some of the professors from the Crimea appealed to their colleagues in Moscow and Petrograd to do something for them. One of the local professors called on the representative of the Crimean government in Moscow. The representative is a young communist, and when the professor said that the professors in the Crimea were dying of hunger, she said, 'What of it, let them die.' " See, Golder to Adams, 2 April 1922, p. 242, GP, Box 33.

[87] Golder met Dzerzhinsky, but completely misjudged him as a capable railway administrator, although accurately describing his commitment to the Bolshevik Revolution. Golder wrote, "Dzerzhinsky is a thoroughly honest, conscientious fanatic who has formed his ideas during the ten years that he spent [in exile] in Siberia. He is about as much fitted to run a railway as I am, but he is better qualified merely because he is a communist. He is like an inquisitor of old: he regards Communism as a religion, and those who disagree with him are heretics to be rooted out." See, Golder to Lutz, 2 April 1922, p. 240, GP, Box 33. See, also, Weissman's view of Dzerzhinsky, portraying him as having a quite friendly and efficient working relationship with Colonel Haskell, *Hoover and the Soviet Famine*, p. 115.

[88] Weissman, *Hoover and the Soviet Famine*, pp. 113–116.

[89] Golder to Lutz, 2 April 1922, p. 240, GP, Box 33.

[90] By 1925, under Golder's direction, the Russian collection at the Hoover Library involved 1,000,000 letters and documents, 20, 340 manuscripts, 127,500 pamphlets, 28,500 printed volumes, 172,000 newspapers, periodicals, and trench papers, 15, 150 posters, photographs, and watercolors. See, Summary of Materials in the Hoover War Library, 4 August 1925, Russian Collection, HIR, Box 156. Lutz wrote in 1923, "[The Russian Collection] covers all phases of Russian history since 1914 and contains inestimable source materials on Russian foreign policy, the overthrow of the Kerensky government, and the Bolshevik revolution. This is

without doubt the most extensive collection which has come out of Russia since 1914 and, together with other Russian materials now here, forms the best archive beyond the Russian borders for a study of Bolshevism." See, Ralph H. Lutz, "The Hoover War Library Grows Yearly in Importance as a Great Field for Historical Research," *Stanford Illustrated Review* (June 1923): 465.

91 Golder to Lutz, 1 April 1922, p. 231. GP, Box 33.

92 Golder to Adams, 3 April 1922, p. 240, GP, Box 33. William Bentinck–Smith, *Building a Great Library: The Coolidge Years at Harvard* (Cambridge: Harvard University Press, 1976), pp. 126–128. One must acknowledge Coolidge's influence on the development of great libraries in the United States, as well as his influence on his students to develop scholarship on Russian history. Byrnes writes, "Coolidge's influence extended throughout the American library world . . . because he educated and excited . . . other graduate students on the role of university libraries, their needs, and programs for enlarging and administrating them." See, Byrnes, *Coolidge*, pp. 129–130. "As the principal founder of Russian studies in the United States, Coolidge exercised profound influence in awakening and then shaping American research and instruction on that country and its culture. Those specialists whom he trained, such as Frank Golder . . . benefited from the depth of his knowledge, the perspective and insights he had acquired. . . ." See, *ibid.*, p. 68.

93 Adams to Golder, 19 April 1922, p. 2, GP, Box 32.

94 Lutz to Golder, 15 April 1922, p. 2, *ibid.*

95 Lutz to Golder, 1 March 1922, pp. 1–2, *ibid.*

96 Lutz to Golder, 15 April 1922, p. 2, *ibid.*

Notes to Chapter VII

1 Golder to Lutz, 4 April 1922, p. 74, GP, Box 32.

2 Four months later, four large crates containing Swiss publications left Berne for Stanford. See, Wilson to Golder, 19 July 1922, p. 1, GP, Box 32.

3 Golder to Lutz, 11 April 1922, misdated 1921, p. 75, GP, Box 33.

4 Ralph H. Lutz, "Hoover War Library," *Army Ordinance* 11 (1930): 333. Golder to Adams, 6 July 1922, p. 269, GP, Box 33.

5 Golder to Adams, 15 April 1922, p. 2, GP, Box 33. Golder also noted that the job of copying the secret Turkish documents at Constantinople had fallen through.

6 Golder to Lutz, 17 April 1922, p. 1, GP, Box 32.

7 On his way to Rome, Golder rode on the train with Colonel James A. Logan. Golder wrote Lutz, "Colonel Logan (by the way he prefers not to be called by his military title and is anxious to forget that he was one of the gang) came down on the same train with me as far as Genoa [to attend the Genoa Conference as an unofficial American observer]. He has had an interesting war and reconstruction experience and has many valuable personal papers. (Logan was assistant Chief of Staff to General Pershing, participated as an unofficial delegate on the Reparations Commission, and headed the ARA Paris office. For several years after the war he was an unofficial U. S. observer at nearly every international conference.) He said something about burning his [personal papers] and I urged him to deposit them with us. The matter should be brought to Hoover's attention and if he asked Logan to do it he would, I think, do it." Logan did give a number of valuable papers to the Hoover Library. See, Golder to Lutz, 24 April 1922, p. 3, GP, Box 32.

8 Golder to Lutz, 24 April 1922, p. 1, GP, Box 32. Golder to Gay, 6 November 1922, p. 1, *ibid.* Golder to Gay, 24 April 1922, pp. 1–2, *ibid.* Gay to Golder, 18 November 1922, p. 1, *ibid.*

9 Golder to Lutz, 24 April 1922, p. 1, GP, Box 32.

10 Golder to Lutz, 30 April 1922, p. 1, GP, Box 32.

11 *Ibid.*

12 *Ibid.*

13 Charles Keserich, "The Political Odessey of George D. Herron," *San Jose State Studies* (February 1977): 85, 87. Cited hereafter as Keserich, "Herron–Political Odessey."

14 Golder to Adams, 31 May 1922, misdated 1921, pp. 95, 93–94.

15 *Ibid.*, pp. 93–94. Herron's motive for giving his papers to the Hoover Library may have been his disillusionment with the Paris Peace Conference. Charles Keserich writes, "Herron believed that Wilson's program would be carried out, that America would become a messianic nation creating a new world without war and a human life approaching the kingdom of heaven." But, in 1919, Herron thought the Paris Peace Conference 'the most catastrophic failure . . . of human history,' [and] had not created a redeeming peace but one of 'squalid controversies, bestial greed, and idiotic revenge.' " See, Keserich, "Herron–Political Odessey." p. 89.

16 Herron had a penchant for messianic philosophy. During his lifetime, he visualized man's redemption through religion, then through socialism, then through Wilsonian liberalism, and lastly

through Italian fascism. Herron also had a notorious past, involving a moral controversy in 1901 for having lived with one Carrie Rand while married to another woman. Herron then divorced his wife and soon after married Rand, a woman of considerable wealth, in an unconventional ceremony: each chose the other as companion. This controversy earned Herron the label of being an advocate of free love and led to his expulsion as pastor of the Congregational Church of Iowa. The controversy also resulted in Herron being pressed to quit his professorship of theology at Grinnell College. Herron then moved to Florence, Italy, where he bought a villa and lived a life without the pressures of economic necessity. He immersed himself in intellectual activity, entertained a steady stream of visitors, corresponded with a wide variety of men and women, and wrote articles for European and American journals. Mitchell Briggs writes, "[Herron had] an acquaintanceship with Europe that was probably unsurpassed by that of any other American." See, Mitchell Brigs, *George D. Herron and the European Settlement* (New York: AMS press, reprinted 1971 from 1932), pp. 11–12. Concerning Herron's controversial past, Golder pronounced him ". . . very sane. I do not fear him on that score." See, Golder to Adams, 31 May 1922, misdated 1921, p. 95, GP, Box 33. See also, Charles Keserich, "George D. Herron: Il Nostro Americano," *Il Politico* XLI (1976): 315–332.

[17] Golder to Adams, 31 May 1922, p. 97, GP, Box 33. Golder also wrote in the same letter, "In the last few days, I have learned so many secrets from Goodrich and Logan as to what is going on behind the scenes that it quite overwhelms me. I am forced to believe that high finance and dollar diplomacy is running this little world of ours." *Ibid.*, p. 95.

[18] Golder to Adams, 25 June 1922, p. 267, GP, Box 33.

[19] *The National Cyclopedia of American Biography*, Vol. 30 (New York: J. T. White, 1944), pp. 76–77. Individuals involved in agriculture tended to favor trade with Soviet Russia.

[20] Goodrich to Hoover, 18 February 1922, p. 3, ARA Russian Unit, Box 276. Goodrich feared that France and Germany would take over the Russian market before the United States had a chance to do so, but thought, "We are the one country which has no selfish purpose in Russia. France is moved by no idealistic motives and cares nothing for the Russian people." *Ibid.*, p. 3. Yet, in another letter to Hoover, Goodrich, writes Weissman, "recommended recognition of Russia as an effective instrument for moderating and finally replacing the Bolshevik regime." See,

Weissman, *Hoover and the Soviet Regime,* p. 109 and Goodrich
to Hoover, 3 April 1922, p. 1, ARA Russian Unit, Box 85.

21 The ARA's generous allotments of food, medicine, and hospital
equipment actually helped the Bolsheviks to increase their authority in Soviet Russia. See, Joan Hoff–Wilson, *Herbert Hoover:
The Forgotten Progressive* (Boston: Little, Brown & Co., 1975),
pp. 197–198.

Hoover wrote to Woodrow Wilson in 1919, "We cannot even re-
motely recognize this murderous tyranny without stimulating ac-
tionist radicalism in every country in Europe and without trans-
gressing on every national ideal of our own." See, Hoover to
Wilson, 28 March 1919, p. 4, Herbert Hoover Archives, Hoover
Institution, Stanford, California, Box 326. Lewis S. Feuer supplies an economic motive behind Hoover's ideological opposition
to the Soviet regime. Feuer writes that prior to World War I,
"Hoover, [a mining engineer], developed in Siberia 'probably the
greatest and richest single body of ore known in the world,' ore
of such quality as 'had hitherto existed only in museum spec-
imens.' He reorganized the Kyshtim mines and smelter works
(which made Hoover a millionaire). Hoover hated the Bolshevik revolution. It deprived him, as he said, of what would have
been 'the largest engineering fees ever known to man.' His staff
of 160 American technicians, which had once been welcomed to
Russia, was deported by the communists . . ." See, Lewis
S. Feuer, "American Travelers to the Soviet Union, 1917–1932:
The Formation of a Component of New Deal Ideology," *American Quarterly* 14 (Summer 1962): 137. Wilson, *Ideology,* pp. 21,
28, 44.

22 Weissman, *Hoover and the Soviet Famine,* p. 135. To bring
Hoover around to the idea of discussions with the Soviets, Good-
rich wrote, "I am certain that Lenin has deliberately embarked
upon his program to do away with the Cheka (replaced by the
GPU), to restore fully the rights of private property in industry
(NEP), and to bring about a situation in Russia that will justify
our country in recognizing them." See, Goodrich to Hoover, 18
February 1922, p. 3, ARA Russian Unit, Box 276.

23 Golder to Hoover, 4 June 1920, p. 1, ARA Russian Unit, Box
276. Golder to H. Eliot, 22 December 1921, p. 1, GP, Box 12.
Golder to Christian Herter, 10 August 1922, p. 1, GP, Box 12.
Golder to Goodrich, 17 September 1922, p. 3, James P. Goodrich
papers, Russia: Golder, HPL.

24 Golder to Adams, 10 June 1922, p. 252, GP, Box 33.

25 Weissman, *Hoover and the Soviet Famine,* p. 124.

26 Fischer, *Lenin*, p. 557. Vladimir Lenin, *Collected Works*, Vol. 33: *August 1921–March 1923*, 45 Vols. (Moscow: Progress Publishers, 1966), pp. 112, 225, 288, 297.

27 Weissman, *Hoover and the Soviet Famine*, pp. 124–130.

28 Hoover to Hughes, 6 December 1921, Frame 907, Roll 181, Warren Harding Papers, Ohio Historical Society, Columbus, Ohio. Cited hereafter as WHP.

29 Robert Murray, *The Harding Era: Warren G. Harding and His Administration* (Minneapolis: University of Minnesota Press, 1966), pp. 348–354. Weissman, *Hoover and the Soviet Famine*, pp. 109–110. Hoff–Wilson, *Ideology*, p. 67. Louis Fischer, *Why Recognize Russia?* (New York: Jonathan Cape & Harrison Smith, 1931), pp. 63–64.

30 Golder wrote, "Radek and I have become quite chummy and he was over for dinner at the Pink House tonight and talked most interestingly to the boys. . . . We are going to keep him supplied with American books of political importance. . . . It is exceedingly important for us to keep in good relations." See, Golder to Harold H. Fisher, 4 December 1922, p. 1, ARA Russian Unit, Box 261. Warren Lerner, *Karl Radek: The Last Internationalist* (Stanford: Stanford University Press, 1970), p. 66. Golder, writing about Radek's willingness to talk, stated, "The Reds have an excellent spy system. Radek told me the other evening that some weeks ago he was in the office of the chief of the Berlin secret police and in talking to him showed him photograph documents from the chief's safe." See, Golder to Lutz, 11 January 1923, GP, Box 33.

31 Golder, Conversation between Governor Goodrich and Representatives of the Soviet Government, n.d., pp. 2–3, ARA Russian Unit, Box 276. Anne Meiburger, *Efforts of Raymond Robins toward the Recognition of Soviet Russia and Outlawry of War, 1917–1933* (Washington, D.C.: The Catholic University of American Press, 1958), p. 80.

32 Goodrich wrote Hughes that the Soviets "[are] exceedingly anxious to reach an agreement with America and show a willingness substantially to meet conditions [of] your note, March 25, could [a] separate agreement be made." See quote in Meiburger, *Robins*, p. 80.

33 Golder to Christian Herter, 15 March 1923, p. 545, GP, Box 33. Lloyd C. Gardner, *Wilson and Revolutions, 1913–1921* (San Jose: J. B. Lippincott, 1976), p. 55.

34 The amount of U. S. private funds available to Tsarist Russia was relatively small. The Imperial government secured enormous

sums of American money, but via private loans to France and Britain. The U. S. showed little concern for the Tsarist debts to other countries. However, the U.S. did expect the Soviets to repay U. S. government credits and private loans to the Provisional Government. See, Press Release Issued by the State Department, 21 March 1923, p. 757, *FRUS, 1923*, Vol. 2. Hughes to Coolidge, 6 May 1922, p. 877, *FRUS, 1922*, Vol. 2. Betty Glad, *Charles Evans Hughes and the Illusion of Innocence: A Study of American Diplomacy* (Urbana: University of Illinois Press, 1966), pp. 312–313.

[35] Many governments, including the United States, have repudiated their war debts. See, Adam B. Ulam, *Expansion and Coexistence: The History of Soviet Foreign Policy, 1917–1967* (New York: Praeger, 1968), p. 148.

[36] Golder, History of Conversation . . ., pp. 4–5, ARA Russian Unit, Box 276. Goodrich to Hoover, 19 June 1922, p. 1, *ibid.* Fischer, *Lenin*, p. 557. Harold G. Moulton and Leo Pasvolsky, *World War Debt Settlements* (New York: Macmillan, 1926), p. 62.

[37] Quoted in Libbey, *Gumberg*, pp. 98–99. Goodrich wrote a long report for Harding, advocating trade with the Soviets. See, Goodrich to Harding, 28 June 1922, Frames 1000 and 1001, WHP, Roll 181.

[38] Other individuals who supported this American commission plan actively and were Goodrich's allies in improved U.S.–Soviet relations, were William Borah, a Senator with agricultural connections, Raymond Robins, a wealthy former miner who was influential in Republican politics, and Alexander Gumberg, who became a banking and Amtorg Trading Corporation advisor for trade with the Soviets. To date, there is no scholarly biography of Raymond Robins, but for an interesting discussion of Robins' political and economic interest in the Bolshevik Revolution's success (Robins headed the American Red Cross in Moscow, 1917–1918, which had more to do with politics than saving peoples' lives) see, Anthony C. Sutton, *Wall Street and the Bolshevik Revolution* (New York: Arlington House, 1974), pp.71–112. For a biography of Gumberg, see James Libbey, *Alexander Gumberg and Soviet-American Relations, 1917–1933* (Lexington, Kentucky: University Press of Kentucky, 1977). For Borah, see Robert Maddox, *William E. Borah and American Foreign Policy* (Louisiana: Baton Rouge, 1969). Goodrich to Golder, 17 July 1922, pp. 1–2, GP, Box 32. Murray, *Harding*, pp. 348, 353–353. Williams, *American–Russian Relations*, p. 198.

39 Hoff–Wilson, *Ideology*, p. 44. William Appleman Williams, *Rise of an American World Power Complex*, pp. 1–19, in Neal D. Houghton, ed., *Struggle Against History: U. S. Foreign Policy in an Age of Revolution* (New York: Simon & Schuster, 1968).

40 Christian Herter to Golder, 8 August 1922, p. 1, GP, Box 32. Herter to Golder, 21 August 1922, p. 1, ARA Russian Unit, Box 261.

41 Golder to Herter, 10 September 1922, p. 2, GP, Box 15. Ray Lyman Wilbur to Hoover, 31 July 1922, p. 1, ARA Russian Unit, Box 261. Herter to Wilbur, 7 August 1922, p. 1, *ibid.* Herter to Kliefoth, 9 August 1922, p. 1, *ibid.*

42 Golder to Herter, 10 September 1922, p. 2, GP, Box 15.

43 Goodrich to Golder, 27 July 1922, p. 2, GP, Box 32. Libbey, *Gumberg*, p. 99.

44 Herter to Poole, 20 June 1922, p. 1, ARA Russian Unit, Box 261. Herter to Kliefoth, 9 August 1922, *ibid.*

45 Golder to Herter, 2 January 1923, p. 5, James P. Goodrich Papers, Russia: Golder, HPL. Golder to Herter, 10 August 1922, pp. 314–315, Box 33. Golder to Herter, 18 August 1922, pp. 322–323, GP, *ibid.* Golder to Herter, 22 August 1922, p. 326, *ibid.* Golder to Adams, 9 July 1922, pp. 1–5, James P. Goodrich Papers, Russia: Golder, HPL.

46 Golder to Herter, 10 September 1922, p. 6, James P. Goodrich, Russia: Golder, HPL. Golder to Goodrich, 17 September 1922, p. 1, *ibid.* Harold H. Fisher, Trip to Odessa, 29 August 1922, pp. 1–14, ARA Russian Unit, Box 84.

47 Golder to Herter, 10 September 1922, p. 4, James P. Goodrich Papers, Russia: Golder, HPL.

48 Goodrich to Golder, 5 September 1922, p. 1, GP, Box 32.

49 Golder to Herter, 20 September 1922, p. 359, GP, Box 33. Houghton to Hughes, 1 August 1922, pp. 829–830, *FRUS, 1922*, Vol. 2. Houghton to Philips, 18 September 1922, p. 834, *FRUS, 1922*, Vol. 2. Philips to Harding, 15 September 1922, Frames 1048 to 1977, Roll 181, WHP. Weissman, *Hoover and the Soviet Famine*, pp. 136–137. In a conversation with Radek two months after the Berlin negotiations fell through, Golder wrote, "We took up Russo–American relations. He assured me that now (perhaps due to Golder's influence) the leading Commissars are convinced that the offer of the American government to send a commission was a friendly act. From this, I was [told] that it was not always so understood. The fact that our government has several times in the course of this year refused a visa to Krassin and other leaders and at the same time asked permission to send an

official commission to Russia with powers to go into any department of the Soviet government and ask for official documents, etc., puzzled him not a little, especially Lenin. It seemed as if we tried to humiliate the Soviets. [Still, the Soviet government] desires nothing better than to tie up with America." See, Golder to Herter, 22 November 1922, p. 413, GP, Box 33.

[50] Golder to Herter, 20 September 1922, p. 359, GP, Box 33.

[51] *Ibid.*

[52] Floyd James Fithian, "Soviet–American Economic Relations, 1918–1933: American Business in Russia during the Period of Nonrecognition," (Ph. D. dissertation, University of Nebraska, 1964), p. 84. Golder to Friends, 8 January 1923, p. 2, GP, Box 15. Goodrich to Golder, 5 September 1922, p. 1, GP, Box 32.

[53] Goodrich to Golder, 18 December 1922, p. 1, GP, Box 32. In early October, Golder had a meeting with Rykov, who had replaced Lenin in the Politburo, and they discussed the American commission controversy. Rykov said that the Politburo had seriously debated the United States commission proposal, but that the Soviets could not understand what other information a United States commission could want since the ARA had plenty of information regarding Soviet Russia's economy. In this opinion, the ARA "is the best informed organization in the world on all questions relating to Russia." Rykov's objections notwithstanding, Golder wrote Herter that Rykov stated, "[The Politburo members] are extremely anxious to bring about relations with the United States. Rykov is particularly eager that American capital should undertake the development of Siberia and the Caucasus." See, Golder to Herter, 4 October 1922, p. 389, GP, Box 33.

[54] Golder to Herter, 16 October 1922, pp. 391–392, GP, Box 33.

[55] Hoff–Wilson, *Ideology*, p. 70.

[56] Golder to H. Eliot, 27 October 1922, p. 2, Box 12. Golder to Adams, 28 October 1923, p. 1, Box 32. Keserich, *Herron–Il Nostro Americano*, p. 315.

[57] Golder to H. Eliot, 27 October 1922, p. 2, GP, Box 12. On this trip to Italy, Golder had an opportunity to view Mussolini's Italy. He wrote, "The Fascists are active. Yesterday they would not let me go to Rome, they would not let me telegraph to Paris. They stand outside of the post office in black shirts and black caps. It is an interesting experiment that they are trying and I trust that it does not prove costly. After seeing the Russian experiment, I am a bit afraid of experiments. I wonder if I can get away today." See, *ibid.*, p. 3.

58 Herron's second wife, Carrie Rand, died in 1914.

59 In London, Golder recorded his irritation with Russian émigrés. He wrote, "When they come across someone who has come out of Russia, they pounce on him with questions, not for the purpose of getting real information, but for confirmation of their preconceived ideas. If you do not agree, then it is proved ipso facto that 'you do not understand the Russian peasant.' The very fact that all this misery exists in Russia might convince these nobles that they do not understand, but it is a waste of words. The point of view of these émigrés almost makes me a Bolo when I am with them." See, Golder to Lutz, 5 November 1922, pp. 383–394, GP, Box 33.

60 While in Berlin, Golder noted Germany's pitiful economy. He wrote, "I have a large room with two beds and a bath which costs 200 marks, plus tax—about fifty cents in all." See, Golder to Lutz, 8 November 1922, p. 399, GP, Box 33.

61 Golder to Lutz, 16 November 1922, p. 401, GP, Box 33.

62 Golder to Herter, 22 November 1922, p. 412, *ibid.*

63 *Ibid.*, p. 413.

64 *Ibid.*, p. 414.

65 Golder to Herter, 2 December 1922, p. 417, *ibid.*

66 Golder to Herter, 21 December 1922, p. 442, *ibid.*

67 *Ibid.*, p. 442. In December 1922, Golder attended the Tenth All–Russian Congress of Soviets. He wrote Herter, "Soviet Russia has the expenditure of a twentieth century state and the income of a nineteenth. Industry and commerce of Russia of 1923 cannot bear much more taxation unless it is more highly developed. To do this, foreign capital must give a helping hand. In his speech, Kamenev indicated that Soviet Russia is kindly disposed towards foreign capital and was ready to go a long way to meet it. Foreign capital need not become frightened at the emphasis laid on the government monopoly of foreign commerce." Golder concluded, "In any case the Soviet is always ready to make special arrangements." See, Golder to Herter, 25 December 1922, pp. 2–3, James P. Goodrich Papers, Russia: Golder, HPL.

68 Weissman, *Hoover and the Soviet Famine*, pp. 132–134. Weissman writes, "The head of the ARA Historical Division in Moscow reported to the home office that Litvinov blamed the 'extreme left communist wing' for the growing hostility within the party towards the mission. In fact, however, even the 'sensitive' Soviet leaders found it increasingly difficult to reconcile wholehearted support for the mission with their deeper commitment to the communist cause. Along with the other Bolsheviks in the lead-

ership, they were compelled toward a Marxist interpretation of capitalist philanthrophy." See, *ibid.*, p. 164.

[69] Golder to Adams, 4 January 1923, p. 2, GP, Box 15.

[70] *Ibid.*, p. 3.

[71] Golder's seemingly perpetual motion in Soviet Russia and Western Europe had taken a toll on him by 1923. He wrote to Harrietta Eliot, "I have read so little in the last three years—time is occupied in reading the early papers, making calls, finding out who is in need, etc. In this manner, the days go fast enough. I have changed a good deal since you saw me but I do not know whether for better or worse. Sometimes I think I understand the realities of life, and sometimes I wonder where I am. I know I am more nervous and restless; whether it will unfit me for future teaching I do not know. When I return I shall come to you for inspection and advice." See, Golder to H. Eliot, 28 Janury 1923, p. 1, GP, Box 12.

[72] Golder to Herter, 1 February 1923, pp. 538, 539.

[73] The RSFSR became the USSR, Union of Soviet Socialist Republics, on 30 December 1922.

[74] Golder to Herter, 20 September 1922, pp. 1–2, James P. Goodrich, Russia: Golder, HPL.

[75] Golder to Goodrich, 17 September 1922, p. 1, James P. Goodrich, Russia: Golder, HPL.

[76] Golder to Herter, 20 October 1925, p. 2, GP, Box 15. Hoff–Wilson, *Ideology*, pp. 44, 67–68, 70. Feuer, "American Travelers to Soviet Union," pp. 139–140. Golder, pessimistic over the Soviet economy in 1922, wrote Herter, "I think it would be better for the foreign capitalist to come now, before the wheels of industry stop running altogether." See, Golder to Herter, 27 September 1922, p. 6, James P. Goodrich Papers, Russia: Golder, HPL. On 2 December 1922, Golder wrote, "Heavy industry is declining and neither Lenin nor all his men can raise it until capital puts it on its feet again. In the *Izvestia* of December 1, there is an article on the condition of the heavy industries in which the writer estimates the value of the production of 1922 (in gold rubles) as one–fifth of that of 1913. The metal industry is at the bottom of the list. Thursday night at the opera, I ran into two of my Bolo friends from Tver (where Golder had recently done a special economic study on the local industries). One is director of the Tver Textile Works and the other is director of all the textile mills of that district. They told me that in some of the mills they had enough raw materials to run until January [1923], in others they may have enough to pull along until May and then they are

through. [If] foreign help should come not too soon, a person traveling in a stage coach from Moscow to Petrograd ten years from now may find small smithies and spinning wheels in each village." See, Golder to Herter, 2 December 1922, pp. 420–421, GP, Box 33.

Regarding Soviet leadership, Golder did not find anyone who would be able to succeed Lenin after his death. Golder wrote, "Lenin's health gives much cause for uneasiness and should he drop out the chances are that there will be a split in the party. Trotsky is next to Lenin, probably the ablest, but for some reason or other he is kept in the background. . . . Radek is one of the cleverest but I do not think he has much influence on internal policies. Rykov, Tsurupa, and Kamenev, the three who have been designated as Lenin's substitutes, are not men of his class. There are all kinds of possibilities and I hope that they will all turn out along the lines of peace and good will." See, Golder to Herter, 2 January 1923, p. 5, James P. Goodrich Papers, Russia: Golder, HPL. In a conversation with Golder, Radek predicted that Stalin would become the next leader of Soviet Russia, a prediction which came true in 1929. Golder wrote Herter regarding Radek's view, but had no comment himself. See, Golder to Herter, 15 March 1923, p. 550, GP, Box 33.

77 Joan Hoff–Wilson, "American Business and the Recognition of the Soviet Union," *Social Science Quarterly* 52 (September 1971): 368. Hoff–Wilson writes, "The policy of non–recognition . . . provides one of the best examples of twentieth century U.S. diplomacy at its worst because it fostered a lack of reconciliation and coordination between economic and political foreign policy. This inconsistency was the direct product of an ideologically based diplomacy that became bureaucratized and obsolete but nonetheless self–perpetuating. As such, it represents an endemic weakness in the subsequent conduct of a U.S. foreign policy that has not allowed the United States to achieve the humanitarian goals it proclaims and that, carried to its logical extreme during the Cold War, became an almost fatal liability in the United States relations with foreign nations." See, Hoff–Wilson, *Ideology*, p. 132. Bennett, *Recognition of Russia*, p. 54.

78 Just prior to his departure for Dagestan, Golder wrote, "I was invited by the President and Mrs. President of the Dagestan Republic to go with them to an operetta. I invited them to go to the opera, but they told me that they were bored by such serious things and preferred light comic opera. I went and was bored." See, Golder to Adams, 12 February 1923, p. 1, GP,

Box 19. Golder to Herter, 8 February 1923, p. 542, GP, Box 33. Golder, *Famine*, p. 273.

[79] Golder to Adams, 13–16 February 1923, p. 7, GP, Box 19.

[80] Golder to Haskell, Trip to Dagestan, 15 March 1923, p. 1, ARA Russian Unit, Box 84.

[81] Golder, *Famine*, pp. 280–281.

[82] *Ibid.*, p. 282.

[83] Golder to Haskell, Trip to Dagestan, 15 March 1923, p. 4, ARA Russian Unit, Box 84.

[84] Golder, *Famine*, p. 282. Golder to Haskell, Trip to Dagestan, 15 March 1923, p. 4, ARA Russian Unit, Box 84.

[85] Golder, *Famine*, pp. 274, 283.

[86] *Ibid.*

[87] Regarding the Dagestanians during the Bolshevik Revolution, Golder wrote, "At first, the population was on the whole anti–Russian on nationalistic grounds; later it split into 'partisan' groups which joined the Reds in driving out the Whites and into different anti–Bolshevik groups, led by religious persons. These two groups fell on each other, massacred each other, [and] demolished each other's villages. . . ." See, Golder to Haskell, Trip to Dagestan, 15 March 1923, p. 4, ARA Russian Unit, Box 84.

[88] Golder, *Famine*, p. 284.

[89] *Ibid.*, p. 285.

[90] *Ibid.*, p. 286. While traveling to Gunib, Golder became a tourist. He wrote, "We passed close to [the] famous Georgievski Bridge, where many noted battles were fought between the invading Russians and the Dagestanians [during the Tsarist period], and where during the civil war about one hundred White officers were made to jump to certain death below." See, *ibid.*, p. 285.

[91] *Ibid.*, p. 289. Golder to Herter, 15 March 1923, p. 1, ARA Russian Unit, Box 84.

[92] Golder, *Famine*, pp. 289–290.

[93] *Ibid.*, p. 290.

[94] *Ibid.*, p. 292.

[95] *Ibid.*

[96] *Ibid.*, p. 295.

[97] *Ibid.*, p. 292.

[98] *Ibid.*, p. 297.

[99] *Ibid.*, pp. 297–298. Golder to Haskell, Trip to Dagestan, 15 March 1923, p. 2, ARA Russian Unit, Box 84.

[100] Golder, *Famine*, p. 298.

[101] *Ibid.*, p. 299. Golder to Haskell, Trip to Dagestan, 15 March 1923, p. 2, ARA Russian Unit, Box 84.

102 Golder, *Famine*, p. 298.

103 *Ibid.*, pp. 299–300.

104 Golder to Haskell, Trip to Dagestan, 15 March 1923, p. 2, ARA Russian Unit, Box 84.

105 *Ibid.*

106 Golder, *Famine*, pp. 303–304.

107 *Ibid.*, pp. 305, 304.

108 *Ibid.*, p. 306.

109 *Ibid.*

110 Golder to Haskell, Trip to Dagestan, 15 March 1923, p. 2, ARA Russian Unit, Box 84. Golder, *Famine*, p. 319.

111 Golder to Haskell, Trip to Dagestan, 15 March 1923, p. 2, ARA Russian Unit, Box 84. Golder, Diary of Trip to Dagestan, p. 32, GP, Box 10. Golder to Harold H. Fisher, 24 March 1923, p. 2, ARA Russian Unit, Box 94.

112 Goodrich to Golder, 2 February 1923, p. 1, GP, Box 32. Goodrich also wrote that "the United States government offered the best of intentions, of good will and charity for humanity, but that 'Hell was paved with good intentions.' " See, *ibid.*.

113 Golder to Herter, 15 March 1923, p. 545, GP, Box 33.

114 Golder to Herter, 22 January 1924, pp. 8–9, ARA Russian Unit, Box 261.

115 Fisher, *Famine in Russia*, pp. 297–298, 300–301, 305–307. Weissman, *Hoover and the Soviet Famine*, p. 173.

116 Golder to Herter, 8 May 1923, p. 584, GP, Box 33.

117 Golder to Adams, 7 May 1923, pp. 574–575, *ibid.*

118 *Ibid.*

119 *Ibid.*

120 While in Sofia, the capital of Bulgaria, Golder noted the behavior of the Allied Commissions there. He wrote, "The French and Italian commissioners have taken for themselves the best houses, have imported furniture from abroad, have cars, servants, staff, etc., all at the expense of these poor people. There is no end in sight. It disgusts one to see these idle carpetbaggers with their fat wives and dogs eating up the earnings of the poor people. Such acts create Bolshevism on the one hand and a disgust in the Allies on the other. Everyone is sighing for America to take a hand, for they believe that we will play fair. We have started something during the last war, and we cannot now let it go. I am glad that we are in a position to save Europe, but the danger and the temptations are so great that in trying to save Europe, we might lose our soul." See, Golder to Adams, 21 May 1923, p. 593, GP, Box 33.

[121] Golder wrote that after this woman had been released from the hospital, "she was greatly worried about the trial of the clergy (the Bolsheviks had nationalized church property and this confiscation placed the clergy in opposition to the Soviet regime) and just as soon as she was able to leave her bed she went to the trial (she, at one time, had been in a convent), and at the end of the trial, as the metropolitan was being taken to the car to be removed to his cell, she, with a number of others, followed him and threw flowers. The police rounded up the whole crowd, of more than 2,000, and took them all to prison. [After she was released from prison], I took her to the Foreign Office, where a communist friend of mine promised to help her to get the necessary papers [to leave the country]. But when she reached there she insisted on telling him that she was for the church and the priests, and I am afraid she will spoil everything. She glows in her martyrdom and is eager to repeat her performance in order to be locked up again." See, Golder to Adams, 24 June 1922, pp. 261–262, GP, Box 33.

[122] Golder to Lutz, 2 June 1923, p. 1, GP, Box 32.

[123] *Ibid.*

[124] *Ibid.*, p. 2.

[125] *Ibid.*

[126] *Ibid.*

[127] Golder to Lutz, 6 June 1923, p. 1, GP, Box 32.

[128] *Ibid.*

[129] *Ibid.*

[130] Golder to Lutz, 7 June 1923, pp. 2, 1, *ibid.*

[131] Golder to Lutz, 9 June 1923, pp. 1–2, GP, Box 32. Golder to Lutz, 12 June 1923, pp. 1–2, *ibid.* Golder to Lutz, 18 June 1923, p. 1, *ibid.*

[132] Golder to Adams, 2 July 1923, p. 1, GP, Box 15.

[133] Golder, Ruhr Diary, 25 June 1923, p. 5, GP, Box 19.

[134] Golder to Adams, 2 July 1923, pp. 3, 5, GP, Box 15.

[135] Golder to Adams, 7 July 1923, p. 2, GP, Box 32.

[136] Golder to Adams, 1 June 1923, pp. 589–599, GP, Box 33. Herron, disillusioned over the settlement of World War I, referred to his condition as "malignant Wilsonitis."

[137] Golder to Adams, 7 July 1923, pp. 1–3, GP, Box 32. Golder to Adams, 26 July 1923, p. 1, *ibid.* Golder to Adams, 15 July 1923, p. 2, *ibid.* Golder to Herter, 13 October 1923, p. 1, ARA Russian Unit, Box 95. Keserich, *Herron–Il Nostro Americano*, p. 329.

[138] Herron's papers at the Hoover Institution dealing with his war and post–war activities at Geneva comprise fourteen bound volumes. In addition to these bound volumes, the Hoover has eleven boxes of Herron's miscellaneous papers and correspondence.

[139] Golder to Adams, 26 July 1923, p. 1, GP, Box 32.

[140] Golder to Adams, 14 August 1923, p. 1, *ibid.*

Notes to Chapter VIII

[1] A. Russell Buchanan to A. G. Wachhold, 28 April 1976, p. 1, Personal Files of A. G. Wachhold, Santa Barbara, California.

[2] Elsie Daly to A. G. Wachhold, 15 June 1976, p. 1, Personal Files of A. G. Wachhold, Santa Barbara, California.

[3] Interview with Charles Burdick, Professor of History at San Jose State University, San Jose, California, 24 August 1976. Golder to Goodrich, 2 February 1925, p. 1, Goodrich Papers, Russia: Golder, HPL.

[4] Interview with Mabel Junkert, Former Secretary for the Hoover War Library, Riverside, California, 23 July 1977. Interview with Graham Stuart, Retired Political Science Professor at Stanford University, Palo Alto, California, 10 September 1977.

[5] Interview with Mabel Junkert.

[6] Golder, *Documents of Russian History, 1914–1917* (New York: The Century Co., 1927), preface, p. vii. Lincoln Hutchinson, preface, p. v, in Gregory Y. Sokolinkov and Associates, *Soviet Policy in Public Finance, 1917–1928* (Stanford: Stanford University Press, 1931).

[7] Golder to Wilbur, 6 December 1924, p. 1, Golder Correspondence, HIR, Box 94.

[8] Golder, A Plan for the Study of the Russian Revolution, 5 March 1923, pp. 1–3, Laura Spelman Rockefeller Memorial Collection, Series 3, Subseries 6, Box 69. Cited hereafter as RMC.

[9] Regarding the Soviet history profession during the 1920s, George E. Enteen writes, "Until 1927, a *modus vivendi* existed between Marxist and non–Marxist historians. But it was a *modus vivendi* in which the non–Marxists effectively dominated the profession: despite hardship resulting from the Civil War and losses through emigration, the so–called bourgeois historians continued their pursuits and retained their leadership in the traditional scholarly institutions," See, George E. Enteen, *Marxist Historians during the Cultural Revolution*, in Sheila Fitzpatrick, ed., *Cultural Revoltion in Russia, 1928–1931* (Bloomington: Indiana University Press, 1978), p. 157. Cited hereafter as Fitzpatrick, *Cultural Revolution.*

[10] Sheila Fitzpatrick writes, "The concept of class war depended on a definition of the old intelligentsia as "bourgeois" and the Communist party as "proletarian." All communists agreed on this definition, but not all thought it necessary to make culture a battleground. In the first ten years of Soviet power, the Communist leadership had tended to avoid outright confrontation with the intelligentsia. Lenin had rejected the idea that cultural power . . . could be seized by revolutionary action. Culture, in his view, had to be patiently acquired and assimilated; Communists must learn from "bourgeois specialists," despite their identification with an alien social class; and refusal to learn was a sign of "Communist conceit." During NEP the leadership as a whole treated harassment of specialists as a regrettable byproduct of revolutionary zeal rather than a mark of developed proletarian consciousness." See, Sheila Fitzpatrick, *Cultural Revolution as Class War*, in Fitzpatrick, *Cultural Revolution*, pp. 8–9. *Ibid.*, p. 29. Isaac Deutscher, *The Prophet Unarmed: Trotsky, 1921–1929* (London: Oxford University Press, 1959), pp. 113, 168. Cited hereafter as Deutscher, *Prophet Unarmed.*

[11] Bennett, *Recognition of Russia*, pp. 68–71. Golder to Goodrich, 11 January 1925, p. 1, Goodrich Papers, Russia: Golder, HPL.

[12] Golder to Wilbur, n.d., p. 10, Golder Correspondence, HIR, Box 94.

[13] Golder to Guy Ford, 8 June 1925, p. 1, *ibid.*, Box 95. Golder to Guy Ford, 15 June 1925, p. 1, *ibid.* Golder to Guy Ford, 25 June 1925, p. 1, RMC, Box 69. Dr. Beardsley Ruml, Memorandum, 18 August 1925, p. 1, *ibid.* J. D. Parks, *Culture, Conflict and Coexistence: American–Soviet Cultural Relations, 1917–1958* (Jefferson, North Carolina: McFarland, 1983), pp. 24–34. Cited hereafter as Parks, *American–Soviet Cultural Relations.*

[14] Golder, Jubilee of the USSR Academy of Science, 5–15 September 1925, pp. 623, 626–627, GP, Box 33.

[15] Golder to Hoover, 2 October 1925, p. 1, GP, Box 15. Golder, The Jubilee . . ., p. 624, GP, Box 33. Golder to Goodrich, 18 May 1925, p. 1, Goodrich Papers, Russia: Golder, HPL. The United States experienced great prosperity during the Roaring Twenties, and Golder, like millions of Americans, played the stock market. He wrote to Goodrich in 1926, "Enclosed please find the three shares of stock of the Union Heat, Light, and Power Co. which you wished forwarded to you. At the same time, I am sending you a list of all my stock. Having stock in many companies which pay dividends at different times make it difficult to reinvest the

dividends. When we were discussing this point you suggested that it might be best to sell this stock and reinvest it in the stock of one or two companies. If you still think so, please let me know and I will send the shares of stock to you." See, Golder to Goodrich, 4 April 1926, p. 1, Goodrich Papers, Russia: Golder, HPL.

16 Golder, The Jubilee . . ., pp. 624–626, GP, Box 33.

17 *Ibid.*, p. 626.

18 *Ibid.*

19 *Ibid.*

20 Golder to Adams, 13 November 1925, p. 2, GP, Box 32.

21 Golder to Wilbur, 15 November 1925, p. 1, RMC, Box 69. Deutscher, *Prophet Unarmed*, pp. 38–39.

22 Kameneva to Golder, 12 December 1925, p. 1, GP, Box 32. Wilbur to Litoshenko, 8 December 1925, p. 1, Golder Correspondence, HIR, Box 94. Parks, *American–Soviet Cultural Relations*, p. 20.

23 Golder to Kameneva, 27 December 1925, pp. 1–2, GP, Box 32. Golder to Wilbur, n.d., p. 2, Golder Correspondence, HIR, Box 95.

24 Golder to Litoshenko, 5 April 1926, p. 1, Golder Correspondence, HIR, Box 95. Golder to Litoshenko, 1 July 1927, p. 2, *ibid.* Interview with Carl Brand, Emeritus Professor of History at Stanford University, Stanford, California, 28 March 1976.

25 Kellogg to Golder, 19 August 1927, Golder Correspondence, HIR, Box 94. Golder to Wilbur, 1 August 1927, pp. 1–2, *ibid.* Wilbur to Golder, 11 August 1927, p. 1, *ibid.*, Box 95. Golder to Wilbur, 20 August 1927, p. 1, *ibid.* Golder to Wilbur, 30 August 1927, Wilbur Papers, p. 1, SUA, Box 65.

26 Golder to Goodrich, 20 August 1927, p. 1, Goodrich Papers, Russia: Golder, HPL.

27 Golder to Wilbur, n.d., p. 1, Golder Correspondence, HIR, Box 95. Parks, *American–Soviet Cultural Relations*, pp. 31–32.

28 Golder to Wilbur, n.d., p. 1, Golder Correspondence, HIR, Box 95.

29 *Ibid.*

30 *Ibid.* Golder had a fairly high opinion of Ossinsky. Golder wrote, "Ossinsky is a clever and able economist and skillful politician." See, *ibid.*

31 *Ibid.* Golder wrote, "It should be said . . . that our study was very inopportune. Just now there is a bitter storm raging in the Communist Party over the agrarian policy. If our study were to be published today, it would furnish ammunition to one or the

other of the combatants. Ossinsky and the men who [have] our affairs in hand [are] too clever politicians to give their approval to the publication of such a book regardless of its merits." See, *ibid.*

32 Susan Gross Solomon, *Rural Scholars and the Cultural Revolution*, in Fitzpatrick, *Cultural Revolution*, pp. 140–143. Deutscher, *Prophet Unarmed*, pp. 38–39, 52, 75, 81, 243, 271–273, 361–362, 366.

33 Golder to Wilbur, n.d., pp. 3–4, Golder Correspondence, HIR, Box 95. Hoff–Wilson, *Ideology*, pp. 69, 101, 102.

34 Golder to Wilbur, n.d., p. 4, Golder Correspondence, HIR, Box. 95.

35 *Ibid.*

36 *Ibid.*

37 *Ibid.*, p. 5. Regarding Madame Kameneva, Golder wrote, "It is hard to understand why the Bolsheviks put such a woman as Madame Kameneva at the head of such an important bureau. She is not a woman of broad education or high character; she has seen little of the world and has had no contact with men of affairs. It is true that she is merely a flunky for those higher up but her position is big enough to make a bad impression on those whom she comes in contact [with] and turns people against Russia." See, *ibid.*

38 *Ibid.*, p. 4.

39 *Ibid.*, p. 6.

40 *Ibid.*, p. 7. Theodore H. von Laue, *Soviet Diplomacy: G. V. Chicherin, People's Commissar for Foreign Affairs, 1918–1930,* in Gordon A. Craig and Felix Gilbert, eds., *The Diplomats, 1919–1939* (Princeton: Princeton University Press, 1953), p. 249. Cited hereafter as Laue, *Chicherin.* Fischer, *Lenin,* pp. 262–275.

41 Golder to Wilbur, n.d., p. 7, Golder Correspondence, HIR, Box 95.

42 *Ibid.*

43 *Ibid.*

44 *Ibid.* Golder, Notes of the Conversation Carried on between Messrs. Rothstein and Ossinsky, Representing the Russians, and Golder, Representing the Americans, on the Subject of Forming a Russian Institute, p. 1, Golder Correspondence, HIR, Box 95. Golder, Agreement between Stanford University and the Society for Cultural Relations of the USSR Regarding the Work of the Russian Institute, 9 November 1927, *ibid.*, Box 94.

45 Golder to Wilbur, n.d., pp. 8–9, pp. 8–9, *ibid.*, Box 95.

46 *Ibid.*, p. 9.
47 *Ibid.*, pp. 9–10. Susan Gross Solomon, *Rural Scholars and the Cultural Revolution*, in Fitzpatrick, *Cultural Revolution*, pp. 144–146. Deutscher, *Prophet Unarmed*, pp. 373–374, 376, 388–389, 391. Golder wrote after he reached New York, "The other day . . . Gov. Goodrich informed me that he had [received] a letter from Ossinsky, expressing his regrets that no agreement had been made." See, Golder to Wilbur, n.d., Golder Correspondence, HIR, Box 95.
48 Golder to Wilbur, n.d., p. 10, Golder Correspondence, HIR, Box 95. Golder to Society for Cultural Relations, 5 January 1927, *ibid.* Golder to Kameneva, 9 January 1928, p. 1, *ibid.*
49 Golder to Kameneva, 9 January 1928, p. 1., *ibid.* Lincoln Hutchinson, preface, pp. vi–vii, in Gregory Y. Sokolinkov and Associates, *Soviet Policy in Public Finance, 1917–1928* (Stanford: Stanford University Press, 1931). Golder, Russo–American Agreement, Golder Correspondence, HIR, Box 94. In 1927, Golder finished an excellent volume entitled, *Documents on Russian History, 1914–1917* (New York: The Century Co., 1927). The same year, Golder came out with another volume entitled, *John Paul Jones in Russia* (Garden City: Doubleday, 1927).
50 Golder to Boris Skvirsky, 1928, p. 1, Golder Correspondence, HIR, Box 94. Golder to Litoshenko, 10 January 1928, p. 1, *ibid.* Golder to Boris Skvirsky, 23 January 1928, p. 1, *ibid.* Golder to Litoshenko, 27 January 1928, p. 1, *ibid.*
51 Golder to Litoshenko, 27 February 1928, p. 2, *ibid.* Litoshenko to Golder, 14 April 1928, p. 1, *ibid.*, Box 95. Golder to Wilbur, 17 April 1928, p. 1, *ibid.*, Box 94. Kameneva to Golder, 4 April 1928, p. 1 *ibid.*
52 Yaroshevsky to Golder, 28 May 1928, p. 1, *ibid.* Golder to Litoshenko, 27 April 1928, p. 1, *ibid.* Golder to Society for Cultural Relations, 13 June 1928, p. 1, *ibid.*
53 Jerry F. Hough wrote, "The history of the Soviet Union cannot be limited to a history of the regime's censorship policy and its purges. The content of substantive policies, the values expressed in them, the interests that they satisfied and failed to satisfy— these too must be part of the political chronicle of the Soviet period, including the Stalin years." See, Jerry F. Hough, *The Cultural Revolution and Western Understanding*, in Fitzpatrick, *Cultural Revolution*, p. 242. For a challenge to the traditional approach to the totalitarian model of Western presentation of Soviet history, see, *ibid.*, pp. 241–253 and Sheila Fitzpatrick, "Culture and Politics under Stalin: A Reappraisal," *Slavic Re-*

view (June 1976): 211–231.

54 Sheila Fitzpatrick, introduction, p. 7, in Fitzpatrick, *Cultural Revolution*. Gail Warshofsky Lapidus, *Educational Strategies and Cultural Revolution*, p. 90, in *ibid.* Jerry F. Hough, *The Cultural Revolution and Western Understanding*, p. 251, in *ibid.* Sheila Fitzpatrick, "Cultural Revolution in Russia, 1928–1932," *Journal of Contemporary History* (January 1974): 34.

55 Golder, *Proposals for Russian Occupation of the Hawaiian Islands*, in Albert Pierce Taylor, ed., *Hawaiian Islands* (Honolulu: Captain Cook Sesquicentennial Archive Commission of Hawaii, 1930), pp. 39–49.

56 This book is, Golder, ed., *The March of the Mormon Battalion* (New York: The Century Co., 1928).

57 Interview with Thomas Bailey, Stanford University, Emeritus History Professor, Stanford, California, 24 August 1977. Albert P. Taylor, *Sesquicentennial Celebration of Captain Cook's Discovery of Hawaii*, pp. 9–53, GP, Box 13. According to Bailey, Golder had been appointed to give Bailey one of his oral exams and this subject was ancient history. Golder showed up late for the exam, and another examiner asked him if he had been reading about ancient history in the encyclopedia. Bailey said that Golder took the joke in good spirits. On another occasion, Bailey had applied to Harvard University for a scholarship, but did not receive one. Golder later asked Bailey if he had been awarded the scholarship. After Golder found out that Harvard had denied him the scholarship, he wrote a letter to Harvard and Bailey soon received a $250 scholarship. See, interview with Thomas Bailey.

58 Golder to Skvirsky, 15 September 1928, p. 1, Golder Correspondence, HIR, Box 95.

59 Edward White to A. G. Wachhold, 20 May 1976, Personal Files of A. G. Wachhold, Santa Barbara, California. Golder to Skvirsky, 15 September 1928, p. 2, Golder Correspondence, HIR, Box 95. Harold Fisher to George Schauman, 19 February 1929, p. 1, *ibid.*, Box 94.

60 Harold Fisher to George Schauman, 22 November 1928, p. 1, Golder Correspondence, HIR, Box 95.

61 Golder to Kameneva, 22 November 1928, p. 1, *ibid.*, Box 94. Skvirsky to Golder, 24 September 1928, p. 1, *ibid.* Golder to Skvirsky, 6 October 1928, p. 1, *ibid.* Skvirsky to Golder, 11 October 1928, p. 1, *ibid.* Deutscher, *Prophet Unarmed*, pp. 454–455. In 1932, Stalin brought the cultural revolution to a conclusion. As early as 1931, Stalin rehabilitated the old technical specialists, and in 1932 they occupied official positions. In

1934, non–Marxist historians, writes George E. Enteen, "were back in positions of eminence and respect in the profession . . ." See, George E. Enteen, *Marxist Historians during the Cultural Revolution,* in Fitzpatrick, *Cultural Revolution,* pp. 186, 244. Sheila Fitzpatrick, *Education and Social Mobility in the Soviet Union, 1921–1934* (London: Cambridge University Press, 1979), pp. 209–233.

[62] Golder to Kameneva, 22 November 1928, p. 1, Golder Correspondence, HIR, Box 95.

[63] Golder to Litoshenko, 28 November 1928, p. 1, *ibid.*

[64] W. B. Beach to Professor Eliot, 23 November 1928, pp. 1–2, GP, Box 12. Sam Seward to Professor Eliot, 2 December 1928, pp. 1–3, *ibid.* W. B. Beach to Professor Eliot, 11 January 1929, p. 1, *ibid.* "Professor Golder Dies After a Long Illness," *The Stanford Daily,* 8 January 1929, p. 4. Burdick, *Lutz,* p. 95. Alexander DeConde, *Herbert Hoover's Latin–American Policy* (New York: Octagon Books, 1970), pp. 15–16.

[65] Interview with Wallace Sterling, Chancellor of Stanford University, Stanford, California, 17 August 1977. Fisher to Kameneva, 30 January 1929, pp. 1–2, Golder Correspondence, HIR, Box 94. Fisher to Chicherin, 4 February 1929, p. 1, *ibid.* Fisher to Litoshenko, 20 December 1929, p. 1, *ibid.* George E. Enteen, *Marxist Historians during the Cultural Revolution,* in Fitzpatrick, *Cultural Revolution,* p. 157. Litoshenko's manuscript was never published nor does a copy exist at the Hoover Institution. Sokolinkov's manuscript did find its way to publication. See, G. Sokolinkov and Associates, *Soviet Policy in Public Finance, 1917–1928,* trans. Elena Varneck (Stanford: Stanford University Press, 1931).

Editor's Bibliography

Unpublished Sources

Adams, Ephraim, Papers, Stanford University Archives, Stanford, California.

American Relief Administration, Russian Unit, Hoover Institution, Stanford, California.

BAEF Papers, Correspondence Series, Golder, Frank, Hoover Presidential Library, West Branch, Iowa.

Byran, E., Papers, Washington State University Archives, Pullman, Washington.

Clark, George, Papers, Stanford University Archives, Stanford, California.

Golder, Frank, Papers, Hoover Institution, Stanford, California.

Golder, Frank, Papers, Stanford University Archives, Stanford, California.

Goodrich, James P., Papers, Russia: Golder, Frank, Hoover Presidential Library, West Branch, Iowa.

Holland, E., Papers, Washington State University Archives, Pullman, Washington.

Hoover, Herbert, Archives, Speeches and Addresses, 1915–1923, Hoover Institution, Stanford, California.

Internal Records, Hoover Institution, Stanford, California.

Jackson, Sheldon, Collection, Presbyterian Historical Society, Princeton Theological Seminary, Princeton, New Jersey.

Lutz, Ralph, Papers, Hoover Institution, Stanford, California.

Lutz, Ralph, Papers, Stanford University Archives, Stanford, California.

Piper, Charles V., Papers, Washington State University, Pullman, Washington.

Robinson, Edgar, Papers, Stanford University Archives, Stanford, California.

Spelman, Laura, Rockefeller Archive Center, North Tarrytown, New York.

Stevens, John F., Papers, Hoover Institution, Stanford, California.

Wilbur, Ray Lyman, Papers, Stanford University Archives, Stanford, California.

Unpublished Government Papers

U. S. Department of the Interior, Alaska Territorial Papers, National Archives Microfilm Publication, 1963, Roll. 79.

U. S. Department of the Interior, Records of the Bureau of Indian Affairs, Alaska Division, Letters, 1887–1908, Record Group 75, National Archives, Washington, D. C.

U. S. Department of State, Political Relations between the U. S. and the Soviet Union, 1918–1929, Record Group 59, National Archives, Washington D.C.

U. S. Department of State, Records of the American Commission to Negotiate the Peace, Record Group 256, National Archives, Washington, D. C.

Warren G. Harding, Presidential Papers, Ohio Historical Society, Archives, Columbus, Ohio, Roll 181.

Published Government Papers

U. S. Office of Education, *Report of the Commission of Education, The Year, 1899–1900*, Washington, D. C.: Government Printing Office, 1901.

U. S. Department of State, *Foreign Relations of the United States, 1918*, Vol. 3: *Russia*, Washington, D.C.: Government Printing Office, 1932.

U. S. Department of State, *Foreign Relations of the United States, 1923*, Washington, D. C.: Government Printing Office, 1938.

Interviews

Bailey, Thomas. Emeritus Professor of History at Stanford University, Palo Alto, California. Interview, 11 April 1977.

Barclay, Thomas. Emeritus Professor of Political Science at Stanford University, Palo Alto, California. Interview, 10 September 1977.

Brand, Carl. Emeritus Professor of History at Stanford University, Palo Alto, California. Interview, 28 March 1976.

Burdick, Charles. History Professor at San Jose State University, San Jose, California. Interview, 24 August 1976.

Fisher, Harold. Emeritus Professor of History at Stanford University, Palo Alto, California. Interview, 3 July 1975.

Graham, Stuart. Emeritus Professor of Political Science at Stanford University, Palo Alto, California. Interview, 10 September 1977.

Junkert, Mabel. Former Secretary for the Hoover War Library, Riverside, California. Interview, 17 August 1977.

Sterling, Wallace. Chancellor of Stanford University, Palo Alto, California. Interview, 17 August 1977.

Personal Letters

A. Russell Buchanan. Mollie Coleman. Elsie Daly. John Daly. Edgar J. Fisher, Jr. Mrs. Samuel Golder. Mabel Junkert. Maurice Mandell. Vincent L. Martin. Charles E. Newell. Louise Overacker. Charles S. Shoup. Mrs. Charles J. Solomon. L. B. Vincent. Edward A. White.

Diaries

Darling, William, Diary, Hoover Institution, Stanford, California.

Fisher, Edgar, Sr., Diary, Ohio State University, Special Collections, Columbus, Ohio.

Memoirs

Allen, Henry T. *My Rhineland Journal.* New York, 1923.

Creel, George. *Rebel at Large: Recollections of Fifty Crowded Years.* New York, 1947.

Francis, David R. *Russia from the American Embassy, 1916–1919.* New York, 1970.

George, David Lloyd. *Memoirs of the Peace Conference*, Vol. 1. New Haven, 1939.

Graves, William S. *America's Siberian Adventure, 1918–1920.* New York, 1941.

Harper, Samuel. *The Russia I Believe In.* Chicago, 1945.

Hoover, Herbert. *An American Epic*, Vol. 2: *Famine in Forty-Five Nations, 1914–1923.* Chicago, 1961.

———. *The Memoirs of Herbert Hoover*, Vol. 1: *Years of Adventure, 1874–1920.* New York, 1951.

———. *The Memoirs of Herbert Hoover,* Vol. 2: *Cabinet and the Presidency, 1920-1933.* New York, 1952.

———. *The Ordeal of Woodrow Wilson.* New York, 1958.

Jones, Stinton. *Russia in Revolution, Being the Experience of an Englishman in Petrograd during the Upheaval.* London, 1917.

Kerensky, Alexander. *The Catastrophe: Kerensky's Own Story of the Russian Revolution.* New York, 1927.

Mendel, Arthur, ed., *Political Memoirs by Paul Miliukov, 1905-1917.* Ann Arbor, 1967.

Steffens, Lincoln. *Autobiography of Lincoln Steffens.* New York, 1931.

Trotsky, Leon. *My Life: An Attempt at an Autobiography.* New York, 1930.

Primary Articles

Bailey, Thomas. "The Russian Fleet Myth Re–examined." *Mississippi Valley Historical Review.* 38 (June 1951): 81–90.

Fisher, Harold. "Frank Alfred Golder." *The Journal of Modern History.* 14 (June 1929): 253–255.

Fisher, Raymond H. "Dezhnev's Voyage of 1648 in the Light of Soviet Scholarship." *Terrae Incongitae* (Society for the History of Discoveries, Amsterdam), 5: 7–26.

———. "Semen Dezhnev and Professor Golder." *Pacific Historical Review.* 25 (August 1956): 281–292.

Goodrich, James P. "Impressions of the Bolshevik Regime." *Century* (May 1922): 55–65.

———. "The Plight of Russia." *The Outlook.* 130 (January 1922): 66–68.

Lutz, Ralph. "The Hoover War Library Grows Yearly in Importance as a Great Field for Historical Research." *Stanford Illustrated Review.* 24 (June 1923): 464–465.

———. "The Hoover War Library: The Great International Archives at Stanford University." *Army Ordnance.* 10 (March–April 1930): 331–335.

Newspapers

The Stanford Daily
Tempe Normal Student

Books by Golder

Golder, Frank, ed. *Bering's Voyages*, Vol. 1: *The Log Books and Official Reports of the First and Second Expedition, 1725–1730 and 1733–1742.* New York, 1922.

——, ed. *Bering's Voyages*, Vol. 2: *Steller's Journal of the Sea Voyage from Kamchatka to America and Return on the Second Expedition, 1741–1742.* New York, 1925.

——, ed. *Documents on Russian History, 1914–1917.* New York, 1927.

——. *Guide to Materials for American History in Russian Archives.* Washington, D. C., 1917.

——, and Hutchinson, Lincoln. *On the Trail of the Russian Famine.* Stanford, 1927.

——, ed. *Paul Jones in Russia.* Garden City, 1927.

——. *Russian Expansion on the Pacific, 1641–1850.* Cleveland, 1914.

——, ed. *The March of the Mormon Battalion.* New York, 1928.

——, Harper, Samuel, and Petrunkevitch, Alexander. *The Russian Revolution.* Cambridge, 1918.

Articles by Golder

Golder, Frank. "A Kodiak Island Story: The White–faced Bear." *Journal of American Folklore.* 20 (October–December 1907): 336–339.

——. "Aleutian Stories." *Journal of American Folklore.* 20 (July–September 1905): 215–222.

——. "A Survey of Alaska, 1743–1799." *Washington Historical Quarterly.* 4 (April 1913): 83–93.

——. "Catherine II and the American Revolution." *American Historical Review.* 21 (October 1915): 92–96.

——. "Eskimo and Aleut Stories from Alaska." *Journal of American Folklore.* 22 (January–March 1909): 10–24.

——. Letter of Kamehemah II to Alexander I, 1820." *American Historical Review.* 22 (July 1915): 833–838.

——. "Mining in Alaska before 1867." *Washington Historical Review.* 7 (July 1916): 233–238.

——. "Proposals for Russian Occupation of the Hawaiian Islands," in Albert Pierce Taylor, ed., *Hawaiian Islands* (Honolulu: Captain Cook Sesquicentennial Archive Commission of Hawaii, 1930), pp. 39–49.

_____. "Primitive Warfare Among the Natives of Western Alaska." *Journal of American Folklore.* 22 (July–September 1909): 336–339.

_____. "Russian–American Relations during the Crimean War." *American Historical Review.* 31 (April 1926): 462–476.

_____. "Some Reasons for Doubting Deshev's Voyage." *Geographical Journal.* 36 (April–June 1903): 81–83.

_____. "Tales from Kodiak Island I." *Journal of American Folklore.* 16 (April–June 1903): 16–31.

_____. "Tales from Kodiak Island II." *Journal of American Folklore.* 16 (April–June 1903): 81–103.

_____. "The American Civil War through the Eyes of a Russian Diplomat." *American Historical Review.* 26 (April 1921): 454–463.

_____. "The Purchase of Alaska." *American Historical Review.* 25 (April 1920): 411–425.

_____. "The Russian Fleet and the Civil War." *American Historical Review.* 20 (July 1915): 1–12.

_____. "The Russian Offer of Mediation in the War of 1812." *Political Science Quarterly.* 31 (September 1916): 380–391.

_____. "The Songs and Stories of the Aleuts, with Translations from Veniaminov." *Journal of American Folklore.* 20 (April–June 1907): 132–142.

_____. "Tlingit Myths." *Journal of American Folklore.* 20 (October–December 1907): 290–295.

_____. "The Tragic Failure of Soviet Policies." *Current History.* 19 (February 1924): 776–783.

_____. "Will the Unrestricted Self–Determination of all National Groups Bring World Peace and Order?" *Journal of International Relations.* 10 (January 1920): 278–288.

Privately Published Articles

Christmas Stories: Golder, Frank:

A Little Journey into the Land of the Monks
Father Herman: Alaska's Saint
Keeping Faith with God
O'Hara

Speeches

Golder, Frank. The Lessons of the Great War and the Russian Revolution. An address delivered before the faculty and students of the State College of Washington on 7 January 1924.

Books

Bentinck–Smith, William. *Building a Great Library: The Coolidge Years at Harvard.* Cambridge, 1976.

Bennett, Edward. *Recognition of Russia: An American Foreign Policy Dilemma* Waltham, Mass., 1970.

Brandes, Joseph. *Emmigrants to Freedom: Jewish Communities in Rural New Jersey Since 1882.* Philadelphia, 1971.

———. *Herbert Hoover and Economic Diplomacy: Department of Commerce, 1921–1928.* Pittsburg, 1962.

Briggs, Mitchell P. *George D. Herron and the European Settlement.* New York, 1971.

Brown, E. J. *The Proletarian Episode in Russian Literature, 1928–1932.* New York, 1953.

Bruner, David. *Herbert Hoover: A Public Life.* New York, 1979.

Burdick, Charles. *Ralph H. Lutz and the Hoover Institution.* Stanford, 1974.

Byrnes, Robert F. *Awakening American Education to the World: The Role of Archibald Cary Coolidge, 1866–1928.* Indiana, 1982.

Chicherin, Georgi. *Two Years of Foreign Policy.* New York, 1920.

Chamberlin, William H. *The Russian Revolution.* 2 Vols. New York, 1965.

Cohen, Stephen. *Bukharin and the Bolshevik Revolution: A Political Biography, 1888–1938.* New York, 1973.

Condoide, Mikhail V. *Russian–American Trade: A Study of the Foreign Trade Monopoly.* Columbus, 1946.

Coolidge, Harold and Lord, Robert. *Archibald Cary Coolidge: Life and Letters.* Boston, 1932.

DeConde, Alexander. *Herbert Hoover's Latin–American Policy.* New York, 1970.

Deutscher, Isaac. *Stalin: A Political Biography.* New York, 1949.

———. *Trotsky.* Vol. 2: *The Prophet Unarmed, 1921–1929.* New York, 1965.

Dwyer, Joseph D., ed. *Russia, The Soviet Union, and Eastern Europe: A Survey of Holdings at the Hoover Institution on War, Revolution, and Peace.* Stanford, 1980.

Ellis, Ethan L. *Frank B. Kellogg and American Foreign Relations, 1925–1929.* New Brunswick, N.J., 1961.

_____. *Republican Foreign Policy, 1921–1933.* New Brunswick, N. J., 1968.

Feis, Herbert. *The Diplomacy of the Dollar, 1919–1932.* New York, 1966.

Filene, Peter. *Americans and the Soviet Experiment, 1917–1933.* Cambridge, 1967.

Fischer, Louis. *The Life of Lenin.* New York, 1964.

_____. *Men and Politics: An Autobiography.* New York, 1941.

_____. *Russia's Road from Peace to War: Soviet Foreign Relations, 1917–1941.* New York, 1969.

_____. *The Soviets in World Affairs.* Vol. 2: *A History of the Relations between the Soviet Union and the Rest of the World, 1917–1929.* Princeton, 1951.

_____. *Why Recognize Russia: The Arguments For and Against the Recognition of the Soviet Government by the United States.* New York, 1931.

Fisher, Harold H., ed. *American Research on Russia.* Bloomington, 1959.

_____. *The Famine in Soviet Russia, 1919–1923.* New York, 1927.

Fisher, Raymond. *Bering's Voyages: Wither and Why.* Seattle, 1977.

_____. *The Voyage of Semen Dezhnev in 1648: Bering's Precursor.* London, 1981.

Fitzpatrick, Sheila, ed. *Cultural Revolution in Russia, 1928–1931.* Bloomington, 1978.

Garner, Lloyd C. *Wilson and Revolutions, 1913–1921.* San Jose, 1976.

Gelfand, Lawrence, ed. *Herbert Hoover, 1914–1923: The Great War and Its Aftermath.* Iowa City, 1979.

Glad, Betty. *Charles Evans Hughes and the Illusion of Innocence: A Study of American Diplomacy.* Urbana, 1966.

Graham, Loren R. *The Soviet Academy of Sciences and the Communist Party, 1927–1932.* Princeton, 1967.

Graham, Otis L., Jr. *The Great Campaigns: Reform and War in*

America, 1900–1928. Englewood Cliffs, N.J., 1971.

Hagedorn, Herman. *The Magnate: William Boyce Thompson and His Times, 1869–1930.* New York, 1935.

Hammer, Armond. *The Quest for the Romanoff Treasure.* New York, 1932.

Hard, William. *Raymond Robin's Own Story.* New York, 1920.

Hasegawa, Tsuyoshi. *The February Revolution: Petrograd, 1917.* Seattle, 1981.

Herron, George D. *Woodrow Wilson and the World's Peace.* New York, 1917.

Hinckley, Ted. *The Americanization of Alaska, 1867–1897.* Palo Alto, 1972.

Hoff–Wilson, Joan. *American Business and Foreign Policy, 1920–1933.* Lexington, 1971.

———. *Ideology and Economics: U. S. Relations with the Soviet Union, 1918–1933.* Columbia, 1974.

———. *Herbert Hoover: The Forgotten Progressive.* Boston, 1975.

Iorga, Nicolae. *My American Lectures.* Bucharest, 1932.

Jessup, Philip C. *Elihu Root.* 2 Vols. New York, 1938.

Joravsky, David. *Soviet Marxism and Natural Science, 1917–1932.* London, 1932.

Kaslas, Bronis, J. *The Baltic Nations: The Quest for Regional Integration and Political Liberty.* Pittston, Penn., 1976.

Kazemzadeh, Firuz. *The Struggle for Transcaucasia.* New York, 1951.

Kennan, George F. *Russia Leaves the War.* Princeton, 1956.

———. *The Decision to Intervene.* Princeton, 1958.

Lang, David. *A Modern History of Soviet Georgia.* New York, 1962.

Lasch, Christopher. *The American Liberals and the Russian Revolution.* New York, 1962.

Lerner, Warren. *Karl Radek: The Last Internationalist.* Stanford, 1970.

Levin, Gordon N., Jr. *Woodrow Wilson and World Politics: America's Response to War and Revolution.* New York, 1968.

Libbey, James K. *Alexander Gumberg and Soviet–American Relations, 1917–1933.* Lexington, KY, 1977.

Lord, Robert. *Some Problems of the Peace Conference.* Cambridge, 1922.

Maddox, Robert James. *The Unknown War with Russia: Wilson's Siberian Intervention.* San Rafael, 1977.

―――. *William E. Borah and American Foreign Policy.* Louisiana, 1969.

Massie, Robert K. *Nicholas and Alexandra.* New York, 1969.

Mayor, Arno. *Politics and Diplomacy of Peacemaking: Containment and Counterevolution at Versailles, 1918-1919.* New York, 1967.

Meiburger, Anne. *Efforts of Raymond Robins toward the Recognition of Soviet Russia and the Outlawry of War, 1917-1933.* Washington, D.C., 1958.

Mock, James and Larson, Cedric. *Words That Won the War: The Story of the Committee on Public Information, 1917-1919.* Princeton, 1939.

Moulton, Harold G. and Pasvolsky Leo. *World War Debt Settlement.* New York, 1926.

Murray, Robert K. *Red Scare.* New York, 1962.

―――. *The Harding Era: Warren G. Harding and His Administration.* Minneapolis, 1966.

Nelson, Keith L. *Victors Divided: America and the Allies in Germany, 1918-1923.* Berkeley, 1975.

Oren, Nissan. *Revolution Administered: Agrarian and Communism in Bulgaria.* Baltimore, 1973.

Palm, Charles G. and Reed, Dale. *Guide to the Hoover Institution Archives.* Stanford, 1979.

Parrini, Carl. *Heir to Empire: United States Economic Diplomacy, 1916-1923.* Pittsburg, 1969.

Pipes, Richard. *The Formation of the Soviet Union: Communism and Nationalism, 1917-1923.* Cambridge, 1964.

Pusey, Merlo J. *Charles Evans Hughes.* 2 Vols. New York, 1951.

Riha, Thomas. *A Russian European: Paul Miliukov in Russian Politics.* Notre Dame, 1969.

Rosenburg, Emily. *Spreading the American Dream: American Economic and Cultural Expansion, 1890-1945.* New York, 1982.

Schuman, Frederick L. *American Policy Toward Russia Since 1917.* New York, 1934.

Seton-Watson, R. W. *A History of Roumania.* Cambridge, 1934.

Solomon, Susan Gross. *The Soviet Agrarian Debate: A Controversy in Social Science, 1923-1929*. Boulder, 1977.

Stewart, Robert Laird. *Sheldon Jackson: Pathfinder and Prospector of the Missionary Vanguard on the Rocky Mountains and Alaska.* New York, 1908.

Strakhovsky, Leonid I. *American Opinion about Russia, 1917-1920.* Toronto, 1961.

Surface, Frank M. and Bland, Raymond L. *American Food in the World War and Reconstruction Period: Operations of the Organizations under the Direction of Herbert Hoover, 1914-1924.* Stanford, 1931.

Sutton, Anthony. *Wall Street and the Bolshevik Revolution.* New York, 1974.

Sworkowski, Witold. *The Hoover Library Collection on Russia.* Stanford, 1954.

Tarulis, John M. *American–Baltic Relations, 1918-1922: The Struggle over Recognition.* Washington, D. C., 1965.

Thompson, John M. *Russia, Bolshevism, and the Versailles Peace.* Princeton, 1966.

Trani, Eugene P. and Wilson, David L. *The Presidency of Warren G. Harding.* Lawrence, 1977.

Trotsky, Leon. *Whither Russia? Toward Capitalism or Socialism.* New York, 1926.

Ulam, Adam. *A History of Soviet Russia.* New York, 1976.

———. *Expansion and Coexistence: The History of Soviet Foreign Policy, 1917-1967.* New York, 1968.

———. *The Bolsheviks: The Intellectual and Political History of the Triumph of Communism in Russia.* New York 1965.

Unterberger, Betty, ed. *American Intervention in the Russian Civil War.* Lexington, 1969.

———. *America's Siberian Expedition, 1918-1920.* Durham, N.C., 1956.

Vernadsky, George. *A History of Russia.* New Haven, 1954.

Wade, Rex A. *The Russian Search for Peace, February–October 1917.* Stanford, 1969.

Weissman, Benjamin. *Herbert Hoover and Famine Relief to Soviet Russia, 1921-1923.* Stanford, 1974.

Wildman, Allan K. *The End of the Russian Imperial Army.* Princeton, 1980.

Williams, William A. *American–Russian Relations, 1781–1947.* New York.

———. *Empire as a Way of Life.* Oxford, 1980.

Wilson, Edmund. *To the Finland Station.* New York, 1968.

Wolfe, Bertram D. *Three Who Made a Revolution.* Boston, 1955.

Zalewski, Wojciech. Unpublished monograph on Slavic collecting at Stanford Libraries and the Hoover Institution.

Articles

Burdick, Charles B. "Aesop, Wilson, and Lenin: The End of the World." Second Annual President's Scholar's Address, 23 April 1975. San Jose State University.

Feuer, Lewis S. "American Travelers to the Soviet Union, 1917–1923: The Formation of a Component of New Deal Ideology." *American Quarterly.* 14 (Summer 1962): 122–136.

Fike, Claude E. "The United States and Russian Territorial Problems, 1817–1920." *The Historian.* 24 (May 1962): 331–346.

Fitzpatrick, Sheila. "Culture and Politics under Stalin: A Reappraisal." *Slavic Review.* (June 1976): 211–231.

———. "Cultural Revolution in Russia, 1928–1932." *Journal of Contemporary History.* (January 1974): 30–52.

———. "The 'Soft' Line on Culture and Its Enemies," *Slavic Review.* 9 (June 1974): 267–287.

Hawley, Ellis W. "Herbert Hoover, the Commerce Secretariat, and the Vision of an Associate State, 1921–1928." *Journal of American History.* 61 (June 1974): 116–140.

Hoff–Wilson, Joan. "American Business and Recognition of the Soviet Union." *Social Science Quarterly.* 52 (September 1971): 348–368.

Hopkins, George W. "The Politics of Food: United States and Soviet Hungary, March–August 1919." *Mid-Century.* 55 (October 1973): 245–270.

Keserich, Charles. "George D. Herron: Il Nostro Americano." *Il Politico.* (1976): 315–332.

———. "The Political Odyssey of George D. Herron." *San Jose Studies.* (February 1977): 79–93.

Lewin, Moshe. "Who Was the Soviet Kulak?" *Soviet Studies.* 18 (October 1966): 189–212.

Maddox, Robert James. "Woodrow Wilson, the Russian Embassy,

and Siberian Intervention." *Pacific Historical Review.* 36 (November 1967): 435–448.

McClelland, James C. "Bolshevik Approaches to Higher Education, 1917–1921." *Slavic Review.* 30 (December 1971): 818–831.

Mohrenschildt, Dimitri von. "The Early American Observers of the Russian Revolution, 1917–1921." *Russian Review.* 3 (1943): 64–74.

Parry, Albert. "Charles R. Crane: Friend of Russia." *Russian Review.* 6 (Spring 1947): 113–127.

Smith, Glen. "Education for the Native of Alaska: The Work of the United States Bureau of Education, 1884–1931." *Journal of the West.* 6 (July 1967): 440–450.

Trani, Eugene. "Woodrow Wilson and the Decision to Intervene in Russia: A Reconsideration." *Journal of Modern History.* 48 (September 1976): 440–461.

Ziegler, Robert H. "Herbert Hoover: A Reinterpretation." *American Historical Review.* 81 (October 1976): 800–810.

Dissertations and Theses

Dixon, Adams Warren. "Revolution, Reconstruction, and Peace: Herbert Hoover and European Food Relief, 1918–1919." Master's Thesis, University of Wisconsin, 1964.

Edmondson, Charles M. "Soviet Famine Relief Measures, 1921–1923." Ph.D. dissertation, Florida State University, 1970.

Finnegan, Edward. "The United States Policy Toward Russia, March 1917–March 1918." Ph.D. dissertation, Fordham University, 1947.

Fithian, Floyd James. "Soviet–American Economic Relations, 1918–1923: American Business in Russia during the Period of Non-Recognition." Ph.D. dissertation, University of Nebraska, 1964.

Goler, Patricia. "Robert Howard Lord and the Settlement of Polish Boundaries After World War I." Ph.D. dissertation, Boston College, 1957.

Hinckley, Ted. "The Alaska Labors of Sheldon Jackson, 1877–1890." Ph.D. dissertation, University of Indiana, 1961.

Paul, Gary. "The Development of the Hoover Institution and Peace Library, 1919–1944." Ph.D. dissertation, University of California, Berkeley.

Poole, Charles P. "Two Centuries of Education in Alaska." Ph.D.

dissertation, University of Washington, 1947.

Reitzer, Ladialas F. "United States–Russian Economic Relations, 1917–1920." Ph.D. dissertation, University of Chicago, 1950.

St. John, Jacqueline D. "John F. Stevens: American Assistance to Russian and Siberian Railroads, 1917–1922." Ph.D. dissertation, University of Oklahoma, 1969.

Williams, William A. "Raymond Robins and Russian–American Relations, 1917–1938." Ph.D. dissertation, University of Wisconsin, 1950.

Index